THE SENTENCE

A FAMILY'S PRISON MEMOIR

Gene Kraig

GREENPOINT PRESS

Printed in the United States of America

Book design by Rob Kimmel Design
www.robkimmeldesign.com

Author photo by Tal Shpantzer
www.talfoto.com

The text of this book is set in Minion, designed by Robert Slimbach, and
ITC Officina Sans, designed by Eric Spiekermann.

ISBN 0-9759760-1-X

Greenpoint Press
A subsidiary of Ducts Webzine Association, Inc.
PO Box 3203
Grand Central Station
New York, NY 10163
www.ducts.org

For my grandchildren,
Andrew Max Kraig
Alison Helene Kraig
Daniel Stuart Kraig
Addie June Nicholas
Michael Jeremy Nicholas

ACKNOWLEDGMENTS

It is with the greatest gratitude that I thank all who gave so much to uplift and sustain me from Jerry's indictment through his sentence and its tragic aftermath:

Susan Antilla, Lilly Ando, Frank Arstone, Margaret (Marvelous) Arthur, Jackie Battenfield, Kate Birmingham, Tanya and Nicholas Bobrinskoi, Deborah Bonelli, Tom Brunn, Andrea Callard, Karen Cantrell, Joan Damankos, Alan Duncan, Lisa Farley, Aurora Ferrero, Stan Frankel, Joseph Gallo, Bill Gunlocke, Gaby Hoffmann, David Holland, Shirley and Freddy Helden, Hank Hentemann, Zena Kaplan, Elroy and Dee Kirsch, Mel Kamens, Stacy Marotta, Jill Lamar, Bob Levenson, Jerry Libava, Shamai Malka, June Marshall, Norma Martin, Dave Pasz, Elizabeth Primamore, Johanna Reiss, Mary Rolland, Susan Rosenzweig, Sherri Sbrocco, Alan Shapiro, Shirley Selhub, Cece Sloan, Frank Sweeny, Ann Stephenson, Somer Stephenson, Judy Stevens, Christine (Hibbs) Steiger, Eric Thompson, Lori Lynn Turner, Marlene Vine, Irv Zaretsky, Mary Zibella. And to Greenpoint Press, Publishers, Charles Salzberg and Jonathan Kravetz, book designer, Rob Kimmel, Publicist Joanna Virello for the best creative team I could have wished for.

Particularly, I want to acknowledge:

Jerry's and my closest friends, Debby and Michael Kaufman, my brother and sister-in-law, Howard and Lee Bayer-Shapiro, my daughter-in-law, Cindy Kraig, my son-in-law, Alex Nicholas. This was my nucleus that made the difference between falling apart and finding the strength to go forward.

My son, Brian's, untiring efforts to keep Kraig and Kraig law practice on its feet was the mainstay of our family's security. He honored his father from the deep well of his heart with unending devotion, respect and love. His concern, love, tenderness and advice guided me through the bleakest days and gave me courage to write this book.

My daughter, Karen Kraig Nicholas, has been my right and left hand, both ballast and thrust. The depth of her giving goes beyond words. I drew motivation from her clear-eyed reality checks. She gave unstinting hours of critiques for seven years. She asked the hard questions and had to relive those hardest of times from the first draft through countless revisions. I owe the writing of this book to her.

THE SENTENCE

A FAMILY'S PRISON MEMOIR

Under a government which imprisons any unjustly, the true place for a just man is also a prison.

—Henry David Thoreau

CHAPTERS

CHAPTER ONE

FIRST VISIT

SEPTEMBER, 1995

The heat and humidity were so high it was as if I were pushing through a barrier of steam as I ran toward a low building, the only one that looked like it was meant for visitors. Once at the entrance, I stopped, quickly combed my fingers through my hair, and then plunged inside, expecting Jerry to be there to scoop me up into his arms.

No Jerry. Instead, there was a crowd milling around the water fountain. He must have been sent back to his unit when I didn't show up on time. Then I realized that I wasn't in the visiting room but an extra-wide corridor, with noise coming from the far end. That had to be where Jerry was waiting for me. I approached a guard stationed at a folding table. "Please, I'm here to see Jerry Kraig."

Without looking up, the guard shoved a clipboard with a pencil on a string attached in my direction. The form had been copied so many times, the lines drawn down the page were so dim they had become broken columns. I began to fill it out: Visitor's Name, Address, Inmate's Name, Inmate's Number. I went weak. What was Jerry's number? I plopped my bag on the table, hoping the letter with his prisoner number on the envelope was inside.

The guard stirred. "No purses allowed," he said and pointed a smoke-stained finger at a flimsy easel near the entrance. All I could make out was a list beginning with bold black 'No's.'

I stared at him, uncomprehending. "What do you mean, no purses?"

"You have to leave it in the car," he said.

Racing back to the parking lot, I damned the place and the heat. I dumped the contents of my purse on the passenger seat. Jerry's letter was sticking out from under my sketchbook. I snatched it up. There it was: 52270-060, Federal Correctional Institution, Morgantown, West Virginia.

I gathered the rolls of quarters that were supposed to have been used for our breakfast and lunch, along with my wallet, which held my ID, and stuffed it all in my pockets, grateful that I'd decided to wear baggy pants instead of the tighter jeans.

Back at the table, the guard shoved the clipboard at me a second time. I flipped through, distressed. "The form I filled out isn't here," I said.

"Oh yeah, you have to do a new one."

"Oh, God," I moaned under my breath and filled it out again.

Barely glancing at it, he asked mechanically, "Do you have any food stuff?"

"No."

He checked a box at the bottom, placed the form on top of a messy pile, and motioned me to the next station. Another clipboard, another form: Inmate's name and number again. Distance traveled? To hell and back. I estimated three hundred miles. How long have you traveled? Counting the three hours lost coming from Cleveland…six hours. What make is your car? Chevrolet. Year? '93. Color? Red. License plate number? I didn't know. I had enough. I made one up. Let them arrest me. I wasn't going back to that lot again.

I continued reading, my heart pumping faster. Do you have on your person food, firearms, illegal drugs, contraband? As if a visitor would check 'yes.' I slashed 'no' through the entire list and handed it to the second guard. He read the form slowly, methodically, as if he had never seen one before. Finally, he cocked his head to the left.

At the threshold of the visiting room, I saw where I was going to have to sustain my marriage for the next two years. But Jerry wasn't here, either. I stood, flexing my fingers that were spongy from retaining water, too frustrated to think.

Off to the right, a female guard sat at a computer inside a partition. She was short; a gelatinous bulge hung over the belted pants of her uniform. I read her name tag: 'S. Stample.' She was displaying a cast on her wrist to a woman leaning on the counter whose pink shirt and coordinated pants were immaculate. I self-consciously tugged my own wrinkled top down.

The woman drawled, "I'm so sorry you're going to be out for surgery. I'll miss you. You got off last week before I had a chance to thank you for getting Don up here so quick." I placed her as a dental hygienist or lab technician. Whoever Don was, I hoped Jerry had nothing to do with him.

"Excuse me," I addressed Stample, "I need to know, how do I find my husband? I'm very late." My tone was urgent.

Stample's expression remained impenetrable, though her eyes registered how upset I was. She asked for my driver's license. I gave it to her and she punched in the numbers and waited, watching the screen. "You're not in the computer," she said, dully. "Are you on his visiting list?"

"Yes." I clenched my hands, forcing patience. "Did you put in my name? It's the male spelling, Gene with a 'G', 'G–E–N–E,' and Kraig with a 'K'. Lots of people make mistakes."

"Your number isn't in here."

"But I sent in the form immediately after he surrendered, three weeks ago. I'm his wife. There's no reason why it shouldn't be there."

She kept staring at the monitor that evidently did not have me on it. Now I knew why they didn't allow firearms. "It's our first visiting day. I had a horrendous trip and there's barely an hour left." I tasted tears in my mouth. My voice shook as I demanded, "I want to see the supervisor in charge."

"Calm down, ma'am," she warned. "Is he a new inmate?"

"Yes, I just told you."

She picked up the phone while still addressing me, "Sometimes it doesn't get in the system but they'll have it in Central."

The woman in the pink shirt moved in so close that I could smell her freshly applied pink lipstick.

"How long did you say you drove?" she asked.

I stepped back. "I didn't." She smiled, waiting.

"About six hours," I said, grudgingly. "I got lost."

Her head bobbed up and down knowingly, "Anxiety. I'm in f.o., Families of Offenders, a support group." She pursed her lips and added, "I'm so glad we don't have children. They really get messed up. Do you?"

"No." Her eyes flickered disappointment. I corrected myself, "I mean they're not children anymore. They're adults. We have grandchildren, but they're too young to understand."

"What's he in for, your husband?"

"It's really too complicated." I turned my attention to Stample, who was still scrolling on the computer.

"Isn't that the truth." She allowed a moment for me to get that we were in the same boat. "What was he charged with?"

Cornered, my mind scrambled. I had to tell just enough to prevent her from probing further. "Conspiracy. He helped a client hide his money from the irs. My husband was an attorney." I didn't bother to add that he was going to win his appeal and be freed from this insanity by October.

"Mine was an irs deal, too," she offered, smiling at me as if I were her best friend. "He was an accountant. He got ten years, eight to go. But we're real lucky 'cause I have a good job. I drive five hours every weekend from Pennsylvania. I stay at Embassy Suites. It's real nice. Where do you stay?"

Stample cut in, "Carol, Don will be back in a couple of minutes. You can go in."

Wrinkling her nose, Carol added honey to her drawl, "I want to thank you, Sue. I won't forget your kindness." Heading into the corridor, she waved at me and said, "Little girl's room. Good luck."

Stample nodded at me, "Yours will be up in a minute, too. Go on in."

The room was lined with rows of tables bolted to the floor, each one with four molded plastic seats attached, like in the cafeteria at the junior high school my kids had attended. Each table spilled over with visiting families and was covered with greasy food containers. The air conditioning in the room couldn't combat the brew of heat from outside and the density of people within.

Suddenly, woozy from stifling closeness combined with the odors of microwaved popcorn and pizza, I was overcome by the urge to leave. But instead, I forced my attention to finding an available table.

It hurt to picture my children here: our daughter, Karen, and her new husband, Alex. Our son, Brian, and his wife, Cindy, their children, our grandchildren, Andrew, three, and Alison, one. If I could prevent them from visiting, I would. The degradation and shame that filled the stuffy room was palpable.

I swallowed guiltily. I couldn't stop thinking about what I should have done differently. "Our mistakes" is how I'd come to think of them. Jerry's sense of loyalty and deep need to please were qualities that many admired in him. But I had seen them as his tragic flaws, too often misdirected and misplaced, sometimes a gash in his self image that shamed me, as if his weakness were mine. I'd seen the potential threat Reuben posed. I'd intuited in some terrible way that he was lethal. There was no denying that I'd seen the train coming straight at us. Yet I'd put blinders on, trusting and believing that Jerry would protect us over everything when I should have stood in front of that train. I squeezed my eyes shut, restraining tears and swallowed. I was Jerry's accomplice. I deserved to be here in this prison's visiting room.

A guard raised the blinds and I was relieved to see the sun glaring off my Blazer's roof. In my frenzy to get back to signing in, I'd neglected to lock it. I couldn't imagine that anyone would steal a car from a prison parking lot, but I felt a moment of elation to be able to keep an eye on it.

Along the far wall, children pumped change into the vending machines. A clamoring line was generating excitement at the microwave. I took a deep breath. I was going to have to get used to the rancid smell. Suddenly curious to see who the inmates were, I began to pick them out in nondescript khaki uniforms. I searched their shirts for prison numbers and I was surprised to find none. The prisoners were so young and fresh faced, they could have been college students, younger Jerrys. At over fifty, he was one of the oldest inmates.

I claimed a table in the corner that I calculated was out of Stample's view. But then I noticed a mirror angled down from the ceiling and saw my make-up and tear-smeared face looking down on me. The tissues were in the car. Sweat and gel had done a job on my hair, spiking it all over. I combed my fingers through it, sorry I had it cut so short. Jerry always liked it longer.

Mirrors aimed down from the other corners of the room as well, and then I saw the guards stationed among the tables, also in khaki uniforms, camouflaged to blend in, the better to watch us. I straightened my back, my hands in my lap under the table. I tore at a cuticle until pain warned. Since Jerry had surrendered, I'd been tearing at them mercilessly.

The loud speaker crackled and a gravelly, male voice boomed, "Kraig out of Carlson, please report to the visiting room."

I jumped out of the seat, looking for Jerry to come out of a door between the vending machines. After a few more minutes of anxious waiting, I deduced he would come up from the outside compound.

Back in the corridor, I pressed myself against the plate glass at an awkward angle to see past a six-foot-high clump of bushes. I shivered. It was at least ten degrees cooler out here. I could see the grounds in more detail. Surrounding a rambling grid of grassy moats were forested mountains that reminded me more of a state park than a prison. Each grid contained a ranch-style, concrete-block, and wood unit with the petunias, zinnias, and geraniums Jerry had told me about. He'd been impressed with how diligently the inmates tended to them. I tried to pick out which unit was Jerry's but couldn't distinguish it by his meager description that it was "near the chapel." Although the population of the prison was over a thousand, it was eerie to see it empty of activity and people, except for a lone tractor lawn mower chugging up the side of a hill toward a weathered barn.

Suddenly, Jerry materialized as if out of a void, bounding up the steep steps and through the door. I called out, "Honey," rushing toward him. But shock and disbelief stopped me. This man wasn't my husband. When I'd left Jerry three weeks ago, he'd had weight around his middle, his shoulders slumped, and his face had the pallor of defeat. This man was straight backed to his full six feet, as lanky as the boy I'd fallen in love with at fifteen. And even more startling, he had a neatly trimmed black beard accented with white that transformed his now dark-tanned face.

"Gene, you're here!" It was his voice, resonant and smiling. My anxiety began to lift. But now Jerry registered shock as a guard seemed to come from nowhere, clamped a hand on his shoulder and steered him away from me down a length of red industrial carpet, saying, "Process down here, buddy."

I watched as Jerry handed his ID to a guard at a folding table. Then he and the other guard turned left and disappeared into a holding room where the inmates were searched before being allowed to be "in contact." It took a couple more interminable minutes and then I was in his arms. I buried my face in his chest, finally safe. The sobs I had suppressed all day let loose. He held me until they subsided, and then we kissed with pent–up longing and fear, afraid to feel too much and afraid to let go. His bristles scraped my face and his smell was not his usual combination of spicy aftershave and Dial soap but the steely-edged odor of a mechanic. Then, aware of a guard's presence behind us, we pulled apart. He looked into my eyes, his voice distraught, "I went out of my mind worrying about you."

"You don't know how sorry I am. You can't imagine. I kept driving and driving because I kept expecting the exit was going to come up. But I'd already passed it! Then a sign said fifty miles to the next exit and I knew I was lost, and it was going to add another hour before I would find out where I was. I kept picturing you waiting. It was a nightmare. I wound up in Hagerstown, Maryland."

"I thought you'd had an accident. I'm just so helpless in here." Jerry's eyes were anguished. "I was outside the chapel all that time, because it's the only place where I could hear the loudspeaker. All the guys are around the unit on weekends and it's bedlam. I knew you weren't paying attention at the Cranberry exit when I told you it was tricky."

"I know. I screwed up our whole day. And then, when I finally got here and I couldn't wait to see you, they wouldn't let me in because I had my bag." My eyes brimmed with tears. "I had to take it back to the car. You'd think they could have sent visiting rules." Tears ran down my cheeks and Jerry tenderly wiped each one with his thumbs. I saw in his eyes how much he needed me.

"There are all kinds of things they don't allow. It's going to be okay. We're both learning." He pulled me close again. I latched onto his arm and we walked into the visiting room.

We sat opposite each other at the table I'd selected. He cupped his hands over mine. Like a parched houseplant, I wanted to absorb the sweat from his palms. A woman's raucous laugh ending in a high-pitched squeal broke the moment. I cringed, overcome by the urge to escape. The room was aboil with people trying to have fun under these restrictive circumstances.

"Feel how worried I was." Jerry leaned toward me. "I'm wringing wet. Why didn't you call Brian sooner?"

"Because I was too anxious to get off the highway to find a pay phone."

"But why didn't you use the cell phone? I even reminded you last night to plug it into the lighter so you wouldn't have to worry about the battery."

"I turned the house upside down and couldn't find it."

"Gene, it's in the glove compartment. I told you I put it there the night before I surrendered."

"Oh honey, God." I wiped my burning eyes and infused assurance into my voice. "Now that I've done the trip, I promise I'll be okay." I tried to picture myself as familiar with the prison as the pink-outfitted woman, her conviviality with S. Stample. She actually looked like she enjoyed being a con's wife. I stiffened with repugnance. That could never be me.

Dark stained the underarms of Jerry's shirt. I drew my finger across his moist forehead as if it were condensation on a mirror that would reveal the husband I had left behind. His newly rugged face and tan turned his hazel eyes greener than brown and were clearer and healthier than they'd been in years. Fine squint lines replaced the puffiness around his eyes, and his cheekbones were once again defined. His face shined with the brightness and good looks that he had in his twenties. "It seems prison is rejuvenating you," I said, wiping at the smudges under my eyes. "I must look like hell."

"Gene, you look wonderful. You don't know how much I've missed you, but now you're here and I can't sit close enough to put my arm around you." He smiled, painfully. "It's harder than the past three weeks of not seeing you."

"It's true. We're not separated by a partition so it's all self-imposed restraint," I said, wishing we could just sit close together.

"That's the method and madness of minimum security. Freedom is always taunting. I have to keep telling myself what I can't do, like walk out the open door and walk in the woods right behind my unit."

For a second an irrational fear came over me that I was losing him. "I still can't get over how much you've changed. You left so down and depleted."

"Strong, my bunk mate, told me I had to get in shape because if you get sick in here, you're sunk. The medical staff is from 'Buy-an-M.D.U.', and he said everyone prays that they don't come down with anything that a bag of salt won't cure or that you won't need more than one aspirin at a time."

"I don't get what salt is supposed to do."

"The medical solution here for everything that ails above the waist is to gargle with salt," he smiled, amused.

"Speaking of medical stuff, what happened at your psych appointment yesterday? We got clicked off the phone last night before you had a chance to tell me."

"It was part of the tests they did for my evaluation. The psych was a grad student, my guess is first year, from the University of West Virginia on the other side of town. The poor kid was so nervous and trying so hard to be professional. She pulled out a new appointment calendar from a new briefcase. I had to have been her first con. Basically, I had to fill out a three-page questionnaire, and I waited for more than an hour while she scored it."

Jerry's face turned sober. He concentrated for a couple of seconds on carefully creasing the corner of an industrial, brown paper napkin he'd pulled from his pocket. "Then she told me, as if she'd just discovered a rare disease, that I'm depressed. I wanted to laugh but then I got angry. I said, 'I'm in prison. I've lost my profession and my son has lost his law partner of five years. There are fines to pay when I get out. I have no income. It's putting my family through hell and my grandchildren have to come to a place like this to see me. If I weren't down, something really would be wrong with me: what else should I be?'

"I could see she didn't have a clue, but she wouldn't agree that my being down was to be expected. She got very nervous and started thumbing through her calendar and said if I wanted to talk she could see me on Tuesdays at ten. Even seeing this student will be a diversion from the monotony, the worst thing about this place. Well, that and no privacy. So I told her to put me in her book."

"I believe in talking. I think you've got a deluge bottled up. What do you have to lose?"

"I've always prided myself on not letting my problems drive me over the edge. But maybe she saw something. It really upset me."

I didn't tell him how depressed I'd been since he left, taking as many as four showers a day, sometimes unaware of undressing and then finding myself under the hot spray.

Jerry sensed what I wasn't telling him. He didn't want to know; it was too hard, too painful, and he was too helpless. He clapped his hands as though to snap us out of it. "I missed breakfast and lunch. I'm starving and you must be too. Did you bring the quarters?"

I rolled my eyes.

"Just checking," he said. We laughed, appreciating that we could and then we walked over to the wall of vending machines, holding hands as if we were going someplace. Only two selections remained, a couple of yogurts and a two-ounce can of fruit cocktail. We fed in almost a roll of quarters, double the price at the store. Jerry ate quickly, checked his watch and stood up. "Good, we still have time for a cappuccino. Strong told me they're great."

Jerry left and moments later he brought back two weaker than instant coffee cappuccinos, a scummy layer of foam on top. We both took a sip. He said, "It's so good. Don't you think?"

I agreed, not wanting to ruin his enjoyment and offered my cup to him, saying, "I'm so thirsty, I would rather have something cold." I took a handful of quarters and headed over to the vending machine. I angrily plunked in the last of the quarters, thinking how Jerry was becoming prisonized. I hated everything about this place, even down to the shined-in scuff marks on the floor.

I came back with a Diet Coke. He smiled apologetically, "So, okay, it's not the

Coffee Bar, but it sure is good to have anything different. The coffee here tastes like the fixative you spray on your charcoal drawings. No wonder all I want to do is sleep. Did I tell you I applied to work at the law library?"

"No…or about the beard or losing weight. And now you're going to work for the B.O.P. (Bureau of Prisons)." Anger flashed through me. Since the trial, I had been filled with revenge. "You were so adamant about not giving anything to the hand that bit you. How could you have changed your mind?"

"Everyone has to work, Gene. The choices were cleaning toilets, kitchen duty, laundry, or maintenance jobs." He opened his hands in a gesture of conciliation. "I met a couple of the guys who work in the library and they said I was crazy not to do it. It's easy, clean, and the supervisor is a woman who's known to be fair. It'll make me feel my life is worth something. The one goal in the joint is to keep busy one day to the next, until you get out." He checked his watch again and looked stricken. "Honey, I'm sorry but I have to go now."

The clock hanging over the guard's platform showed 2:40. Confused, I checked behind me to see if something had happened. Most tables had emptied. "But we still have twenty minutes," I said.

"Strong told me the guards strip-search the last inmates to go in," Jerry said and looked down, his face flushed with embarrassment.

We stood behind a brick post in the corridor and kissed good-bye. His beard scratched, but I didn't care. Then he said softly into my ear, "Please take care of yourself for me."

"You too," I said, clinging tightly as we kissed again.

He pulled away. "I really have to go now," he said.

He opened the glass door for me to leave and watched as I headed up the path to the parking lot. I looked back and waved. His face was locked and grim, unreachable again.

Worried about the strip search, I started to run back to the car. Before I got in, I looked back, but Jerry was no longer there.

CHAPTER TWO

THE BEGINNING OF OUR DESCENT

JULY, 1984

The garage door rumbled open. Jerry was home early. He came into the kitchen, his summer blazer rumpled, his tie loosened at the neck. He leaned against my back and kissed the side of my neck. "Mmm, *eau de turpentine.*" I smiled. It was a good sign; he was in a joking mood. I turned my head and caught the corner of his mouth with my lips. Reaching over my shoulder, he grabbed a lime out of a bowl of fruit on the counter, brought a frosty bottle of vodka out of the freezer, and set it down with an attention-getting clink.

He tossed the lime, plucked it out of the air, and grinned as if he'd caught a fly ball. Slicing wedges, he said, "I had a very interesting day."

"Interesting" was not a word Jerry would use to describe a promising new personal injury case. "Interesting" implied a case that he would call creative; one that would turn out to be a time waster and ultimately a loser, but worth taking for the "challenge." He scooped ice into our glasses, poured generous slugs of vodka and added jiggers of Rose's lime juice. He squeezed the larger wedge of lime into my drink—I liked it that way—and fit a thinner slice onto the rim of my glass. Smiling like a magician, he handed it to me with a flourish.

"What are we celebrating?" I asked, knowing he needed a substantial fee to end what he underplayed as a "little slump" of disappointing verdicts and low settlements.

He sipped, let out an appreciative, "Ah," but watched me warily, anticipating the need for damage control. "Reuben Sturman invited me for lunch today," Jerry said, sounding defensive, yet impressed with himself.

I took a large swig of my gimlet, its acidic liquid going down harshly. "I thought you said something good happened." I sipped again, this time for the drink's harsh heat. "I was expecting you to tell me you signed up the case of your dreams." I faced Jerry sideways, swishing my hand in the bowl of cold water holding potato slices, which swam around my fingers like slippery coins.

Jerry leaned against the counter. "Hon, just listen, okay? I need to talk to you about this."

"Okay, what?" I wiped my hand on my paint-crusted shirt.

Jerry smiled, satisfied that he had my attention. "This is important. There's a hungry prosecutor, Bruce Taylor, who's formed a vice squad with the sole purpose of raiding and prosecuting Reuben's stores, and there's no let-up in sight. Reuben's very worried."

"Well, he should be. You saw yesterday's headline. 'The Czar of Pornography' took up half the page and the photo under it wasn't meant to get him sympathy, either. What was he doing leaving the courthouse wearing a Groucho Marx mask?"

"Reuben said Groucho Marx was his hero because he made fun of everything."

"Then the editorial was right. Reuben was "taunting the law." He deserves what he's getting," I said with finality, wishing the conversation were over. Shade was heading over the tennis courts at Thornton Park on the other side of our yard. It would be much more productive to get some exercise before dinner than to engage in another frustrating argument over Reuben, as had been happening too often over the past month every time he made the news.

Jerry sipped. I sipped. The drink went down much mellower now. I started to suggest tennis, but Jerry, his tone gilded with the authority of an insider, said, "Actually, since Larry Flynt was shot by that anti-pornography fanatic, Reuben's nervous that he'll be next. Flynt's paralyzed now." Jerry gazed out the window at the backyard. "It's so shocking to see this huge guy with an enormous appetite for life confined to a wheelchair. Reuben said security's tighter at Hustler than a maximum-security prison and Larry's constantly surrounded by bodyguards."

I tightened my hand around my drink, wanting distance from this whole conversation. "Since when did you become Reuben Sturman's confidant?"

"I've known him for thirty-three years, and for eleven of them he was as brotherly to me as Joe, sometimes more."

Reuben's brother, Joe, who was fifteen years younger, was one of Jerry's best friends since sixth grade. "That was when you were an impressionable kid and Reuben sold comics and candy, not girlie magazines."

Jerry added a slug of vodka to his drink, looking deflated. "I can't talk to you when you get like this. I've been out in the heat in this jacket all day. I was at two arraignments in two different courts and an arbitration. I missed the loop bus and had to walk up to Lake Erie Plaza. I'm all sweaty. I'm going to change." He left the kitchen.

"I'm sorry," I said, too softly, after I heard him go upstairs. I needed to change, too, but first I wanted to finish preparing the potatoes for the grill. With Jerry's jazzy whistling coming from the upstairs bathroom, I recalled how my husband had come to know Reuben, which was in the top ten of Jerry's fondest recollections.

Joe had begun to work for Reuben at Premium Sales, his wholesale magazine, new and used comic books, and candy business. When Reuben needed more help, Joe recommended Jerry, an enterprising kid who was always on the prowl for lucrative ways to fill his pockets. Jerry gladly gave up scavenging pop bottles for redemption and grabbed this "real job" working with Joe. From age twelve through the first couple years of college, Jerry bought his own clothes, dated, and saved money for his first car, all as a result of his earnings working for Reuben after school, on weekends, and during most of his school vacations, even after he went to college.

Jerry's parents were relieved to have their son practically paying his own way. Though his father, Max, earned a living as a house painter and paperhanger so that Jerry's mother, Helen, didn't have to work, frugality was a necessity. Times were rough for everyone in our old Cleveland neighborhood, filled with uneducated immigrant Jews and Italians without silver spoons. Jerry and I both grew up on 140th Street and Kinsman, just six apartment buildings between us, with Stein's Grocery smack in the middle. Though both sets of our parents were first-generation Americans, they were still coping with the hardships brought on by the Depression followed by World War II.

Unknown to me, Jerry was my crossing guard on Able Street when I came home for lunch from kindergarten, and I must have stood next to him at Stein's Grocery waiting to pay for a loaf of Wonder bread or a bottle of milk. Because our parents weren't in the same crowd and because of a five-year age difference, we didn't know each other. Jerry's younger brother, Bobby, occasionally showed up and joined my small troop of friends in a game of Red Rover or dodge ball. But he was known in the neighborhood as wild and rough. My mother didn't approve of him as a playmate, and I was happy to keep my distance.

I will never forget hearing my mother tell my best friend Debby's mother, Ida, about Jerry's mother. Ida was watching my baby brother, Howie, and me while my mother went down to the corner to pick up Passover chickens from the live poultry market. When my mother returned, she could hardly wait to exhale the smoke from her Camel before she began. Appalled, she reported seeing Helen Kraig at noon, her hair tied up in a rag like Carmen Miranda with a cigarette dangling from her mouth, shamelessly standing on her porch in a negligee as she shook a mop over the side of a rusty railing. She wore glamorous, high-heeled satin slippers, and her toe nails were painted the same deep red as her lips. Then, my mother said, stubbing out her cigarette, Helen yelled like a common washerwoman for Jerry and Bobby to come home for lunch, while she waited for them as if she had nothing to do but stand there all day. Debby and I exchanged thrilled looks. News from the street like this didn't come along every day. What extraordinary new material to spark our imaginations when we played house.

Besides the negligee scene, Helen and Max Kraig were known to throw wild parties, at which drinking and dancing went on into the wee hours. For my parents, Ida and Max, and our other neighbors, big nights together included lots of cake, coffee, and tea, mah-jongg for the women and gin rummy for the men. If the pot got as high as a dollar, they were living on the edge.

I first met Jerry on a blind date, Memorial Day weekend, 1957. I was fifteen and he was twenty, but he liked to say it was the reverse: I was as mature as a twenty-year-old and he was as immature as a fifteen-year-old. Though five years' difference pushed the limit, it wasn't out of the realm of possibility for me and my girlfriends to date older boys. I was more mature than most of my friends. That same year I taught Hebrew at temple to twenty-eight second graders after high school two days a week and Sunday school to kindergartners. I thought of myself as an independent thinker and an adult, and by August Jerry and I were gaga in love. We knew we wanted to spend the rest of our lives together. The depth of our shared roots seemed, fatefully, to bind us together. That and my parents.

We moved from 140th Street when I was twelve. My family joined the exodus from the Kinsman neighborhood to the suburbs. With loans from relatives, we bought an older colonial house in Cleveland Heights, a working, middle-class neighborhood. Jerry's family, one of the last to leave, stayed until he had graduated from high school. Then they moved to Willowick, a faraway eastern suburb where his father, Max, was foreman for a construction company building tract housing. One of the tiny bungalows became theirs.

My mother fell for Jerry the first time he entered our house. He was tall, handsome, with an accepting broad smile. Despite the reputation of his family, Jerry was at ease with himself and possessed a casual kind of refinement that said "winner." Both my parents jumped right in, reminiscing about the old neighborhood. My father was in the middle of appreciatively remembering the time Max had helped him change a flat tire when I came downstairs in a gingham blouse and skirt that whirled over layers of crinolines, the outfit my father had taken me to the wholesaler to buy. I was surprised to hear the swell in my father's voice, the embracing tone he used to charm someone he wanted to impress. I was going to go out with someone my father looked up to, which was rather amazing. My mother asked after Helen as if they had been bosom buddies who had lost touch. Her memory seemed to have expunged Helen's notoriety, which she and her friends had enjoyed at Helen's expense.

Jerry was never a guest in our house. He belonged. He ate hundreds of dinners at our table before we married. My mother catered to his taste as if he were her first-born son. Summers, I sat on the porch steps watching while he threw endless pitches to Howie. It wasn't until dark that I finally got my boyfriend to myself and we'd go for a drive for ice cream and then park at Shaker Lakes to make out.

Jerry introduced us to pizza and played his records of musicals and jazz. But most remarkable was how he joked around with my father as no one else could, bringing him out of his many bad days as a door-to-door salesman. My father liked to say that Jerry was a 'Joe College,' and couldn't have been prouder that he was soon to enter law school. My parent's unvoiced message was that Jerry was the man they trusted to provide a beautiful future for their daughter.

I was a year out of high school and Jerry was in his second year at Cleveland Marshall Law School, later to become Cleveland State, when we were married. Almost immediately, we faced mounting bills and then the pressures of being new parents once Brian was born eleven months later. I taught preschool and took college courses at night. Jerry was an insurance adjuster and attended law school nights. Brian was three when Karen was born, and Jerry became an associate lawyer in a small Cleveland firm. My father immediately put out the word to his customers and so, from the start, Jerry had his own clients. The demands of everything seeming to happen at once were buffered by my parents' support of regular dinners and baby-sitting.

Over the years, Jerry reminisced about his days as a stock boy at Premium Sales. With sentiment mellowed by fond loyalty, he said Reuben was like a cool uncle, turning him on to jazz, playing records, and telling jokes while he and Joe filled orders and replenished inventory. Saturdays, he recalled, Reuben drove Joe and Jerry to work, stopping at a mom-and-pop doughnut shop to pick up a couple dozen for their breakfast, and he treated them to salami sandwiches for lunch. Jerry had never known anyone as freewheeling with money as Reuben or as generous. He was delighted to accept Reuben's offer of tickets to the Cleveland Browns and seats behind home plate for the Cleveland Indians games.

Jerry loved pranks and quick wit and was schooled in the ways by Reuben, who joked and teased to win over customers. Reuben sealed deals with handshakes, and Jerry was impressed by the trust others placed in him. But he respected Reuben most for helping people who came looking for employment, hiring them, even when it meant creating a position. And Reuben dipped into his pocket, giving to the many who came to him in financial distress, never asking questions, or to be paid back.

In the early 1960s, several years after Jerry stopped working for Reuben, Premium Sales closed the door on comic books, Wrigley's gum, Oh Henry! bars, and Life magazine. Instead, Reuben changed the name to Sovereign News and the company went X-rated.

Reuben's parents, immigrants and card-carrying Communists, were an embarrassment to their son, who just wanted to be an ordinary American boy. Rebelling, Reuben took on capitalism with a vengeance. While Reuben's primary motivation was money, he embraced the ideal of freedom of expression for all. The renegade nature of sex as a commodity attracted him, and when Reuben discovered the lucrative rewards of sex for sale, it was as if he had fallen into the American capitalist's pot of gold. Flexing his entrepreneurial muscles, he rapidly expanded, opening X-rated 'adult' bookstores spanning national and international markets. He not only sold every kind of hardcore printed matter, he published it, produced adult movies (later videos), and was the innovator of the twenty-five-cent peep show booth. Money flowed in from all fronts.

With the first headline lambasting Reuben, Jerry and I got into it. Though I hated pornography, I underscored that I agreed with him about First Amendment rights. I was against censorship of any kind, including pornography being censored. Prior to becoming an artist, I'd been a freelance journalist and strongly believed that without freedom of expression, my work and everyone else's would be rendered meaningless. But I was suspicious of Reuben's motives and I believed he was using the First Amendment as a smokescreen to amass his own wealth and power, in other words greed was his motive.

Jerry surprised me by his vehement support on Reuben's behalf. His cheeks flushed as he asked me pointedly, didn't I know Reuben just won a landmark decision in the Supreme Court that would benefit anyone who wants to publish? Because of the backlash in the press against pornography, it was easy to misread Reuben's motives. When he had worked for Reuben, Jerry passionately said he witnessed firsthand how deep Reuben's commitment was. He remembered Reuben's crusade for William Gaines. In Jerry's senior year in high school, Reuben was distributing Gaines' *Entertainment Comics' Tales from the Crypt*. The cover of the first issue showed a shockingly gruesome illustration of a man hanging himself. Inside were corpses, dismemberments, and vivid stabbings.

Gaines was denounced by the press as depraved and immoral, and prosecutors warned him to tone down the illustrations. But he made the next issue even gorier, saying defiantly that nobody was going to tell him what to create. Jerry stood in awe of Reuben's refusal to buckle under the pressure to drop distribution of the magazine and of his donation of vast amounts of money to Gaines's defense fund. Reuben saw literary merit in Gaines' work; yes it was violent, but it had redeeming value. He appreciated its ironic humor and bizarre liberal morality. The day the Supreme Court agreed to hear the Gaines case, Reuben took it as an affirmation, and when Gaines won, he claimed his share of credit for the victory.

I recalled when Jerry had selected to debate the Gaines case in his constitutional law class, his first year at Cleveland Marshall Law School. I was seventeen, a high-school junior. Jerry's fraternity pin's presidential gavel dangled over my heart, engaged-to-be engaged. The Saturday night before his debate I timed him in the living room. I was babysitting Howie and he had come downstairs in his pajamas. Jerry was more of a big brother to Howie than to his own brother, Bobby, and Howie was attached to Jerry like a barnacle.

Jerry displayed the magazine to Howie and dramatically played to his young, captivated audience of one. "Look how innocuous this magazine is. Think of the books that have been wrongfully banned." Howie nodded, though he had no inkling what Jerry was talking about. He pulled himself up importantly as Jerry took one book after another out of a beat-up briefcase and handed them to him, reading each title, "*Alice In Wonderland, The American Heritage Dictionary, The Grapes of Wrath, Mother Goose, The Bible!*"

Reading was the mainstay of my life, and pride swelled inside of me; this was what it meant to have the weight of freedom in your hands. Jerry picked up *Tales from the Crypt* again and rustled its yellowed pages saying, "We must never impede a person's First Amendment rights." He was wired with conviction. I was utterly impressed and fell in love with him again that night, convinced he could become anything he set his heart on, even a Supreme Court judge, his 'long-shot dream.'

I was startled when Dave Brubeck blasted out of all four speakers in both the den and the living room. Jerry adjusted the volume and came back into the kitchen in faded green shorts and a Cleveland Indians T-shirt. I got a whiff of talc. He stroked his freshly shaved face on my cheek, dry and smooth. "Nice?"

"Very."

"Hon, I really need to tell you what happened at lunch."

Suddenly, the reason for Reuben's surprise luncheon invitation popped into my head. "He hit you up for a donation to his porno defense fund. No," I corrected, "his First Amendment defense fund. If you gave him a dime, don't tell me." I turned and dumped the bowl of potatoes into a colander.

"For once, you couldn't be more wrong. He doesn't want me to give him anything. He's going to pay me to be his First Amendment coordinator." Jerry lifted his shoulders as if he had just received an award. "Because of the raids, Reuben has had to hire lawyers all over the country and he needs someone to oversee the First Amendment litigation and manage fees. It's an administrative position but it would put me in the thick of the decision making. I think it's a tremendous opportunity to work with some of the best legal minds."

I was as astounded as if he had just announced he was going to leave me. "I can't believe you just gave up your practice and didn't even talk to me first. Well, Brian's going to be devastated. Not that I haven't said it'd be better for him to build his own career instead of coming into your practice."

"Gene, for God's sake, stop and listen." The green glints in Jerry's eyes flickered angrily. He snatched up a book of matches, slid open the patio door and said, "You always want me to talk to you, but I can never tell you anything."

I hastily seasoned the potatoes, made a tin-foil packet and went outside, rebuffed. It took a lot for Jerry to show a temper. He was right, I hadn't heard him out. He'd turned the gas on the grill too high and flames shot out of the grating. He concentrated on the fire settling and looked at me, half grimacing. "I'm not giving up anything. The practice will still be there for Brian. It's been a dream for both of us since he started working for me on Saturdays. Some day he's going to be the best partner I've ever had. Taking the position with Reuben will only make the practice more financially secure. He's hiring me on a fifty-thousand-dollar retainer." Jerry leveled his eyes at mine. "He'll lease a new car for me and give me an office at Sovereign. That was my one demand. I want to keep Sovereign and my practice separate." Jerry grinned, disarmingly. It was a done deal. I handed the packet to him and sat on the picnic bench.

Through the woods that divided our yard from the community pool, I could hear the lifeguard boom into a megaphone, "Stay off the ropes." How many summers had Brian and Karen cut through the woods to the pool and tennis courts? We'd bought the house because of the woods. Probably the only thing Jerry and I had agreed on unequivocally.

"Congratulations," I said, half meaning it, feeling that maybe I'd been too harsh.

Jerry dropped the packet over the hottest briquettes. It hissed. He closed the grill's lid, pulled a lawn chair up to the bench and placed a placating hand on my thigh. "Hon, Brian's going into law school and Karen's on her way to Ohio State in a month. Reuben's retainer will give us the financial security we've never had. Do you know how many cases I have to settle in a year to make fifty-thousand dollars?" I nodded, guiltily. "I thought you'd be happy. Isn't this what you wanted, for me to be under less pressure?"

"You know I do. You're almost fifty and already you have seriously high blood pressure. Your father died from a heart attack at sixty-two." I searched his eyes for understanding that I was against Reuben not him. But his mind was elsewhere.

"I've been feeling very selfish lately," I admitted. His attention returned. "We're paying out rent every month for my studio and let's be realistic, my art might not ever be worth anything. So, what if I get you off the hook?" Jerry's eyebrows lifted in skeptical curiosity. "I'll go to work for you and you can get rid of Doreen. I can learn how to sign up a case, do the court filing, and answer the phones. You'll pay me Doreen's salary and benefits and that'll really pay both of us. Then you won't need Reuben's retainer." I was so carried away by my own virtuosity and the rightness of the solution, I was already picturing myself as a professional in a conservative light grey suit, more than just the receptionist. "I think I could be a big asset."

Jerry smiled the way he did when Brian used to throw a wild pitch and it beelined into the bushes. "I'm touched that you care so much. But you wouldn't work out at the office any more than I could teach your kids art class on Saturdays. And there's the fellowship you just got that'll easily cover your expenses for a year. Your first show is coming up in New York. You've worked so hard to get it, and I want that for you. Hon, you couldn't stop making art any more than I could stop being a lawyer."

A cheer rose from the pool. The voice on the megaphone congratulated a winning swimmer. Amused by the timing, I smiled. I hadn't known until this moment that Jerry felt so deeply about my art. I had thought he put up with it because it wasn't in his nature to thwart anyone's dreams, least of all mine.

"But, I want to help," I repeated though my heart knew he was right.

"Even without Reuben we aren't in trouble like that."

"But I thought the retainer was what this is all about."

"Hon," Jerry said, searching for the right words, "What I need you to understand is that I want to take the position. I need to do something that's going to challenge me in a different direction. I'm flattered that Reuben asked me. I can't emphasize enough the excellence of the lawyers who represent him. They're the most respected legal minds in the country and I'll be sitting in on their arguments before the Supreme Court, contributing. This is the art I need to do." He smiled, astonished, as if he'd arrived at a revered destination and was going to make it his.

"The cause is one thing, but what about Reuben the man?"

"I defend murderers and rapists. You've never asked me not to represent them. And Reuben isn't a criminal; he's a businessman selling a commodity that a small but committed segment of the population doesn't approve of. I agree that Reuben shouldn't cave in because they want to put him out of business. He's the same man who always let me come back to work when I was broke, even if he didn't need me.

He's asking me for help now...."

Smoke was pouring from the grill. I went to it and lifted the lid. The packet was stuck. I picked it up with tongs and charred bits of potato slipped through the grate. Disgusted, I threw the tin foil mess on the picnic table. "The potatoes are burned. We can order pizza or go out. Karen's working, so she won't be home for dinner."

"I hope she's baby-sitting across the street so she won't need to be picked up at Baskin and Robbins."

"It's your lucky night. She is baby-sitting." I said, sullenly.

Jerry pulled me close. "Let's not fight anymore, okay?" His shirt was sticking to his back. His voice pushed for acceptance. "Hon, I have a good feeling about this."

I couldn't let myself relax in his arms. "I hope so. Really, I do."

$\sim$

By the end of the first month Jerry was at Reuben's, I'd set my reservations aside. In part, that was because the fifty-thousand dollars a year Jerry could count on freed me in a new and important way. I stopped buying cheaper student-grade oils and splurged on deeper-hued professional Windsor Newton. My painting seemed to come alive as I experimented with larger canvases. And Jerry was invigorated in a new way, though his workload had doubled and he should have been dead tired. He was juggling two full-time jobs, driving back and forth several times a day from his law office in the cast-iron Rockefeller Building at Public Square up Superior to Sovereign at East 40th Street and Kelly Avenue, a light-industrial section interspersed with run-down houses and gap-toothed lots. If he had to be in court, he scheduled around it.

As Reuben's first First Amendment coordinator, Jerry eagerly threw himself into developing the job as it went along. He came back from sitting in on a hearing in the Memphis appellate court that had been argued by one of Reuben's most venerable attorneys and pored over several legal pads filled with blue-inked notes. Even as the "fly on the wall," he said, "Being privy to First Amendment law as it was being made, excites me even more than I anticipated."

An impromptu trip sent Jerry to Miami for one day. Reuben wanted him to sit in on a trial concerning an adult video store near the Hialeah dog track. Jerry called my studio from the airport at the end of the day and gave me the news of the trial. Though they lost the trial, they were going to appeal. Jerry was pleased to learn that Reuben never wanted anyone to spend time in jail. His policy was to pay all legal fees for the accused clerk and post the money bond. But Jerry's new red Chrysler convertible wouldn't start and was being towed. The lawyer he'd traveled with would drop him off at Reuben's. Could I pick him up on the way home?

"Of course I'll pick you up," I said.

My art studio was on a floor with ten others, in a converted warehouse-factory building at 26th and Superior Avenue, equidistant from Jerry's law office and Sovereign News. I had imagined Reuben's headquarters as a strange admixture of ideals whose basis was sleaze. I pictured it plastered with lewd pinups everywhere; Reuben's office, the inner sanctum of iniquity, with lots of red, his favored porno star leaning her cleavage into him as she lit his Havana cigar and making a show out of refilling his tumbler of scotch.

The gated 'guest' parking lot was empty. Newly laid blacktop was slashed with freshly painted yellow diagonal lines that radiated an electric sizzle under the late afternoon sun. I pulled in next to the building, a nondescript, aged, beige-brick warehouse. It was strange to recognize it as having been a women's clothing outlet where I used to bargain hunt in the late seventies.

As I searched for the buzzer at the entrance, I heard a click, and the door released. I watched myself crossing the threshold in a surveillance monitor directly overhead. I was wearing paint-spattered shorts, a blue T-shirt and tennis shoes drenched in green enamel. Not exactly the image I would have chosen to meet Reuben for the first time.

Inside, the warehouse was an echoing, bare-bones concrete interior. Its expansive center housed a twenty-foot-high, maze-like barricade of pallets stacked with cargo-sized cartons filled with 'adult' merchandise. Rock music blared from somewhere. Forklifts entered and exited as if they were performing secret maneuvers. Three of them scuttled toward the shipping department at the far end, where men were loading tractor-trailers that would transport the adult payload to Reuben's stores throughout the country, as well as his other warehouse hubs in Chicago, Miami, Detroit, Houston, Los Angeles, Pittsburgh, and New York.

A lone worker, copying some information into a beat-up notebook off of a carton, directed me to the offices, which were opposite the shipping department. I climbed a rigged wooden staircase to partitioned cubicles that reminded me of a used-car dealership. I was surprised to find Jerry's office was only big enough for a worn desk and a metal-framed visitor's chair. He was on the phone, laughing at something his secretary, Doreen, had just told him, writing down the last messages of the day from the law office. He gave me a welcome grin and motioned for me to sit.

With the exception of a legal pad and one file on Jerry's desk, there was no indication he worked there. The starkness rattled me. It was so unlike him not to have anything around. His law office abounded with what he held near and dear. From floor to ceiling behind his desk were photos of the kids at every age on numerous beaches and also photos of Jerry in front of every courthouse we passed, which he insisted on taking everywhere we vacationed. Word had gotten out that Jerry's astrological sign was Leo, and after the first plaster lion was placed next to a stack of Ohio Revised Codes, clients and friends had kept them coming. Jerry's 'sign' threatened to overrun every available surface.

By the looks of his office, one would think Jerry was either the busiest or the least-organized lawyer in the world. His leather sofa was covered with files, as was his desk and coffee table. Yellow post-its with hurriedly scrawled notes denoted each file's progress. And where there weren't lions, there were golf doodads, a silver tee business-card holder next to the phone, a putter along with several other irons jumbled in a corner. On the wall was a poster-size photo of Pebble Beach, the most lauded of his twenty-five annual golf trips with Joe Sturman and two other colleagues, Bob Garfield and Alan Shapiro.

Jerry hung up the phone, looking satisfied. He swept the desk clean of the legal pad and file, put them under the contents in his briefcase, and snapped it shut. "I don't want anything here that could be confiscated or construed as evidence against me if or when there's a raid. Reuben's accountant's office was raided in Detroit and his charges for a vacation to the Cayman Islands on his personal credit card were used as evidence against him. The government alleged he was using it as a tax shelter for Reuben because Reuben opened an adult store there recently. The case got thrown out, but it cost Reuben a lot of money and time."

For a moment, I felt relieved to see that Jerry was thinking ahead defensively, protecting himself and us. But seeing my speculations of the risk he was taking by working for Reuben confirmed didn't ease the trepidation I felt. I now understood why he had been so adamant about keeping Reuben's work separate, though it made logistical sense for him to handle everything from his law practice. Disturbed, I thought Jerry was fooling himself. The prosecution authorized raids and indictments the way commercial fisherman used ghost nets, catching the minnows to snag the king salmon. They sacrificed the indefensible for the most valuable catch. Words were on my tongue, "Quit now before it's too late," but I held them back. He didn't want to hear it. All it would do was make him keep things from me, and I needed to know what was going on. Jerry had the kind of intelligence that saw the loopholes in arguments. He was prudent and not a risk taker. My heart softened; he was charged with a new air of competence. He would never do anything that would put us in jeopardy.

Before we went home, he needed to drop off some documents at Reuben's office. He pointed across the hall and said, "I'm sorry everyone in the art department's gone for the day. You'd get a kick out of meeting them. They're all artists."

"You mean porn illustrators," I said, annoyed.

"That's their job, but they all went to art school. John makes very intricate pen drawings of trains."

Jerry tapped on the door of the 'czar of pornography's' den. Reuben called out, abrupt and annoyed, "Yeah, okay." If Jerry weren't with me, I would have forgone the satisfaction of my curiosity for a more opportune time.

Inside, there was plush red carpet. I was right about that. But the walls weren't flocked, sateen, or leather but paneled a dignified dark mahogany. It was disappointingly subdued, everyman executive.

Reuben tipped back in a leather chair on the phone at a corporate desk. Chewing on an unlit cigar with a Diet Coke in one hand, he gestured for us to sit with the other. The only hint of titillation was a twenty-something exotic looking woman reclining on a tufted leather sofa. Jerry half waved but smiled familiarly, "Hi Naomi." Her lips lifted slightly at the corners but she didn't speak.

Reuben's ex-wife, Esther, had been a hardboiled transplanted New Yorker who was all business. She'd taken over managing Premium Sales after she and Reuben married and immediately tightened the reins, beginning with the installation of a time clock. When Reuben wasn't there, she clamped down on all the horsing around. But Reuben had still indulged Joe and Jerry with food, jazz, and free tickets. Jerry hadn't minded Esther. She added to Joe's and his fun, they were always finding ways to circumvent her. After the divorce, Reuben impressed Jerry by remaining devoted to Peggy, Esther's daughter from her first marriage, whom he'd adopted. Their two sons, Lee and David, now ran different divisions of the pornography business.

Reuben hung up, barely got out a clipped hello to me, and he and Jerry exchanged folders. The phone rang. Reuben scowled, told us it was important and dismissively waved for us to leave.

Heading to the stairs, I said, "I never would have known you had this cool-uncle stuff going on with this guy. With an ego that big you should never trust him."

"Gene, that's just how Rube gets when he's under a lot of pressure," Jerry said, dismissively.

We detoured around the pallets. The forklifts looked abandoned mid-job, giving the warehouse the appearance of a haphazard parking lot. Jerry pointed to a 'Cleveland Rocks' bumper sticker pasted on the back of a forklift near the loading dock. "Guess whose that is? Remember Philly Cohen?"

I shook my head. My curiosity had turned to aversion.

"You know Philly; he lived at Abel Street? Short, a little on the pudgy side. I guess that's what happens when you live across from a candy store." Jerry half laughed, amused by the memory. "He had a sister Estelle…a year older than you."

"Oh yeah, the dirty kids."

"Philly came to work for Reuben when I went to college. All those guys from Kinsman are still here. They'd never make the kind of money Reuben pays them anywhere else. They have houses in Beachwood and Pepper Pike bigger than ours. He takes good care of everybody."

"You make him sound like the Godfather."

"I guess that makes me Michael Corleone."

Jerry took the keys from me and we got into the car. "Hon, Reuben's not forcing anyone to do what they don't want to do. Right now the government's plowing millions of dollars into putting pornography out of business. But a lot of Reuben's lawyers were talking at FALA (First Amendment Lawyer's Association) about how this latest Supreme Court ruling has the Feds revving up to change tactics, and they're going to go after Reuben on taxes. That would mean the First Amendment defense would be over. It could happen tomorrow or in a year. I see my position here as temporary."

"I can only hope," I said softly.

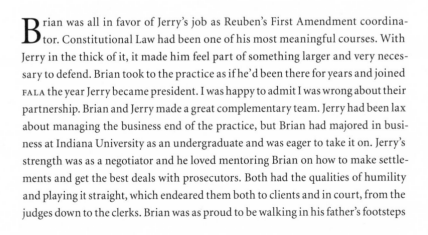

Brian was all in favor of Jerry's job as Reuben's First Amendment coordinator. Constitutional Law had been one of his most meaningful courses. With Jerry in the thick of it, it made him feel part of something larger and very necessary to defend. Brian took to the practice as if he'd been there for years and joined FALA the year Jerry became president. I was happy to admit I was wrong about their partnership. Brian and Jerry made a great complementary team. Jerry had been lax about managing the business end of the practice, but Brian had majored in business at Indiana University as an undergraduate and was eager to take it on. Jerry's strength was as a negotiator and he loved mentoring Brian on how to make settlements and get the best deals with prosecutors. Both had the qualities of humility and playing it straight, which endeared them both to clients and in court, from the judges down to the clerks. Brian was as proud to be walking in his father's footsteps as Jerry was to have him.

Two years stretched to five and Jerry and I maintained an uneasy truce. Casting only an occasional dispersion at Reuben, I slipped into the security that Jerry's position afforded and it turned out to be a blessing in disguise for Karen and me. When she graduated in June from Ohio State University as an art history major with aspirations to write, she set her heart on moving to New York. At the same time, I was about to have my first solo exhibit there. And I'd become aware that to keep the momentum of my career going, the city was where I had to be. At the end of August, Karen and I sublet a loft in SoHo, and for six week stints from September to June, the New York art season, I planned to live with her.

Jerry was thrilled to have a place in New York, too. It was the one city we'd never tired of as tourists, having gone for weekend excursions with and without the kids since Karen was born. Jerry was proud to be in a financial position to make this dream possible for his daughter and me. He continued to travel in and out of town for Reuben, and there were more trips once he became president of FALA. And although there was geographical distance between Jerry and me, it was also the most gratifying period in our marriage.

All was rolling along smoothly until, as Jerry and others had anticipated, when the government couldn't get Reuben on pornography, after ten years of trying and twenty million dollars, the IRS took over. They blitzed Reuben's enterprises with evidence-gathering raids, attempting to establish tax fraud. Reuben had married Naomi after she got pregnant with their daughter, Erica. He spent most of his time with them at their family home in California. In 1987, coincidentally, just as the First Amendment work had all but dried up, Jerry's office got the Edwards case. It was the most challenging personal-injury case of his career and would require his full-time attention. He handed Reuben his resignation. And I gave a sigh of relief.

CHAPTER THREE

THE HERRING

1991

Three years after Jerry quit working for Reuben, we had a second encounter over him in our kitchen. In the same midsummer heat, I was again getting dinner together, and Jerry came home early with a proposition from Reuben, who had called Jerry's law office that afternoon. His problems had escalated: the Feds had raided Sovereign's Cleveland headquarters and confiscated anything that smacked as evidence, from every corporate paper to newspaper clippings, ad hoc memos, and personal photos. Reuben's IRS trial was looming at the end of the year. He was grim: this was nothing like the intellectual argument defense of the First Amendment. The IRS was a whole different animal; if they wanted you, they would get you. Reuben was desperate to form Gemstone, a trust that would ensure his children's security should he go down. He asked Jerry to do him a favor: fly to Switzerland to meet with associates and his business partner, Edvard Stockli, to vouch for the legitimacy of the formation of the trust.

This time, Jerry wasn't seeking my understanding and acceptance. He'd already agreed to go to Zurich the next weekend and wanted me to come with him. He coaxed, "We'll go back to Kronenhalle. Reuben's going to pay all the expenses." Kronenhalle was a restaurant we'd discovered on vacation years earlier, and we'd had a magical night. I'd worn a white Victorian-cotton nightshirt I bought from a flea market that afternoon. We'd drunk lots of wine at the table that had been James Joyce's favorite, which thrilled me. But for Jerry, the trip stood apart from all of the others because of the appetizer he had at Kronenhalle, which were herring fillets laid out on a chilled slab of marble, with two mounds of chopped apples and onions, served with a dollop of thick sour cream.

"Flying all the way to Switzerland and flying back, getting airsick, for two days in Zurich isn't worth it. I barely managed the one-hour flight to New York."

Assuming my response meant the subject was over, Jerry turned to leave the kitchen to change.

"You know," I said, stopping him, "sticking your neck out for the First Amendment was one thing, but putting it on the chopping block to vouch for some trust is crazy. How do you know Reuben's not trying to pull a fast one on the government?"

Jerry's eyes flickered in irritation. "Because Bob Garfield worked on it. He's the tax expert and my friend! If he thought it was questionable, he would have told me."

"Yeah, but didn't he also quit?"

"That was because Bob said the work was taking too much of his firm's resources and Reuben was late in paying," Jerry said dismissively. "Look, what's it going to hurt if I can help Reuben? I understand the pressure the government is putting on him. I'm going to say I was there when Reuben wanted to form Gemstone, Alfaro in Panama did the initial work to set up the trust and Bob Garfield took over. There were problems transferring the ownership of the properties back to Reuben in order for him to get clear title and that's it."

My head swam for a moment with legalese. "At this point I don't think you have any business helping Reuben."

"Listen, hon, I just think it would be great to do something crazy. Come on, I'll make a reservation for Saturday night."

"You're going for the herring, aren't you?" I said, getting it.

"Herring at Kronenhalle…" Jerry rubbed his stomach. "Yep."

"I don't care if it's the Taj Mahal. You shouldn't go," I said, aggravated that we were even discussing Reuben and with a sense of foreboding about the folly of it all.

Jerry went the next weekend. He attended Reuben's meeting and told his brief history of Gemstone, which only took an hour, and had his herring at Kronenhalle, which was just as wonderful as the first time. The only downer, he said, was wishing I were there with him.

Then Jerry had no further contact with Reuben. Three years later, 1993, Reuben was convicted of tax evasion and sentenced to a minimum-security prison in California, though the IRS was never able to tie it in with Gemstone. Reuben was in his sixties and was looking at ten years in prison.

Though the federal government still believed Reuben was hiding his money, they had been willing to take their pound of flesh and let it rest. But Reuben ignited their fury all over again by executing an amateurish escape from prison that didn't put him on a plane to Argentina or Israel, where he would have had immunity but to an apartment close to his California home, where he was caught within a couple of months.

Jerry's explanation was that Reuben had turned a corner and finally wanted to be punished. What followed proved Jerry right. When the Feds found Reuben and brought him to trial, his behavior took an even more bizarre turn. He came up with a scheme to bribe the judge and convinced Naomi to bribe a juror with sex in exchange for a vote of not guilty. Though the juror didn't comply, the attempt, combined with Reuben's escape, got him a ticket to maximum-security prison where he would live out the rest of his life.

CHAPTER FOUR

INDICTMENT

1995

I was in New York, making the extra effort to finish the paintings for my show in April, so I could be in Cleveland for the winter, the first time in seven years of commuting back and forth from New York. It wasn't that anything had gone wrong or was particularly worrisome, but I'd been detecting a plaintive quality in Jerry's voice when we'd recap each day on the phone. Often he was too tired or uninspired to go into anything of substance but just satisfied the minimum check-in. My intuition told me that perhaps our being apart was getting to him. I was glad that we were leaving with Karen and Alex the next morning for Lake Placid, treating them to four days of cross-country skiing between Christmas and New Year's.

Jerry arrived at our New York apartment looking worn-out. In the six weeks since I'd last seen him, his fifty-eight years seemed to have caught up with him. He was puffy eyed, and I was surprised to see that he'd gained weight, something he'd always been careful about. I wondered if he had suspended his weekly tennis games and was snacking too much. He had called December 'lawyer-hell month,' the season when he was always rushed by year-end settlements. But this year, he was also preparing for the unusual confluence of three back-to-back trials beginning the first of the year. The velour pullover I'd bought for him the last time we'd been together, at Thanksgiving, had had plenty of room to spare, but now stretched over a paunch. I vowed to cook healthfully when I got back home as I helped him unload the elevator of all of the ski paraphernalia he'd brought from home for the trip. Cross-country skis, boots, bags of sweaters, my parka, and his duffle and briefcase filled most of our apartment's 600 square foot living area.

Our first day on the trail, we were out from sunrise and stopped only for a quick lunch at the ski chalet. Our muscles rebelled around 4:30, so we called it a day and headed to the car, ravenous. Jerry thumped his chest like Tarzan, flushed and beaming from exertion. "You're looking at a new, improved man. I needed this," he flashed me a grateful smile.

We gave ourselves an hour to shower before heading out for an early dinner at a four-star restaurant that the bell-captain had recommended to Jerry.

I gave Jerry first dibs in the shower and volunteered to take out the dog. Alone at dusk in the hush of full-blown winter, I felt more peaceful and content than I had in a long time. Macabee tugged at the leash, yelping to be set free. It hadn't been easy to find a lodge that allowed pets. My dog loved snow. Feeling sorry I had penned him up in the room all day, I gave in and let him go free. His ten pounds of jet black fur, like smoke shot from a cannon, streaked through the powder, reminding me of the release and excitement I felt every time I went back to New York.

My mother had disapproved of my idea to commute from Cleveland, when I told her my plan at lunch. That day, Jerry was going to pick me up to take a late-afternoon flight to New York. We were going to spend the weekend together, then I would stay on in New York for six weeks: our new routine. Jerry had consulted a headhunter to look into the possibility of getting a position at a New York firm and had been told to forget it unless he could promise a minimum yearly billing of a hundred thousand dollars: a sheer impossibility. He had also batted around the idea of becoming a public defender but soon dropped it. We accepted that we'd live with the commute: he'd come to New York for a weekend or two every month and we'd make daily phone calls.

My mother's waning lung capacity had been steadily sapping more and more of her ability to get around on her own. The steroids she was on, so vital for her breathing, were wreaking havoc, weakening her bones and making them brittle. She had become so shrunken and fragile, I was afraid to hug her. Merely bending down to pick up her robe off the floor had cracked her rib and she was in terrible pain. Her mind, though, seemed to be compensating for her declining health, becoming sharper than ever, and I was grateful for that.

At lunch, she'd taken enough pain pills to make it into the kitchen. We ate crackers, hers with thin slices of salami and mine with cheese. She was in a particularly empowered mood and as I poured us coffee, she let fly the accusations she had been harboring: Didn't I realize that I was neglecting Jerry by taking advantage of his wanting me to be happy? Hadn't I grown up seeing how much she had struggled? If only she could have had what I had: a husband who was a successful lawyer, respected by everyone who knew him. Everybody loved Jerry. Neither the children nor I wanted for anything. How could I be so selfish? She claimed solace that my father, already taken by lung cancer, had been spared seeing what I was doing to my marriage. She saw nothing wrong in art as a hobby, even having a studio downtown, but running to New York like a yo-yo was irresponsible, asking for trouble. It was only a matter of time before my life would be out of control. Did I have any idea what would happen to me if I lost everything?

She had intimated some of this before, but now I felt as if I were under a burning spotlight. Her breath rattled in her chest. And though I hated myself for pushing her further, I asked, "Are you insinuating that I'm driving Jerry to cheat on me?"

"No," her eyes played coyly on my face, "but you're making it convenient."

"Mother, if that's what he's looking for, my being in Cleveland or in New York isn't going to stop him." My tone was bratty, something I'd never have braved as a kid. "Look at the statistics. What is it, half the marriages end in divorce? I'm sure the reason isn't because of wives commuting out of town to work." I was angry with her for forcing me to defend my life and at myself for falling so short of her understanding and approval.

"You can look at statistics all you want," she said. "I'm looking at you. You make choices in your life, and they have consequences. You're handing Jerry freedom on a silver platter."

"Good! I believe in freedom. It's even better then that he's chosen me."

She pressed her lips tight and concentrated for a moment on rearranging some crumbs next to her plate. She was wheezing but her iron will persisted. "You're too arrogant to see that you have to guard freedom or it's taken away from you."

I felt we were at a stalemate. "You don't understand."

Her eyes penetrated through me. "I understand plenty."

After that lunch, I continued to commute a dozen or more times over the next two years, but we never spoke about it again.

The dog had become a dot in the distance. I clapped my gloved hands and yelled, "Macabee, come!" but he kept going. I should have never let him off the leash. I yelled again, and he stopped, deliberated, then made a slick turn back. "Good boy, good boy," I encouraged, as he bounded back and plopped next to me. "Close call, buddy." I scratched the top of his head. He had left a wake of calligraphy in the snow. I thought of the unwritten, the unspoken: Jerry's and my togetherness. No matter what our differences, how my art life and his practice had sent us on different tracks, nothing had and nothing could break our bond. I wished my mother were alive so that I could tell her this now.

The sun suddenly dipped below the mountain, and just as suddenly the afterglow from skiing was gone with it. Where I had been too warm most of the day, now my sweaty clothes felt damp and icy.

I came into the room ready to jump in a hot shower, hoping Jerry was still in it. But he was on the phone, a towel wrapped around his expanded middle. The hairs on his legs were slick and wet. His feet bled two wet footprints on the carpet. This was so typical of him. His idea of being away from the office was to call twice a day for messages and return all of them. I impatiently motioned him to hurry it along, but then I noticed that something else was going on. His shoulders that had lifted with renewed vigor after skiing were slumped down and forward, and his high color took on a purplish tinge, the flush of anxiety. My heart quickened, I mouthed, "What happened?"

Jerry shook his head. I couldn't tell if he meant I was interrupting an important call from a client, or that something terrible had happened to one of the kids. I watched him, afraid to move. He pressed the phone tightly to his ear, as if he were trying to prevent what he was hearing from escaping. He said, "No, I think I'm just so shocked. I can't believe it."

I shivered. Although it was supposed to be a nonsmoking room, an undercurrent of stale cigarette smoke assaulted my nose. Jerry had drawn down the bedspread and propped the pillows against the headboard the way he always did when he wanted to catch a score on TV before he showered. An uncorked bottle of Merlot was on the dresser with two water glasses next to it.

Jerry placed the phone down carefully and, with his head down, continued regarding it. When he looked up, his eyes were dulled with a gravity I had never seen before. "That was Louie Serkin," he said.

"I thought someone had died," I said, pulling my arms out of my sweater. "What could be so earth shattering that he had to call you here?" I asked, angrily, as I continued to inch the sweater over my head, trying not to smell the damp wool.

Jerry's voice was muffled, "Louie got word that I'm going to be indicted by a grand jury."

I dropped the sweater to the floor. I couldn't have heard him correctly. "You mean another rumor's floating around?"

Jerry's mouth tightened. "This time it's not a rumor. Louie heard it from a prosecutor. An indictment's coming down."

"But you said at Thanksgiving nothing would happen: the Feds were just stabbing in the dark and pointing fingers everywhere."

"I know, but now they've stopped at me."

"What are they saying you did?" I asked, belligerently. It seemed as remotely possible as him being picked out of a lineup as a serial killer.

Jerry rubbed his eyes. "Louie didn't have any details."

"Well, the prosecutors have obviously made a mistake. You haven't worked for Reuben in…." I began to calculate.

"Seven years," he said flatly.

"But, Reuben's in some prison in California, isn't he?" Jerry nodded. I reached for his royal blue velour robe he'd thrown over the back of a chair and wrapped myself in it. "This is just crazy."

"It is, but unfortunately it's true."

My mind ran to a safe corner where Jerry took clients through legal mazes and brought them safely through all the time. "Okay, so when is this supposed to happen?"

"After the first."

"Well, you'll have to get a continuance. You're starting the Keane trial on the first."

Jerry sat on the edge of the bed and rubbed his day's stubble of beard, then cupped his chin in his hands and closed his eyes. His words came slow and foggy as if he were talking in his sleep, "My beard was up so nice from the steam…I just stepped out of the shower when the phone rang." He looked up at me. All I could see were his eyes, as if he were calling for help from deep inside a well. His voice was strained, "Gene, there are no continuances for indictments."

"But you get continuances all of the time."

"Actually it's an arraignment," he rubbed his eyes as if they hurt, "really a formality. The grand jury is a rubber stamp for the prosecution. The accused pleads guilty or not guilty and the judge sets bond, or if the crime is serious, the person's put in jail pending trial. The accused assumes the burden of proving his innocence. That's the beginning and end for a lot of people." His brows knit together as if his words had struck him. "I feel so thrown because I can't imagine what they think they have against me."

I pulled Jerry's robe tighter, chilled to the bone. I needed a hot shower.

"Think."

"Gene, what do you want from me? I don't know, okay?" He aimed the remote at the TV.

"Jer, how serious can it be if you don't know what you've done?"

Hockey scores blared as Jerry watched the screen.

I blared louder, "How can you care about some stupid scores?"

Jerry turned around and faced me. "How come you can't understand that being a lawyer is who I am? Any charge against me can ruin me. No matter what the outcome, this is serious."

I slid my hands up the opposite sleeves and grasped my forearms. "It's like a deep freeze in here."

The phone rang and we both looked at it. After three rings, I was the one who picked it up. "We're ready," Karen piped energetically, "should we pick you up?"

"Not yet. I have to shower."

"Mother, we're starving. This is no time to be frisky."

I looked at Jerry. His color had drained. He looked pasty, as if he'd gotten sick. "I wish. Listen, give us a half an hour, okay?"

I took the shower's hot spray full on my face, trying to reign in the onslaught of unknowns, until the water went cold. Stepping out of the tub, I heard Karen in the next room. "Dad, it's an inferno in here."

"Mom was cold," Jerry said.

"You look kind of pale. Are you all right?"

I dried quickly and wrapped myself in a fresh towel, grabbed some tissue and wiped a clearing on the weepy mirror.

"I'm fine. It's just that I got some disturbing news," Jerry said, downplaying, as he reiterated the phone call. When he was finished, he added, "I'm just a little thrown because I never thought it would happen. It's so unexpected."

"Unexpected! It's like a bomb," Karen's voice surged. In the mirror, my eyes stared back at me, glassy green. I was stricken by my responsibility. Jerry should have never taken the retainer with Reuben in the first place. I should have stopped him. "Dad, what are you being accused of?"

"Louie just said something to do with Reuben."

"Wait a minute. Who's Louie?"

"Remember Mapplethorpe's pornography case at the Cincinnati Art Museum? Louie won it in the Supreme Court."

"So, how does he know what's going on with the grand jury?"

"A prosecutor told him."

"But the prosecutor didn't tell him what the crime is?"

"Look Kare," Jerry paused, "all I know is that the government still believes that Reuben's got money hidden somewhere. And they've been prosecuting people associated with Reuben, like his accountants. They are hell-bent on recovering it. They haven't come up with any winners so far and I think they're very frustrated. And they have to justify all the money it's costing the government. All we can do right now is wait to find out."

By now I'd finished applying my makeup. My face, blushed and eye shadowed, looked reassuringly like the one I always put on for the public. I had my hand on the doorknob when Karen's voice stopped me, "Know what I think? I think Reuben cut a deal with the prosecutor and made you his scapegoat. Isn't that what happens?"

"I'm the last one he'd use. Reuben wouldn't set me up."

"How do you know? Maybe he's looking for parole. He is a pornographer," her voice spiraled angrily, "who knows what he'd do to save himself?"

"Reuben isn't in a position to deal unless he forks over the money they say that he has. He did himself in when he escaped from minimum security, and then Naomi was caught trying to bribe a juror. When I knew him, he believed in fighting the law using the judicial system and he wasn't a bad man. But, sadly, he's become everything the government said. He's seventy-three and he is going to die doing hard time. I feel sorry for him."

"It seems to me it's time to start feeling sorry for yourself, Dad. The guy's scum. Or, maybe it's a ploy by the Feds to scare off the lawyers who represent pornographers." I came out of the bathroom. The same thought had just flickered through my mind. I locked my eyes with my daughter's hard-edged blue eyes.

"Well, I can see how this is a very political issue," Alex said. "I think someone's running for senator."

I took our coats out of the closet. "I think Alex is right. The Feds just want to make their political point. They don't want you, Jer," I looked at Jerry, whose color had begun to return. "Nothing's going to come of this. I can feel it," I said.

"Mom's instincts are usually right," Jerry said, with renewed energy. "I'll talk to Brian tomorrow. We'll file to have the indictment dismissed on the grounds of speculative evidence. I was Reuben's First Amendment coordinator. I wasn't his lawyer." Jerry held open my coat and kept his hands on my shoulders as I zipped it up. "But let's not talk about it anymore tonight. We're going out for a great dinner."

The Monday after New Year's Jerry delivered his opening statement at the Keane trial. At lunch recess, he walked up Superior Avenue to his own arraignment in Federal Court. He had sloughed off my request to go with him, saying it was only a formality, that nothing would happen. Too anxious to paint, I watched the clock in my studio, berating myself for not insisting on going. Karen called, hoping to hear what happened before she got tied up in a meeting at the talent agency where she was a junior agent.

My studio opened into an entry space where the artists on the floor hung paintings. I sat on a peeling leather sofa, claimed from a dumpster, doodling on some scrap paper, waiting for Jerry's call. The relic of an elevator was still run by an operator, John, one of Jerry's long-time clients. The inner chain door had clanged open and shut so many times, at first I didn't cue into who John was talking to when I heard him say, "I got in an accident this weekend. Nothing too serious. But my wife's back is hurting. I'll give you a call next week."

The bell trilled. I startled and ran to open the door. Jerry smiled but his eyes were somber. He carried his briefcase in one hand and a brown bag in the other.

I pulled up two paint-splattered, plaster-flecked school desks, also dumpster finds, and set out the lunch he'd picked up. "Was the indictment so bad that you needed a Slyman's corned beef?" I asked, while keeping my eyes on my lunch, tuna on rye with lots of mayo.

He bit into his sandwich, chewed, then swallowed. "It was pretty hard being the one charged...." He sipped cream soda from the can, took another bite, and opened the briefcase that he'd placed on the floor next to the desk. He pulled the indictment out. "My charge is co-conspirator." He proceeded to read: "Attempting to conspire to impede the collection of taxes of Reuben Sturman from the IRS." He paused, "So there it is. They're lumping me with Reuben's partner in Zurich, Edvard Stockli, and his attorney from Panama, Heratio Alfaro. It's all about Gemstone, the trust Reuben was trying to establish for his kids...and Gemstone was perfectly legal...." Jerry paused, processing the impact of the information. "Okay, and here's the thing that was like being hit in the stomach. Mel Ginsberg would have been the third co-conspirator, but he turned witness for the prosecution."

"Wasn't he your replacement after you stopped working for Reuben?"

"Not exactly. Reuben had become obsessed with finding a lawyer to collect rents from his stores and to complete the transfer of his properties into Gemstone. I knew Ginsberg wasn't doing very well, so I had occasionally referred collection clients to him. I recommended him for the job. Everyone who had the opportunity to work for Reuben thought they were falling into a pot of gold, so Ginsberg was thrilled to take it. But he was in way over his head from the beginning. Remember how he used to call me constantly, asking questions."

"How could I forget? He drove me crazy, calling you at home all the time." I stared out the window, behind Jerry, where a freighter was out on Lake Erie's horizon, moving so slowly it looked immobile. I wanted to push it forward.

"Well, he's more than a nuisance now. He's given me to the Feds in exchange for immunity and probation," as Jerry said this, his eyes fixed on a ragged red area on my painting, a kind of misshapen target. I was too appalled to respond. He added, more to himself, "He must have been pretty scared."

"Scared. I'd like to show him what scared is." I kicked loose a hardened lump of plaster on the floor, picked it up, and threw it at cardboard stacked against the wall. It hit short but slid under, a fast, clean getaway.

"You know, anyone can be a conspirator and not know it." Jerry's voice was frighteningly hollow. "My client, Juanita Thomas...all she did was take phone messages. But drugs were in the house when it was raided, and she's doing ten years in the Ohio Pen." Jerry opened his arms wide in a gesture of surrender, then playing it off, he slipped the indictment back in the briefcase.

Prickles of fear skittered up the side of my face. "Are you saying you could get ten years?"

"No...Actually, I want you to know that I feel better. It's a little worse than I expected but we're going to straighten it out." Jerry dug into the other half of his sandwich, and I unwrapped mine. Tuna seeped out from under soggy lettuce. It was a mess. I let it sit. The freighter on Lake Erie had barely made it to the next window bay.

"At least I know what I'm up against." Jerry wiped mustard from his thumb. "No matter what Ginsberg says, there has to be evidence to back up the indictment and there isn't any. The shock is still sinking in. But we're going to be fine."

"Fine," I repeated, grasping it as if it were a lifeline that had been snapped in two, Jerry and I at the shorter end. Strength infused his voice, "But, you know, it felt good to look the judge in the eyes and plead not guilty. He released me on a five-thousand-dollar personal bond. That's good."

After Jerry left, I called Karen, but she wasn't back from her meeting. Brian was in court and also unreachable. I rambled up and down the hall, needing to talk through the anxiety contracting and expanding inside my chest, hoping my one studio confidant, Margaret, would show up. Out of ten artist studios, I was the only one there. Like the freighter inching on the horizon, the judicial system was a world onto itself and I knew this was going to be an agonizingly long haul.

The kids were over for dinner. Jerry and Brian wanted to discuss Jerry's defense away from the office. The court had denied Jerry's petition to overturn the indictment. As if they'd expected it, Jerry and Brian took it in stride. I, on the other hand, had hoped for a miracle and felt let down all week.

I noted the picked-over dinner plates. No one had much of an appetite but Jerry, who had overeaten and was now pouring himself a second glass of wine. Brian, sitting next to Andrew, was waving half a grilled cheese sandwich in his son's face. "You're not getting down to play with Macabee until you eat one more bite," he said, as if his fatherhood depended on it.

Alison wriggled on Brian's lap, demanding, "Down."

Tension bounced off all of us. Brian finally gave up, "Okay, both of you go play." Andrew's booster seat clattered to the floor in his rush to catch the dog. Alison whipped after them both, screaming.

Out the oversized picture window, I watched the bright jacket of a child coasting down whatever snow was left on the hill at Thornton Park, slivering past the jagged spaces in the bare woods. It couldn't have been only two weeks since we were at Lake Placid. Ohio was in the throes of a thaw. Soot flecked the last of the snow that had drifted up along the layered flagstone edging of the terraced lawn.

Cindy snatched up a protesting Alison, saying she had to change her diaper.

With two kids under three, she was going to feel the brunt of the disruption. Cindy was a private person who shrank from the limelight, and it was inevitable that Jerry would make the paper. Anything about Reuben was fodder for a front-page headline. There would be no place to hide from the focus of that kind of spotlight. The buzz about Jerry's case was already out, a word-of-mouth brush fire. Cindy had been an elementary-school teacher but had stayed home since Andrew was born. Our security was intertwined. A splinter of pain caught in my chest as I realized the penalty my daughter-in-law was going to pay for having married into our family, the family she had taken for granted. It was supposed to be the secure, professional, upper-middle-class lifestyle she had hoped for. The law practice was bound to lose clients and its high regard among colleagues in and out of court. Jerry was right. Even if the charges were dropped, the damage could be considerable.

Having changed Alison, Cindy sat with her on the couch cajoling an interest in Dr. Seuss. "Look Ali," she said, wedging her daughter in, "Fox in sox and sox in box...." Alison kicked a wiry leg and wound a strand of her mother's long brown hair around her finger, engaged for the time being. Anyone watching would envy us, a typical happy family together on a Sunday afternoon. I felt as if someone were watching and knew the truth. I began to stack the plates, needing to do something useful.

Whenever Jerry and Brian talked about cases together they shared a collabora-tive closeness beyond that of partners, they used shortcuts of expression, gestures: the intuitive knowing between father and son. "I've been talking with Louie and he was very positive. He's really fired up. He doesn't think the government has a case against me. All they could have as evidence is a paper trail of the legitimate work I did as Reuben's coordinator. Louie knows what I did for Reuben. He wants to try the case and he has complete confidence we'll win." Jerry excitedly caught my eye. "Someone has to stop the government from railroading freedom of speech through the back door of the judicial system. I'm thinking Louie should represent me." I felt a sense of expanse. This was about democratic freedom.

Brian's eyes widened as if a car were barreling toward him. "Dad, I thought we decided you were hiring Messerman. He's the biggest gun federal defender around and Louie's inaccessible. He's in Cincinnati."

"That's why I wanted you to come over. After the deposition yesterday, I met with Messerman." Brian's brows furrowed like Jerry's. "Here's the picture. First of all Messerman runs his own ship. I would be his client, period. He wouldn't allow us to be involved in my defense. His fee is one hundred thousand dollars minimum; that's without going to trial. You know I don't have that kind of money. But the most crucial thing is he prefers to negotiate deals. He wants me to change my plea to guilty, and he practically guaranteed that if I give the prosecution someone, he could get them to agree to the same deal as Ginsberg. I told him I don't have anyone to give, but he said, 'It's obvious Reuben got his hands dirty. There's always someone to give.' I told him, 'Brian and I want to be involved and I've thought about it. I still don't have anyone to incriminate and I can't plead guilty.' Messerman shook my hand, wished me luck, and said if I changed my mind I shouldn't hesitate to call. Now, on the other hand, Louie indicated that his fee would be around thirty-five thousand dollars, and he's eager to have both of us work with him as part of the defense team. You'd be an attorney of record."

"I definitely think it's important for me to be an attorney of record," Brian nodded, "and without a doubt we should work on it. Who cares more than us, or knows more than you?" Fight was in his eyes. "I also agree that you shouldn't plead guilty. It would be the end of…you'd get automatic disbarment. We'll all go down. I guess," Brian faltered, "it seems Louie is the best choice." Andrew climbed onto his lap. Brian kissed the top of his son's honey brown hair as Andrew picked up a roll and he spread butter over it. "I hope we're making the right decision. Messerman…" Prone to vacillation, Brian could rehash pros and cons for days.

Jerry cut in, "Maybe this will help you feel better. Just wait a minute." He left the table and went into the den.

"What do you think, Mom?" Brian's eyes searched my face.

It felt as if a large stone lodged inside my chest. "Well, Dad and I talked about it for a long time last night. And under no circumstances do I want him to plead guilty. *A*, I can't imagine he'll lose. *B*, we need a lawyer who gets it. And Louie does…."

Jerry came back and set a legal pad on the table before Brian. Leaning over his shoulder, he said, "Last night I worked on priorities. Right now, it's crucial that we petition the court to get my trial separated from Alfaro's. He's also pleading not guilty. I agree with Louie that it's too risky for a jury to hear both Alfaro's and my case as one. It'll be too complicated for them to keep the evidence straight, and there's the issue of Alfaro's AIDS. I feel badly even alleging this in the complaint but the aspect of AIDS as a sexually transmitted disease and that Reuben was a pornographer…it's no stretch that it could backlash on us."

For the first time Cindy entered the conversation, "Was his AIDS transmitted homosexually?" She asked markedly, but her expression was unreadable. I wondered what else she was thinking.

"No, and it's so ironic. He came from Panama to Miami for heart surgery and was infected by a blood transfusion. When he returned to Miami for treatment, that's when the Feds nabbed him and he was indicted. What a double whammy. The Feds wouldn't even let him post bond to go home. He's been wearing electronic bracelets and kept under house arrest for the past six months in an apartment in Miami. They're transferring him here for the trial, and his disease is in the terminal stage. I feel so bad for him. He's spending the last days of his life separated from his family and country."

Feeling the impact of this travesty, I grasped the edge of the table. "What possible outcome could the Feds expect from a jury trial that could be worse than what they have already inflicted on that poor man? He's already facing a death sentence." Then, I met Cindy's eyes above Alison's head on her shoulder. "What do you think about Brian being on the defense team? It'll mean even less time that he'll be home."

"It's up to Brian." Cindy said, rubbing Alison's back. "I know how much he wants to, and Jerry would do it for him."

"I want to push it through as fast as possible," Jerry said.

"The faster it's behind us, the better," Brian agreed.

"My goal is for it to be over by Mom's opening, and that's in four months." Jerry cut a wedge of apple cookie pie and motioned for Brian to come with him into the den. "Let's see how the Browns are doing."

I thought of Jerry telling Karen and Alex about the indictment in the hotel room and my intuitive reaction that nothing was going to come of this. Here were Jerry and Brian going to sock into the Browns game like any other Sunday. They weren't treating Jerry's case differently from any other serious case they brainstormed over. The heaviness inside my head lifted.

R euben had hired Alfaro to establish Gemstone in Panama as a blind trust for his children. Alfaro worked on it over a year but was never able to form the trust because of complications with the transfer of Reuben's properties. The court denied Jerry's petition to grant a separation of Alfaro and his trials based on a simple conclusion: co-conspirators, co-trials. Jerry was disappointed but still hoped Alfaro's lawyers would file their own petition and the court would allow him to go home to Panama to die.

Meanwhile, for weeks Louie and Jerry, Brian, and other assistants were locked in the prosecutors' offices in downtown Cleveland as they sifted through hundreds of file boxes of the government's alleged evidence, confiscated from Reuben's headquarters, stores, and warehouses around the country. They hoped to cull from the tax forms, old trial testimonies, personal papers, and documents the evidence that the government claimed would find Jerry guilty. Most crucial was to find the memo Jerry had sent to Mel Ginsberg that the government declared Jerry's "battle plan" and was alleged to prove that he was the "mastermind" of the conspiracy.

Three weeks into the search, they found the dreaded memo. Jerry barely remembered writing it but recalled his intention was to help Ginsberg understand by describing the situation as he saw it. Jerry had warned him not to proceed with the transference of the properties, considering Reuben's precarious situation. With this laid out for Ginsberg on paper, Jerry hoped to put an end to Ginsberg's barrage of phone calls asking him for help.

After combing the memo for its damning evidence, Jerry came home elated. "There's nothing in it that I wouldn't say again. If this was what they're calling my "battle plan," there was no army or artillery."

But there was another smoking gun: Bob Garfield, one of the foursome on Jerry's annual golf trips, who Jerry regarded as his best friend. Joe Sturman had introduced them shortly after Bob and his wife moved back to Cleveland, Bob's hometown. He had worked for the IRS in Washington, DC, and established a law career, specializing in estate and tax law. By the time of Jerry's indictment, he had lunched regularly with Bob for thirty years. Often, Bob had confided money problems. He and his wife lived beyond their means: they belonged to the best country club, lived in the wealthiest neighborhood, and had all that was required to sustain a high-end lifestyle. Jerry always said Bob was intelligent with a great sense of humor and was a devoted friend. Initially, Jerry and I had seen the Sturmans and Garfields socially, but as I had become more and more serious about my art, I'd withdrawn. Bob's status seeking turned me off. His wasn't a friendship I shared with Jerry.

A week after Jerry hired Louie, he met Bob for lunch. Bob was panicky, saying he'd been called to testify before the grand jury. The prosecutor had given him an ultimatum: either Bob would be indicted for conspiracy or he could opt to be a witness for the prosecution and testify against Jerry. Bob was terrified. He said he couldn't risk going to prison; he wouldn't be able to take it. All the prosecutor wanted him to say was that Jerry was Reuben's 'point man.' He wanted Jerry to understand that he had no choice but to do it.

If I was outraged over Ginsberg, I blew up over Garfield. "'Point man!' He's linking you directly to Reuben as next in command, the one calling the shots. And what does he mean he has no choice?"

"He's scared, Gene. I'm scared too. I've had clients willing to turn in their brothers to stay out of prison," Jerry said.

"Okay, so people sell their souls all the time. But Garfield had a choice! He chose to testify against you, his best friend." My voice was derisive, condemning. I clenched my fists. "I would never turn in Debby, my best friend, to save my skin. I wouldn't be able to live with myself. I hope Garfield's conscience kills him, but then he probably doesn't have one. You could have hired Messerman and coughed someone up. But you didn't!"

"First of all Gene, I don't know what went on after I left Reuben, and I don't know that Reuben hid any money. I became suspicious of Gemstone at a meeting in California, but that's all, and I wasn't working for Reuben then. I think Reuben was tapped dry. The store owners had gone on a feeding frenzy, stealing from him after he was indicted on tax fraud. They have yachts, homes all over the globe. Second, I would have to plead guilty to make a deal and I can't do that. I'd have my license taken away and most likely it wouldn't be reinstated. That would be worse than going to prison."

"Your friend Garfield doesn't think so, the bastard. You better have told him, no more whining to you over lunches about having to give up his precious country club."

Jerry twirled his wedding band around his ring finger and my heart wrenched.

I felt as if we were being torn apart by a force too large to reckon with. "I don't bear your animosity toward him," he said.

"What do you bear?" I asked, angrily, wanting him to stop being fair for once and see my side.

"He's a coward, and what's worse, he knows it." Jerry's mouth pulled grim. "I pity him."

"Think of the weight a testimony against a best friend will have."

"Gene, I'm upset too. But we'll make sure the jury knows that Bob's testimony hinges on a plea bargain. We'll neutralize it."

April 17, the Sunday night before the trial, Jerry, Louie, Jerry Hirschorn, a jury selection specialist we had hired on Louie's recommendation, and I went to see Heratio Alfaro where he was confined at a Marriott Hotel not far from our house.

His Panamanian attorney led us into a sitting room, saying, "Heratio is very weak from the flight from Miami. He needs to rest a little longer. I hope you understand." Jerry offered to return in an hour, but the attorney said, "No, no. Let us begin in the meantime without him."

The atmosphere was somber. We lowered our voices as if we were in a hospital. Alfaro feebly entered the room, leaning heavily on a cane. He struggled into a chair prepared with pillows and sunk in. He was emaciated, his dark skin hung from his prominent bones, a regal but dying bird. His silk shirt and wool trousers, also loose, were simply cut and elegantly tailored. It took several minutes for him to gather enough strength to speak. He first asked his nurse to order food and drink for his guests, as if we were visiting dignitaries. After he made sure we were served coffee, pastries, and fruit, his voice gathered some strength and he rasped, "The government offered me probation if I would plead guilty, but I refused. How could I die and leave this blot of disgrace on my family? If I must stand trial, and should I be found guilty, they could still hold their heads up with dignity; with the knowledge, you see, that I had fought for the family's good name."

"I understand. I feel the same," Jerry said, so softly the quiet in the room deepened. "I was the first in my family to go to college. When I became a lawyer, it was as if I became a king in my family's eyes. It would be a betrayal of their pride to plead guilty."

Alfaro and Jerry regarded each other warmly. It was as if the rest of us weren't there. Alfaro wiped his forehead with a handkerchief. His breathing was labored. He said weakly, "I have petitioned the court for a continuance to be allowed to go home until I am physically able to stand trial."

His attorney nodded at Alfaro and asked "May I?" Alfaro nodded. His attorney continued for him, "We have received an answer from the court. Before it will agree to rule, it requires that Heratio undergo a medical examination by their doctors to confirm his incapacity."

"I'm so sorry," Jerry said.

"We are, as well. Delays at this time are critical. The government already possesses Heratio's records, including prior examinations by their doctors. But we hope for tomorrow. Perhaps the judge will have a change of heart."

Despite our empathy, we needed Heratio's petition to be granted.

CHAPTER FIVE

TRIAL BEGINS

1995

It was a brittle sunny April morning. We pulled into the nearly empty underground parking garage of the Sixteenth Circuit Federal Courthouse in Akron, Ohio, an hour early. We hadn't spoken much during the forty-minute drive. I was seized by worry that I didn't want to transmit to Jerry, who'd wandered through the house most of the night worried about the judge's decision to grant the postponement of Alfaro's trial.

Last night, after seeing Alfaro, Louie had made an offhand remark, "Tomorrow morning's the biggest hurdle. The judge has to grant separation of the trials. A not guilty verdict is all in his hands." After we got home, an attorney friend called, trying to convince Jerry that it wasn't too late; he should plead it out and make a deal. It would have been like calling off our wedding, Jerry's decision was that inviolable. He said he came from people like the ones who would make up his jury: humble, working people, many who would be skeptics of the IRS. He believed they would see through the testimonies of the plea-bargained witnesses. By morning, though bleary eyed, he was charged and ready to go.

I got out of the car and searched for Brian's car. He and Jerry planned to meet up with the defense team for last-minute prepping, but he hadn't arrived yet. I felt an intense need to see my son; I could tell him how nervous I was and that I wished Karen were with me. Jerry was humiliated to be on trial. He'd talked to Karen, his brother, his only remaining but favorite uncle, Louie, and several close friends out of coming, insisting the testimony would be dry tax stuff. He promised to report in every night by phone. My eyes met his over the roof of the car and the automatic electric door locks clicked ominously. His expression said this is it. Inside the building, we kissed good luck and Jerry went off to find his defense team.

I stepped into the courtroom waiting area, which was ringed with chairs around faded grey, stained carpet. It felt too conspicuous to sit there. When I had passed the coffee cart by the newsstand, the smell had turned my stomach, so going down to the commissary for the hour wait was out. With nowhere else to go, I pushed tentatively at the courtroom door and it swung open. I hesitated, fearful of breaking some rule and looked around for someone who might give me permission.

But I was alone in silence so resounding, it was as though I had entered the government's church. A center aisle divided sleek glossy benches. The prosecutor's table was on the left and the defendant's table on the right. Our table, I thought, but it felt so remote as to be impossible. A burnished gold seal of Ohio beamed out over the raised judge's bench, and two huge flags, the American and the state of Ohio's patriotically rippled from the air coming out of a vent. In religion the presumption of sin prevails. Here, the courtroom proclaimed guilt. Its power emanated like heat waves. I had observed all this with a strange detachment. I wondered if, now that the day was here, I was numb. I decided to sit in the tenth row on the side of the defendant's table, a few spaces in, distant, but close enough to sense what was going on.

Remarkably, I'd only been in a courtroom one other time, shortly after Jerry passed the bar, maybe his second trial. It was in East Cleveland, a dingy, chaotic municipal court that had overflowed with noisy, downtrodden people, howling babies, and young children. Jerry had been so eager and clean-cut in his new and only 'trial suit.' He'd rushed from his client to bailiff to prosecutor as if he were competing in legal Olympics and justice was the gold medal. As a junior lawyer, his boss had thrown this and other early trials to him as 'losers' to learn from. I tried to remember if he'd won in East Cleveland. It wasn't likely, but it bothered me that I couldn't remember. It was just as well I hadn't attended any of the others. Jerry said he became too self-conscious having me there, and I didn't have the temperament for it either. I found I had to clamp down on my natural inclination to second-guess every word, gesture, and pause.

Soon, people started rustling in. Several, in a group, noted me, and took places on the prosecutor's side. They whispered to each other in profile. I shifted uncomfortably, feeling like the enemy. Everyone wore suits, including the women. This morning I had pulled out the most conservative clothes I owned: navy blue pants, the material too loose and flowing, the short-sleeved print blouse bared my arms, and with my choppy, short haircut, the first impression I must be making was too offbeat. I felt wrong. How could I have not thought of it? Jerry hadn't said anything, either. But little slips could add up. I pulled at a hangnail. Tonight I would go and buy court clothes.

Our defense team filed in, exuding the confidence of a well-equipped infantry.

Jerry's shoulders were back and his head tall; he emitted an aura of warmth and compassion that drew people in. You'd never guess he was the defendant. As he passed, he extended his hand to me. I detected a glint of fear in his eyes.

He took his place at the defense table. The attorneys were performing a pantomime. Like surgeons laying out instruments, they angled opened briefcases just so and positioned papers, legal pads, and manila folders in horizontal order.

Brian left the defense table and slid in next to me, patting my shoulder. "How ya doing, Mom?"

"Okay. Nervous. My hands are freezing." I touched his cheek. "I didn't expect to be so nervous."

"I talked to Karen last night. Now that the trial is beginning, she was so upset about not coming she was ready to get on a plane."

"I know. We must have talked to her right after you. Dad reassured her that it'll be over by Thursday, and we'll be with her in New York on Friday for my opening. So that calmed her down. But, right now, I'd airlift her out here if I could."

Off to the side, behind the bench, the door to the judge's chambers opened. Alfaro's lawyer pushed him out in a wheelchair, his legal team following. He looked even more feeble than he had last night, propped up with pillows, a camel hair blanket over his lap.

Brian stood up. "I'm going to find out what happened."

He came back beaming. "Mom, it's great. The judge granted Alfaro a medical continuance. He's going home."

I filled with optimism. Alfaro's wheelchair reached my row. I touched his arm, groping for words to express my overwhelming desire for him to make it. All I could manage was, "Good luck, Heratio."

"To Jerry and you too, Mrs. Kraig."

I turned to Brian. "This is great."

He squeezed my shoulder. "We needed this. It's a very good sign."

I glanced at my watch. It was nine. As if on cue, the bailiff addressed the court. "Everyone, please stand. Here ye, here ye, the Honorable David D. Dowd presiding."

The chamber doors opened and Judge Dowd took the bench. The bailiff placed a bound sheaf of papers before him and he slowly thumbed through them. I searched his face for insight into the judgment behind the judge, but his expression was devoid of any emotion. His only distinguishable feature was a shock of yellow-gray hair that fell with a boyish aplomb over the left side of a prominent forehead that I hoped was a sign of open-mindedness.

Judge Dowd had presided over the Sturman trials for ten years. After Jerry's, there would be one more and then he was planning to retire. Bad timing. Jerry always tried to get his trials scheduled when the judge wasn't due to go on vacation because he believed his attention would already be out on the first tee. How was Dowd going to focus on testimony he'd heard argued inside and out with one foot out the door?

Judge Dowd peered at us as if he were a theatrical producer checking the tally of a full house. With a satisfied smile, he lifted his robed arm and proclaimed, "So say the court." He cracked the gavel. The trial began.

As the first round of juror candidates entered the jury box, I eyed Hirschorn, our jury specialist. He was wearing a conservative enough suit, but I zeroed in on his cowboy boots, the same ones he'd worn at the meeting the night before with Alfaro. They seemed to put on airs and could be perceived as disrespectful. The jury pool was being selected from a rust and bible belt of small Ohio town within an hour of Cleveland but worlds apart. Over the last fifteen years the area had become more and more economically depressed as the steel and rubber factories shut down, forcing the workers into other means of earning a living, mostly rank-and-file jobs. Hirschorn leaned casually on the juror's box as if it were a backyard fence. His educated drawl probed and reprobed each of the prospective juror's lifestyles and conscience. I kept expecting the prosecutors, Craig Morford and James Wooley, to object but they sat back casually, almost disinterested. Their only reactions were nearly imperceptible nods. I worried that the jurors would see us as outsiders, a team of slick, liberal Jews.

The prosecutors alternated questioning the potential jurors. They asked nothing of anyone's background. All they wanted to know was each person's name, address, and employment. Their methods were the same, unanimated and routine. In the meantime, Hirschorn furiously scribbled notes. Several times he jumped to his feet, objected, and dismissed jurors. The process was over in an hour.

We broke for recess before the first witness would testify. Around the conference table, Louie said, "Great. A school teacher. A couple of salesmen." He directed a laudatory smile at Hirschorn, "You picked well. The woman, the one in the back, her brother was in prison. She'll be careful about convicting."

"They all seem fair. That's all we can ask for," Jerry said, remarkably subdued.

Hirschorn slipped papers into his briefcase. "I'm very pleased." Latches snapped. He shook hands around the table. Job done. There was silence for a moment after Hirschorn left.

"Don't you think it was strange how the prosecution didn't seem to care who Hirschorn picked," I asked, looking at Jerry.

"A little, but you have to realize they're a well-oiled machine at this point."

I wanted to ask, what do they know that we don't? But Jerry's attention had shifted to his legal pad. He put on his reading glasses and said to Louie, "There are some points I think we should cover." I looked at Brian, peering over his father's shoulder as he sipped his coffee. I reassured myself; he would have said something if he thought there was reason for concern.

Recess was over. I took my place on the bench and was surprised to see the rows pretty much filled around me, all men. I wondered, uncomfortably, if they were overflow from the prosecutor's side.

Craig Morford's opening statement seemed to be taken straight off the indictment. He saved the clincher for last, saying, "The government will prove Jerry Kraig was Reuben Sturman's point man and the mastermind of the conspiracy behind Gemstone, the trust that Reuben Sturman formed to defraud the IRS of taxes."

I had a clear view of Morford: the back of his head still and straight, his shoulders pulled back so taut, I felt the strain in mine. I bit at a piece of skin on my lip, then stopped myself. It made me appear anxious, unconfident. I went for my cuticle instead.

Morford sat down and James Wooley took over. He called Bob Garfield to the stand. I trembled as he came down the aisle. When he reached my row, I braced my hands on the bench to steady myself, willing him to see the contempt in my eyes. But he stared straight ahead.

Bob lifted his arm to swear the oath, straining his double-breasted suit jacket. His face was deeply flushed, though the air conditioning blasted out frigid air. He blotted his large domed forehead with a handkerchief, careful not to disturb his toupee, and deposited himself in the witness chair.

Brian joined me as Wooley was establishing Bob's credentials: senior partner at a law firm specializing in real estate and tax law for twenty years, and one of Jerry's closest personal friends. He asked Bob to describe how he had taken over the formation of Gemstone at Jerry's recommendation. Bob went through the history perfunctorily and I wondered if the jury was listening. Morford took over, continuing elegantly and seamlessly. He wanted to know who named Gemstone? What, I wondered, was he up to? I crossed and uncrossed my legs, wishing I could ask Brian to explain, but his attention was fixed on Garfield, who was putting elbow grease to his speculation that it was most likely Reuben but his voice glossed with sincerity. Then again, he said, it could have been Jerry. It was a long time ago and he didn't exactly recall.

But Garfield didn't have to recall anything. I clutched Brian's sleeve and whispered, "He knows Dad didn't name Gemstone."

"Mom, Dowd will expel you if he catches you reacting. Stay calm, all right?" Wooley kept Garfield expounding on Jerry's role as the go between when he hadn't been able to reach Reuben, Jerry as the mediator of the payment of his fees when Reuben was late, and when he had doubts about the legality of Gemstone and wanted out, Jerry had taken the file and returned it to Reuben.

Wooley was our enemy. He was out to nail my husband. But I couldn't help being impressed by his finesse with every question, the astute coupling of 'Jerry and Reuben,' 'Reuben and Jerry' that showed proximity and access, right hand

and left: men of the same mind, same goal—the same crime. I inhaled and my breath shuddered coming out. So this was their 'battle plan.'

The prosecution had no more questions for Garfield.

Judge Dowd addressed the court, "We will take a one-hour recess for lunch. Trial will resume at 1:00 PM." The gavel resounded on wood.

In the conference room, I circled the table, too agitated to sit down. Everyone else was bunched at the end. Jerry picked up on my nerves. "I don't think Bob's testimony was significant one way or the other."

"He said you named Gemstone," I said, my hands clenched.

"Garfield did what we expected," Louie intercepted, speaking rapidly. "But what he didn't say was that Jerry was the point man. That was a big gift. Quite frankly I don't get it," he half chuckled, "after Morford made a point of it in his opening statement. All Garfield said was that Jerry was Reuben's contact, which was innocuous." Louie's lips were wet with a little kid's excitement over an anticipated easy win.

"But, Louie," Brian said cautiously, "don't you think it's important when you get Garfield on cross to emphasize how Jerry was completely separate from Gemstone?"

I caught Brian's eyes and nodded my agreement. I felt calmer. My son wasn't letting anything slip through.

Louie reached for a sandwich.

Jerry turned toward me. "He didn't say that I did anything illegal, which is crucial."

"But it was Wooley's show," I said. "He used Garfield to navigate you in and around Reuben's dirty dealing and he's making sure the jury will have all the rope it needs to hang you."

"Hon," Jerry said gently but with an undertone of warning that I shouldn't push this. "We know their strategy and we're going to attack it. The piece we have to clarify is that I knew the owners of the properties Reuben wanted to transfer into Gemstone because of the First Amendment litigations that I was managing. I knew everyone. That was part of my role as coordinator." He dug into the wrapper and pulled out a turkey on rye, fumbled with the packet of mustard, got it open, and concentrated on squeezing it evenly over his sandwich. His appetite was a good sign. He eagerly lifted the sandwich to his mouth and said before he bit into it, "I could tell Bob was shaken."

"I'd like to have seen him shake until the rug fell off his head."

Everyone laughed. I felt exonerated now of being the voice of doom. Jerry raised his coffee cup. "That's my wife."

Brian raised his can of soda. "Here, here, that's my mom."

Chips were passed around. Everyone was relieved to leave Garfield's postmortem. They weren't worried. I needed to take their lead and take it all in stride as they were; just another typical day in the old courthouse. Optimism and trust waylaid my fears. We were going to win. Suddenly, I was starving. I reached for my sandwich, too.

~

We assumed the same places in the courtroom. Brian asked me if I was all right. I assured him of my renewed confidence. He looked at me apprehensively for a second before he went up front to sit with his father. The air conditioning was cranking out an arctic chill, but I would rather have it too cold than too warm. I wanted the jurors alert for Louie's cross-examination of Garfield.

Bob was back on the stand, seemingly more at ease. His color was normal and he'd stopped sweating. Louie reestablished that Jerry had no background or experience in tax law and that Bob had joined Reuben's team as the expert. So far so good. Louie then referred to Bob's grand jury testimony. "I'm reading from page fifty-two." There was some confusion while Judge Dowd located his copy and gave the signal to go ahead. Louie read from it, quoting Garfield, "The beneficiary of the trust would be a foreign trust." He asked Garfield, "Whose idea was that, Jerry Kraig's or Reuben Sturman's?"

Garfield warily admitted that it was his own idea. Louie then established that Garfield had then assigned the file to an associate at his firm, Joe Motta. There was nothing of consequence here; I wondered where Louie was going. Garfield explained that Motta's work was to clear the property titles by getting a compilation of all Reuben's holdings, in whose names they appeared, provide legal descriptions for each, and then deal with state and federal tax issues. Louie accepted this information as a matter of course. I inhaled tensely, though it was going okay.

Then Louie asked Garfield, "And who did you go to get that information?"

"I would go to…my point man would have been Jerry Kraig."

'Point man!' Out of Garfield's mouth. I felt as if an electric current was burning down the side of my face and neck. We had just been blown up by our own land mine. What had slipped past the prosecutor our own attorney got him to say.

I searched the faces of the jury, thirteen blank faces. I latched onto denial that the significance of Bob's testimony had gone over their heads. Maybe I was overly sensitive. I sent a silent plea to Brian to come back to me and tell me that I was overreacting. Louie was proceeding as if nothing happened.

Garfield continued, "I never felt from either my brief contacts with Reuben Sturman or my many contacts with Jerry Kraig, that they were asking me to do something that would create a tax problem." The skin on my face felt too tight. Please let it be over.

Louie turned over the page of his legal pad. "The defense rests, Your Honor."

Thank God.

Judge Dowd ordered Garfield to step down, and as he passed the table for the prosecution, a flicker of satisfaction passed between Morford and Wooley. Dowd announced that the trial would resume tomorrow morning at 9 AM. He tapped the gavel, swiveled his leather chair away from the bench and left.

The defense table was a huddle of suits, their hands were chopping the air in a fury. We're not going to lose, a voice in my head commanded. Jerry had always said that when he tried cases, the balance tipped back and forth. One day gloom and doom. The next, he was fighting for all he was worth and hitting all the marks. That's what he loved, feeling he was on top of everything, and the client knowing how much he cared. That was why he could never give up being a trial lawyer.

In the conference room, Louie backpedaled, "A point man can be construed as the one in charge, but in itself it's not damaging testimony. We'll turn it around in final argument." His lips were so wet they looked slippery. "We'll show that you did nothing more than any conscientious attorney, making referrals and going to meetings."

"It wasn't good that the 'point man' thing came out because the prosecution twisted it to sound criminal. But I've never been that concerned about it. I'll clear it up when I take the stand," Jerry said.

I directed my eyes at Louie, "We're still on track, right?"

"Absolutely, no bolts out of the blue. We're doing fine." He clicked open his briefcase and brought out some papers.

Jerry's eyes darkened. "What has me nervous is Ginsberg's testimony tomorrow."

At nine the next morning, Ginsberg took the stand and the courtroom seemed to take on an unclean presence. His greasy hair flopped over his sallow forehead. A smirk was pasted on his mouth and he lunged forward in the witness stand as if he if he relished squealing.

The way Morford launched into how Ginsberg went to work for the Sturman 'organization,' it sounded as if Ginsberg had joined the mob. Then changing pace, Morford asked softly, "And who hired you to take the position?"

"Jerry Kraig," Ginsberg answered matter-of-factly.

I craned around the person seated in front of me to see Louie sitting at the defense table, business as usual, the eraser tip of his pencil resting on his legal pad. I pressed my back hard against the bench to deflect my need to yell out, "Louie, object! Jerry didn't hire Ginsberg. It was a referral." I tried to read Jerry's back for a tremor, a knot of tensed muscle, nothing. And Brian's back offered only blank blue serge.

Ginsberg was now filling in the details. "Jerry gave me two or three boxes, some general files for example, and a specific file for each property that would be purchased by Gemstone."

My mouth was dry and cottony, and I swallowed. I pictured the files barricading us off from any sense of normal.

Morford changed his tone to one slightly tougher yet still kindly, "As a result of your work for Sturman involving Gemstone, were you indicted in this case?"

Ginsberg nodded, but Dowd admonished him to answer. "Yes," he corrected, loudly.

"And," Morford continued, "how did you plead in this case?"

"Guilty," Ginsberg said, proudly.

Why was Morford bringing up the plea bargain? We were going to expose his testimony against Jerry to save himself?

"And are you, in fact, guilty of conspiring with others to obstruct the IRS in your work for Gemstone too?"

"Yes."

"Now, was there a plea bargain?"

"Yes, there was." Ginsberg raked his fingers through his hair.

I swallowed, confounded.

"Have you been sentenced yet under the terms of your plea?"

"No."

"And could you explain to the jury what promises the government made to you that will take place when you are sentenced in this case based on your truthful testimony here today?"

It was as cold in the courtroom as a morgue. I hunched into myself, my arms around me like a straitjacket.

"Well, the government has made no promise," Ginsberg's voice oozed earnestness. "The agreement was that, depending on my cooperation, meaning my testimony at trial and in the investigation, they would recommend to the judge a downward departure on the sentencing guidelines. But it was made clear to me that any ultimate decision on sentencing was to be made by the judge in this case."

Morford had brought Ginsberg's skeleton out of the closet, accounted for the rattle of its bones, and in doing so established the authenticity of his testimony. Fear clutched at my chest. The prosecution didn't need home runs. A series of run-scoring hits would do just as well.

I pulled my arms even tighter around myself. I was shaky, as if I'd lost my balance.

"So," Morford said, "there was a memo that was sent to you by Jerry Kraig...."

Finally. Here it was. I was almost relieved. I released the stranglehold of my arms. We were prepared for this.

Morford addressed Dowd, "Your Honor, before we go ahead and read the memo, we have a blowup of the document so the jury can follow along as well."

The bailiff displayed a large easel before the jury box: the enlarged memo stood there, extra-large type blaring its irrefutable importance. Morford turned the pages as Ginsberg read Jerry's words: "The government alleges that Reuben Sturman is the nominee of Gemstone Realty and therefore they can attach Gemstone's income to satisfy the Sturman lien. Suit is being prepared to attack the government's claim. The suit will have to allege that Sturman is not the nominee of Gemstone and proof will have to be offered. The easiest way to prove the case would be for someone to come in and prove that they own Gemstone."

Judge Dowd interrupted, "Slow down."

Ginsberg continued, "Another way to win would be to show that Gemstone is fully owned by an irrevocable trust in which Sturman is not the beneficiary. If the trust were established before the tax lien and is for the benefit of others, even Sturman's children, the government would not be able to attach the funds, because Sturman can't get the funds himself. Gemstone was established by attorney Alfaro in Panama. I was instructed by Reuben to send him a fee of fifteen hundred dollars."

I shuddered. Nothing could sound more conspiratorial than this. Ginsberg paused, grimacing as he stretched his neck. Judge Dowd asked him to continue. "Alfaro forwarded all corporate documents to Treufit Limited Trust Company in Zurich. Treufit is operated by attorney Wehinger in Zurich. Since the stock issue from Panama is bearer stock, Treufit is the holder of the stock, but we do not know who they hold the stock for. Before we go on, we have to have to know the answer to this."

I hadn't heard the memo before, only what Jerry had paraphrased. It's legal language sounded like a complicated maze made even more complicated. Brian was writing furiously on his legal pad, as was Louie.

Ginsberg read on, an obedient drone, "What we would like to do: Have the answers to the above and take the deposition of attorney Alfaro explaining that he organized the corporation and sent the papers to Zurich. Then depose Wehinger and have him identify the owner of the stock. I anticipate that under Swiss law, Wehinger will not be able to reveal the owner of the stock. However, if he can't reveal who the owner is, perhaps he could state who is not the owner, in other words, Sturman. Or, if the property is held in a trust, assert that the trust is irrevocable and that Sturman is not the beneficiary. At that point, the burden should shift to the government to rebut the proof and or offer proof that Sturman is the owner of Gemstone. We believe they have no such proof and are merely shooting in the dark. However, because we have the burden of proof, we must be able to present a case that establishes that Sturman is not Gemstone."

"We must be able to present a case" repeated in my head. I knew what Jerry meant: he'd been on the team, always the team player. Now, 'we' emitted the odor of a back-room deal in which Reuben's cigar puffed out orders of aggression borne out of fear. I scanned the faces of the jury, almost expecting to find their nostrils flared, accosted by the smell. I caught the eyes of a woman in front. She could be the teacher, with her blouse primly buttoned at the neck. The faces of the others could have been those of any bored audience. Ginsberg droned on, "Some anticipated tactics by the government: One, they will want to depose Sturman; Two, they will want a denial of ownership from him under oath; Three, they will want full discovery from Alfaro, Wehinger, and me. Before we proceed with the lawsuit, we must have the answers."

The blowup of the memo was removed, signaling the end of direct. I shifted on the bench. The worst was over and I felt sick; it all looked so incriminating. But I consoled myself that Jerry and Louie hadn't seen it that way. Jerry hadn't acted as counsel for Gemstone, but as a lawyer he had tried to explain the situation to Ginsberg as he'd understood it. He'd clarify all of it to the jury when he testified.

Louie's cross-examination followed immediately. His main line of attack was Ginsberg's credibility. He wanted him to admit that he'd given a false affidavit to Reuben's tax attorney, DeSantis, stating that a Mr. Kummer in Switzerland was the rightful owner of Gemstone though he knew it wasn't true.

"I lied. I mean, I'm not going to deny it." Ginsberg practically bragged, "This whole Gemstone mess was—I was out of my area and I shouldn't have been involved, and that's why I'm here today," he shrugged. "I admit it. It's like I didn't see the forest for the trees and that's exactly what happened."

Louie led Ginsberg through the muddle of faxes and Jerry's memo all over again: more figures, a scramble of names and dates. The good thing was that Ginsberg didn't peg Jerry as the mastermind of Reuben's organization, and he admitted that Jerry hadn't been paid by Reuben out of the funds Ginsberg was authorized to disburse to everyone else who'd been involved.

With Ginsberg established as a liar, what did that mean for Jerry? My mind couldn't assimilate the complexities. Guilty innocence. Jerry had said that he hadn't wanted to be paid because he didn't want the government to tie him to Reuben anymore. Who was going to believe that he went to meetings for Reuben gratis? Where was one attorney in history who had worked for a rich mogul for nothing? Unfortunately, that one attorney was my husband. I swallowed bitterly. Lucky me.

I wished I'd been indicted. I would plead guilty for this debacle: my oversights and neglect, the mistakes that had seemed to be the snags of spousal disagreement were now threatening to unravel the fabric of our lives.

As Ginsberg stepped down, his head hung like a fallen limb, as if he had banged into one of those trees he hadn't seen in the forest.

Tomorrow, I steadied myself, Jerry would take the stand. His character would impress the jury enough to take him out of the thug category. It had to. He was going to have to disconnect every link the prosecutors had made tying him to Reuben. It was what he didn't do, not what he did. That, and his character witnesses: a judge, a sheriff, a former law partner, two respected colleagues, Brian, and me. I had rehearsed my testimony in my head since the trial began. All I needed to do was show the jury how human Jerry was, given the situation of his history and loyalty to Reuben. He'd gotten on a crooked path, but he wasn't responsible for the direction it took. As his wife, I would give credibility to Jerry's misjudgment but not his misdeeds. But then, what weight does a wife's word carry? My head pounded with the urgency to make everything right.

Jerry was driving us back to Cleveland. Louie and Brian were in the back seat. Instead of picking apart Ginsberg's testimony, we'd withdrawn into our own thoughts, in my case, fears. Breaking the silence, I said to Jerry, "The line in the memo about your sending Alfaro Reuben's check of fifteen hundred dollars…it made you sound…" I searched for the right words, not wanting say 'guilty,' "very involved."

Keeping his eyes on the rush-hour traffic, he said, "I know. But that was the prosecution's tactic: to present the memo to look like a battle plan and magnify everything I said. Actually, I'd handwritten it on my personal stationary. And I sent fees to lawyers all the time. It was right before I quit and Reuben was in California." He rubbed his eyes and placed his hand back on the steering wheel, gripping hard. His shoulder nearest me, lifted in a half shrug, "Reuben asked me to send a letter of instruction to Alfaro so I did."

"Nothing there that can't be explained," Louie agreed dismissively.

I retreated into myself, half paying attention as Louie continued on about lawyers testifying, until I heard him say, "I've changed my mind about Jerry taking the stand tomorrow."

I snapped to attention as if a shot had been fired. If I heard right, he had to have lost his mind. Louie was sitting directly behind me. I whipped my head around to look at him, but constrained by the seat belt I only glimpsed the tip of his nose and his mouth moving, talking fast. "In my opinion Jerry's testimony won't make our case stronger because the prosecution's already done the job." I glanced at Jerry. His face was set hard but absent of the protest that was swelling and about to burst inside me. Louie was rapidly ticking off his points, "Garfield hasn't significantly hurt us. Ginsberg's been established as a liar and most important I got him to admit in cross that Jerry was never paid except for travel expenses. What does that mean? Truth to logic: Jerry wasn't working for Reuben!" Louie's voice rose so triumphantly I expected him to bow. "So why put Jerry in the vulnerable position of allowing the prosecution the opportunity to open other doors, damaging doors, that we might not expect?"

"What do you mean? Jerry has to take the stand!" I pounded my fist in my lap like a gavel.

"Yeah, Dad. Mom's right. You are your own best character witness. You're the one who has to straighten out the picture the prosecution has painted of you. You have to counter that." Brian turned to Louie, "It's the biggest thing he has going for him."

Jerry searched my face for a second. "Louie's right. I've been thinking about it, too."

"Then why have you been up for the past three nights working on your testimony?"

"Because I've been nervous about it. Lawyers make the worst witnesses. They have trouble refraining from taking over their own defense by getting argumentative and offensive and that makes them come across guilty. I haven't been able to sleep because I've been going over and over what I want to say so I won't make those mistakes."

"It's always better not to complicate with unknowns," Louie said.

"If I lost and I hadn't taken the stand…" I blurted out.

Jerry's eyes taunted but they were hurt. "You think I'm going to lose?"

"No, but what I mean is…you know, how can you not speak up for yourself?"

Louie repeated his reasoning, his words slurry, and then he paused and said, "Jerry, it's not only my opinion. I had a conference call with everyone else at the office last night…we went over all of the evidence again and they agreed that you're more at risk if you take the stand. You can explain paying Alfaro and going to the meeting in Florida. But Morford's just waiting to nail you on Switzerland, especially since you saw Stockli and he's your alleged co-conspirator. You weren't working for Reuben, but it's a hard nut for the jury to swallow. We want you to sit it out."

"It was the goddamn herring," I said.

"A fine kettle of fish I got myself in," Jerry said, his self-deprecating smile turning into a grimace, his face shamed red.

"Maybe you should sit it out, Dad," Brian said.

I turned to look at my son. He was drained of color and too haggard for his age. I placed my forehead against the cold window smeared with Macabee's licks. Brian would carry the weight of whatever happened the rest of his life. I closed my eyes, shutting myself off from the feeling of futility. I didn't know what was right anymore. Maybe I was wrong. I certainly wanted to be. This was how they got you. As Louie said, "with the unknowns."

At home, during dinner, we thrashed it over. Jerry said he'd seen this situation many times. Some clients insisted on testifying and some didn't. Either way it had never worked in their favor when they'd gone against his advice. He knew he could explain it all best. He spread butter on a piece of bread and then let it drop on top of his omelet, the cheese on top hardened. His eyes begged for me to be on his side. "I don't trust my own judgment. I'm shot. I have to put my faith in Louie." I wasn't hungry either. I'd put Macabee in the kennel for the week so I wouldn't worry about taking him out. I wished he were here now so that I had an excuse to leave and go for a long walk. The house seemed tired.

After we went to bed, I stared up at the ceiling as if it would reveal the answer. Finally, I convinced myself to go over to Louie's side. I rolled over and hugged Jerry's back. I could tell by its tenseness that he was still awake. "I'm afraid of Switzerland too. Who would ever believe you went there for dinner? The people on this jury would think going to Cleveland for dinner was extravagant."

"Thanks, honey. I need you to be with me," Jerry said.

I felt his tension ease. He rolled over and took me in his arms. His breath was against my cheek, "I still believe we're going to win."

CHAPTER SIX

OKLAHOMA CITY BOMBING
AND *DAY ONE*

Wednesday, the third day of the trial, Morford was about to call his first witness of the day when the bailiff approached Judge Dowd and whispered something to him. Looking stricken, he combed his fingers through his hair several times and said, "We have just received very disturbing news. The Alfred P. Murrah Federal Building in Oklahoma City has just been bombed. It's not known who set it off. Hundreds are believed injured and killed."

Exclamations erupted through the courtroom. Brian was next to Jerry and the ten rows between us felt like an impassable divide. Judge Dowd stood and ordered us to clear the court until further notice. He cracked the gavel as an afterthought, and before we had a chance to stand, he was gone. For a few seconds everyone stayed put in silence. Then, as if a current had rushed through, we emptied en masse into the waiting area, our faces mirroring each other's shock.

I spotted Jerry and Louie at the window that gave a view of traffic innocently flying past on the freeway. I longed to be in one of those cars. I plucked at Jerry's sleeve. He drew me close. "Those poor people just went to work and look what happened," he said.

Joining us, Brian said, "At the water cooler, I overheard the bailiff talking to a deputy. He said that all of the federal buildings and courthouses in the country are being searched for explosives. I'm worrying we're sitting ducks in here." He'd looked so crisp and bright when we got here an hour ago. Now he'd loosened his tie, a water spot looked like a fallen tear.

The red exit sign over the stairwell door captured my field of vision. I pulled away from Jerry. "I think we should get out of here."

"We can't go anywhere until the judge orders or we'll be held in contempt," Louie said.

"Contempt or dead? I choose contempt," I said.

"If there were any real threat we would have been evacuated immediately," Jerry said and smiled weakly. "We're okay, I promise." I leaned back into him, my head turned toward his chest, needing to soak in his solidity.

"I hate to sound cold, but I can't help thinking the timing couldn't be worse for us. The federal government has just become the victim of a conspiracy. It's bound to influence a jury who's about to deliberate on a conspiracy trial," Louie said.

"Louie's right. It's an exacerbated disaster," Brian said.

Jerry looked at Louie, back to Brian, and pointedly kept his eyes on him, "I don't think we should be drawing dire conclusions. This is Dowd's second-to-last trial. He's going to be very careful to guard against outside influences. He has a reputation of wanting a clean record."

The threat of our building blowing up seemed to be over as the crowd began to disperse, though the elevator and exit door to the stairwell were still being guarded and we couldn't leave the floor. Jerry jingled coins in his pocket. "Might as well check in at the office." Louie took off with Brian to the conference room.

I remained, listening to reactions. Anxiety had worked up appetites. There were lots of speculations about lunch. The woman court reporter next to me was talking about the variety of restaurants to choose from at the Quaker Square Mall. She was hoping the judge would call a recess for the day. Her friend vied for a restaurant at the Summit Mall. When else would they get the chance to get paid to shop? she wanted to know. They giggled like school girls. I toed the carpet, envying their carefree moment.

The bailiff's voice bellowed over the talk and laughter, "Court is recessed for lunch. Trial will resume at precisely 1:30."

At 1:30 on the dot, Judge Dowd brought down the gavel, a commanding smack. He made no further mention of the bombing. The jury lined the two rows inside the box like complacently placed candies. Pastel colors on the women, faces with freshly applied lipstick. I'd carefully removed smudges of eyeliner under my eyes and reblushed my cheeks. For some reason, there was comfort in grooming.

Morford and Wooley alternated calling their last three witnesses, business as usual. Another plea bargain, a woman, Stephanie Friedman, who had worked for Reuben in California and had driven the getaway car when he escaped from the minimum-security prison. She was in the prosecutor's witness protection program, had an alias identity and received seventy thousand dollars yearly income from the Feds. Not a bad life for a twenty-something ex-office assistant. She testified that Jerry had delivered a Gemstone file from Cleveland for her to give to Reuben. The next day Reuben and Jerry met. She tried to guess that it concerned Gemstone but Louie objected. The jurors were instructed to disregard the testimony and it was stricken from the record.

I detected a glimmer in the woman juror's eyes in the front row. I hoped it meant she saw the folly of plea-bargained testimonies. All it took was one staunch juror to be on our side. The other two witnesses were tax attorneys whom Reuben

Gene Kraig

had hired to work on Gemstone but who had quit when they'd run into snags. Nothing new: Jerry had met them but hadn't worked with them. He'd only provided background about Reuben's need to form the trust and had recapped how it had progressed to that point.

Jerry and I drove home drained from the day in court and distressed about the bombing. But the testimonies, if we could ever have imagined testimonies could be the bright spot of the day, we agreed, hadn't hurt us. And as the prosecution had rested, we wouldn't agonize all night about what damage tomorrow's witnesses might cause. We expected the prosecution's final argument not to last very long and, even better, to hold no surprises.

Jerry suggested the Italian bistro on the corner for dinner, guessing rightly that I had no energy for cooking. We ate our pastas quickly, passing on wine, not saying very much. There were still all the phone calls to make: the nightly check-ins with family and friends, starting with Karen.

The phone was ringing when we walked in. Jerry answered and I went to change into sweats. Jerry called upstairs, "Hon, it's Karen."

I picked up the phone on my nightstand and sat on the edge of the bed. Jerry said from the downstairs phone, "Go ahead Kare, tell Mom."

"I just talked to Brian. He was so upset you weren't home he called me. There was a message on the machine at the office. You know *Day One*, the news show on ABC?"

"Yeah, what about it?" All I could think was how good it would feel to stretch out on the bed and not move or say another word until morning.

"What, that's the fifty-thousand-dollar question. Tomorrow at 10 PM, Forrest Sawyer is going to be interviewing none other than our very own prosecutor, Morford, and our very own pornographer, Reuben Sturman. I know production. I'm in the business. This was filmed at least a month ago. The prosecution had to have been very aware that it was going to air now. They're worse than Sturman."

"Oh, my God," I said. Jerry was so quiet I couldn't tell if he was still on. "Jer?"

"Uh huh, I'm here."

"What are you going to do?" Karen's voice ripped.

"I'm going to see if it's true. If it is, then I'll try to find out what we can do to stop it from airing," Jerry answered.

"You'd think I could do something, but I'm only an agent for commercials. I have to call Daphne. She lunches with everyone in the industry," Karen said.

"Maybe you could find out exactly when the show was taped. If it was premeditated to air now...it's important to know."

We hung up.

Jerry called Brian, who called the client whose son was a production assistant at Day One who'd called with the tip but he couldn't disclose any of the production information. He was afraid of compromising his job. Five calls back and forth to Louie, during which the main topics of conversation were: the bombing of a federal building in Oklahoma City and a television program about Reuben in prison the day before the jury was going out. We speculated on the slant it would take. There was a grab bag of Reuben's exploits against the law to expose, the most egregious being his escape from prison and his attempt to tamper with the jury and bribe the judge. Without doubt Reuben's criminal behavior would cast the worst dispersions on Jerry. We sat in the den after the last phone call too down to move. Jerry's face, his eyes closed, was in his hands. He was thinking. Finally, he folded his arms over his chest and looked at me, "Maybe, just maybe this will work in our favor."

"What do you mean?" I asked, feeling a twinge of hope.

"Well, if Dowd doesn't sequester the jury tomorrow night, there're grounds for a mistrial."

"What if he does sequester them? Can it still work in our favor?

"No." He got up and flipped on the news. The screen lit with the smoking rubble of what had once been the federal building. Sirens wailed. The voice-over said, "Suspects Timothy McVeigh and Terry Nichols, both known antigovernment extremists, are in custody." Louie had called that one. The jury's sympathy was bound to be biased toward the government, seen in the glaring spotlight as the victim of a conspiracy. It wouldn't be a stretch for the jury to seek vengeance against Jerry as another dangerous perpetrator.

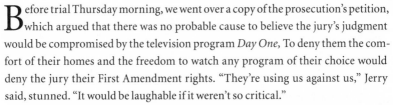

Before trial Thursday morning, we went over a copy of the prosecution's petition, which argued that there was no probable cause to believe the jury's judgment would be compromised by the television program *Day One*, To deny them the comfort of their homes and the freedom to watch any program of their choice would deny the jury their First Amendment rights. "They're using us against us," Jerry said, stunned. "It would be laughable if it weren't so critical."

Brian's eyes met his father's. "They are as ingeniously deceptive as an espionage unit."

Our petition asked the court to sequester the jury that night. We argued that should the court allow the jury access to watch *Day One*, it would deny Jerry his constitutional right to a fair trial.

The courtroom was packed as we awaited both sides to finish petitioning the judge in chambers. This morning, the air conditioning blasted out of control. I huddled inside the sweater I'd worn over a tailored long-sleeved silk blouse. Brian slid in next to me. I inched closer. "Do you know anything?" He shook his head as we all stood for the judge to take the bench.

Judge Dowd swiveled around to face the jury. Highlighting the gravity of the situation, he held his eyes on them for a couple seconds then spoke, "For reasons I can't divulge…I want you to turn off every television in your house before ten tonight and keep them off until morning. That means the ones in your kid's rooms, kitchen, basement. You get the picture. Not to do so, you will be held in contempt of this court." He smacked down the gavel. His voice followed like an echo, "It is so ordered."

Brian hit the top of the bench in front of him. He whispered vehemently, "What's the first thing any person with normal curiosity would do? Turn on the TV and watch. I would!" I wanted to soothe him and I wanted to scream at the judge.

Jerry slid in next to Brian. Louie followed, leaning into our row. "All we've got now is cause for appeal."

"Cause for dismissal?" Jerry asked, tentatively hoping but knowing the answer.

Louie shook his head, "Sorry, Jer, no," he smiled grimly, "but definitely appealable."

"Don't we have to lose to appeal?" I asked.

Louie spread his hands as if he were offering something but nothing came forth. "Let's see the program tonight and we'll regroup in the morning. I'm still confident. There's still no evidence."

Karen called as we walked in the door to our house. "Where were you? I've been calling every five minutes."

"At the drugstore picking up Dad's blood-pressure pills. What's wrong?"

"I saw a promo on TV at seven o'clock, just after the news, and there was Reuben in his cell talking about sending his slut wife to offer sexual favors to a juror in exchange for an acquittal. I can't believe how twisted this is." I pictured her eyes burning blue with anger, her foot swinging furiously.

Jerry had picked up the extension phone in the den. "You're right, it is twisted.

We didn't think of promos running before ten o'clock. Anyone on the jury could have seen it with impunity." His voice was flat.

"Dad, isn't this cause for a mistrial or something?"

"If only it could be, but our luck doesn't seem to be going in that direction."

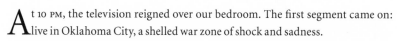

At 10 PM, the television reigned over our bedroom. The first segment came on: live in Oklahoma City, a shelled war zone of shock and sadness.

We watched, tensely waiting for 'our' segment. Jerry sat on our bed on top of the quilt, cross-legged, in jockey shorts, bare chested and straight backed, looking like a noncombatant warrior, unconscious of his strength. I was under the quilt, hugging my pillow on top of me as if it were a shield against the onslaught.

There was a commercial and Diane Sawyer filled the screen. "We will return to the Oklahoma City bombing at the end of this program. Now, we're going to turn now to a *Day One* investigation. We're going to tell you what prosecutors don't want you to know: how easy it is for criminals to tamper with a jury. You're going to learn why it happens so often and how little you have to lose if you're caught. The fact is: all you need is one juror to hold out, as you know, and you'll have a hung jury. Take the case of one of Cleveland's most notorious citizens, Reuben Sturman. Forrest Sawyer learned that when the stakes are high, often the criminal's last, best hope is jury tampering."

FORREST SAWYER   *You're the biggest in Cleveland.*

REUBEN STURMAN   *In the world. I was the biggest in the world. Ever since. Never will be another.*

FORREST SAWYER   *Over thirty years Reuben Sturman built a multimillion-dollar sex empire offering everything from adult movies, magazines, and the biggest seller of all, peep shows. For most of those years scores of government agents tried and failed to crack Reuben Sturman's X-rated empire. They indicted him for obscenity ten different times.*

REUBEN STURMAN   *I beat these guys sixteen ways from Sunday. Every one of them. They all hated me like poison. Because of the fact they could never win.*

FORREST SAWYER   *The only way they could get you was taxes.*

REUBEN STURMAN   *As it turns out.*

CRAIG MORFORD   *This case was really about greed; a man who had millions and millions of dollars but refused to pay his fair share of taxes on it… those dollars.*

FORREST SAWYER   *Reuben Sturman thumbed his nose at you. He dared you to catch him.*

CRAIG MORFORD   *No, he thought he was above the law.*

FORREST SAWYER   *Assistant U.S. Attorney Craig Morford was on the team of ten prosecutors and seventy-five agents who finally came up with an indictment they thought would stick, tax evasion.*

CRAIG MORFORD   *In terms of trial schedule…there were thirty, forty bank accounts. Millions of dollars going overseas. Money being carried over in briefcases. Gold being loaded up on dollies run across from one bank to another in Switzerland. It was a massive conspiracy involving millions of dollars.*

FORREST SAWYER   *Right through the trial Sturman kept on displaying contempt for the government. He began to realize he was being buried under a growing mountain of evidence. As the trial went on, it surely became increasingly evident you were losing and losing badly.*

REUBEN STURMAN   *Not losing bad but I could see I wasn't going to win. As bad as you can get.*

NAOMI STURMAN   *He said that…he would lose the case without my help.*

FORREST SAWYER   *Had he ever asked you for anything before?*

NAOMI STURMAN   *Never in my life.*

FORREST SAWYER   *Naomi Sturman has lived with Sturman since she was nineteen years old. Now she says he was pressing her to join his plan to beat the government one last time.*

NAOMI STURMAN   *He wanted me to offer twenty-five thousand dollars to this particular juror and um….*

FORREST SAWYER   *And if the bribe didn't work?*

NAOMI STURMAN   *Do whatever it takes to sway this juror.*

FORREST SAWYER   *All it takes is just one juror to hold up, to vote not guilty, and hang the case. Is it a big risk to bribe a juror?*

REUBEN STURMAN   *I was willing to take that chance.*

FORREST SAWYER   *You were looking at…*

REUBEN STURMAN   *I had no idea.*

FORREST SAWYER   *Years? Maybe even the rest of your life?*

REUBEN STURMAN   *Possible.*

FORREST SAWYER   *How much time?*

CRAIG MORFORD   *Probably a maximum of one hundred years on sixteen counts.*

FORREST SAWYER   *And for jury tampering, what's the maximum?*

CRAIG MORFORD   *Five years.*

FORREST SAWYER   *Five years versus a hundred.*

CRAIG MORFORD   *Exactly. And he decided at that point tampering with a jury was worth the risk.*

FORREST SAWYER   *Naomi Sturman looked for a juror right where she could find him. In the courtroom.*

NAOMI STURMAN   *And he was in the front row. Right in the middle and I just remember looking up at the jury and he was staring right at me.*

CRAIG MORFORD   *She was making eyes with the juror—kind of winking and smiling, coming on to him.*

FORREST SAWYER   *You had a juror up there drooling. You never noticed?*

CRAIG MORFORD   *Never crossed our minds.*

FORREST SAWYER   *Just before the jury was to start deliberations, the juror received a note with an imprint of a kiss with an invitation to meet at the Pier W Restaurant that night.*

CRAIG MORFORD   *The game plan was to use her wiles, if you will, to get that juror confused. Mess with his head and ask him—to get him—to do anything it took to get* him to acquit her husband.

FORREST SAWYER   *Greg Hoffstaeder would not speak to* Day One. *It wasn't until three years after the trial that he would talk to a grand jury about his date with Naomi. About what he expected that night, he answered, 'sex.' Were you willing to do what was necessary for this juror to vote not guilty?*

REUBEN STURMAN   *I think so. I imagine.*

FORREST SAWYER   *What did you offer Greg Hoffstaeder?*

NAOMI STURMAN   *To sed—*

FORREST SAWYER   *Seduce? Actually you started to say it. What he wanted you to do was seduce him?*

NAOMI STURMAN   *Yes.*

CRAIG MORFORD   *We had a fifteen-year investigation, a ten-week trial, and it almost all comes crashing down over drinks and dinner at the Pier W Restaurant with the defendant's wife and one of our jurors.*

FORREST SAWYER   *And that could happen anytime?*

CRAIG MORFORD   *Yes. Absolutely.*

FORREST SAWYER   *1988, one of the reputed members of New Jersey's crime family,*

> the Luchese Family, was acquitted after a juror was paid off. 1987, New
> York crime boss John Gotti and his associates, on trial for racketeering,
> bribed a juror and walked. Again in 1988, South Philadelphia, Little
> Nick Scarfo, one of the most violent mob bosses in history got away
> with murder. Is there anything that can be done to prevent jury tam-
> pering?
>
> CRAIG MORFORD   Our only recourse when a jury comes back with an acquit-
> tal and we suspect jury tampering is to do a thorough investigation of
> each juror.
>
> FORREST SAWYER   Reuben Sturman is now serving nineteen years in a max-
> imum-security prison. He and Naomi were divorced in 1991. As for
> Reuben Sturman, he is serving the twenty-seven months he was penal-
> ized for jury tampering.

Jerry leaped out of bed and punched the air. "Did you hear what Morford just said? 'A jury that comes back with an acquittal of someone they suspect of jury tampering goes through an investigation.' He just tampered with ours. What juror will have the courage to acquit after hearing this? Of course they're not supposed to be watching, right?" He said, livid, his color blanched.

"And, if that wasn't bad enough, they made the tie-in with the mob." My heart was hammering. I clicked off the TV and got out of bed. The king-size mattress became an island separating us. Jerry moved quickly to pick up the phone as it rang. I could hear Karen's voice raised out of control.

Jerry said, "It's Morford's First Amendment right to speak to the media." He listened. "Right. I know, but there's nothing illegal about saying what he would do in light of the law." He listened, pacing the carpet along my side of the bed. "That's true but it's very hard to prove malice, especially against the federal government. I'm disgusted." He listened. "Yeah, we sure couldn't have foreseen this one. Listen, honey," Jerry rubbed his eyes, "the jury's holding the cards now. My only chance for acquittal depends on whether they peeked at the hand. Either way, Mom and I will be coming straight to the gallery. We'll see you tomorrow. Can you just tell Alex I have to call Brian? I love you too."

It rang again. Brian's yells sounded as if he were in a bullring, like a fighter who wouldn't be put down. Jerry listened and said little. After he hung up, it was as if I were seeing him concede. My heart sank. Whatever fight he'd had left went out of him.

He sat down on my side of the bed, rubbed his face with his hands, and kept them there as I was stretched out on my side. The quiet was stark, abstract, glass-like. I was afraid to break it. He laid down and we still remained quiet. Nothing to say. Too much to say. He turned to me and spoke into the curve between my neck and shoulder, "We can appeal but we don't have a case against them. The First Amendment would prevail."

Protest expanded inside my chest. "I can't just take it."

He rolled onto the pillow, settling in half-fetal position for falling asleep, but we kept contact, his back against mine. "If only I could start again," he said barely audibly.

My mind sought the starting place. From where? Deciding to work for Reuben? Deciding not to go to the meeting in Switzerland? Hiring the biggest federal defense attorney in the country? Not having an alcoholic mother and a father who taught him to deny what was happening? Not needing to please others at the risk of his own well-being? My not paying enough attention? My not running in front and blocking him until he quit Reuben?

Jerry had fallen asleep on his back. Little sputters of breath came from between his lips as if he were being jostled in a car driving on a rutted road. I rolled onto my back and stared up at the ceiling. I pictured Jerry's mother; first as the most beautiful woman I had ever seen when I was a little girl; then her bloated face, puffy eyes holding tears of pride at his law school graduation as he received his diploma; her son the attorney. Tears trailed down my cheeks and neck, itching and irritating as insect bites. But I didn't let myself wipe them. I fell asleep with the image of their dried salt residue as veins of retribution.

CHAPTER SEVEN

VERDICT

APRIL 21, 1995

Our side and Morford and Wooley met in Judge Dowd's chambers. I waited, forcing patience, in the same place on the bench I'd been occupying for four days. Finally, our side came out single file, one sober face after the other. Taut lines etched downward from the corners of Jerry's mouth. A sharp pang warned inside my chest.

We all rose for the judge's entrance. His hair flopped over his forehead, unruly. I braced for the whack of the gavel, but it didn't come. Instead, he addressed the jury, calling the first juror's name. Squaring his eyes at him, he asked, "Did you or anyone in your family watch television after 10 PM last night?"

"No, Your Honor."

The woman who I figured was the teacher, who I had high hopes for, said the same, her eyes giving nothing away. The others followed, link by link in a chain of compliance with the judge's court order.

"So satisfies the court." The gavel cracked down like the shot of a pistol. I sucked in air. "Before Mr. Sirkin delivers his final argument," the judge focused his eyes directly on Jerry, "I will ask Mr. Kraig at this time if he wishes to reconsider and testify."

Jerry and Louie made eye contact and Louie shook his head no. Dowd's telling you to do it. For God's sake, Jerry, take the stand. I silently begged him over the heads in front of me. He stood and hesitated, then pulled his shoulders back and said, "No, Your Honor," his voice almost too soft to be heard. Dowd rubbed his head vigorously and worked his mouth as if he tasted something sour. His upper lip curled angrily above his teeth. There was a beat of silence and he said, "Let the court convene."

Louie's final argument was a confusing reiteration of the points and counterpoints of the testimonies. If the jury saw Jerry at the edge, I couldn't see where Louie was convincing them to pull him back.

When it was Morford's turn, he seemed to erupt out of the robotic control he'd presented throughout the trial. He hurled out his winning points with preacherly and moral indignation: Sturman the tax cheat, pornography, Jerry Kraig, point man, and mastermind of the conspiracy. All eyes in the courtroom seemed to be riveted on Morford. Jerry had not fought back, and now it was too late. The blood pounded in my temples. I was overcome by the hopelessness of the powerless.

10 AM, exactly twelve hours since *Day One* had been on TV, and the jury was sent out to deliberate.

We set up camp in the conference room to wait for the verdict. I separated myself by going to the window. The others jumbled around the opposite end of the conference table. Their ties were loosened, their bodies looked rumpled, like a fraternity bash gone sour. The conference room was on the second floor, but a derelict parking lot outside appeared to be on the same level, creating the odd illusion of being able to walk out the window onto its wasteland of compressed landfill. Scrubby weeds spiked out of an infinite web of cracks. Somehow, I found satisfaction in this forlorn scene.

"We made the right decision," Louie's voice jolted through my anguish.

"Something happened to me," Jerry said. "I caved in." He rubbed his face. Less than an hour had passed, but it could have been a year. The talking stopped. The silence was edgy. Brian brought out the *Plain Dealer* from his brief case and retreated behind the sports page. I brought out Solzhenitsyn's *Gulag Archipelago* from my overloaded bag and sat down with it by the window. I'd browsed at the half-price bookstore after dinner, the second day of the trial, and it had leapt out at me. I showed it to Jerry. He read the cover, "The main sources are Solzenitsyn's own prison experiences and those related to him by 227 other survivors," and aversion had crossed his face. I saw he was upset that I wanted to read a book about torture, neighbor against neighbor, brother against brother. But, during lulls in the trial, I had found in these pages the strength of survival, survival over the worst treatment imaginable. Now, the words were more than I could handle, so instead of reading I took comfort in its weight in my lap, like a pet, and sat fingering the pages. My mother's sad, angry eyes filled my mind. Her accusation began with my name, "Genie," and I answered, "Stop. We did what we knew." But my mind stopped there. I didn't have any more heart to think what that meant.

One by one we left the conference room and scattered to wait for twelve people from Akron, Ohio, to determine Jerry's, our children's, and my own fate. Jerry went to call the office and return messages on the pay phone. I guessed he was glad to have the distraction. I worked the waiting room, pacing around the seating area while keeping my eye on the courtroom door, my heart lurching every time anyone went in or out. The next group of anxious looking defendants emptied out of the elevator and busied themselves with the selection of chairs. Jerry came back from the phone and I suppressed my need to grab and hold him as if he'd been away on a long trip. "Everything's good at the office. It's a quiet day," he said, a slight lilt in his voice, still connected to ordinary life. We walked to the courtroom doors, holding hands.

I rested my head on his shoulder. "How could it take this long?"

"Could be another hour or the whole day," he said, his voice softly authoritative. He liked these kinds of questions.

"The longer it takes, the better chance we have, right?"

He shrugged. "Everyone has a different theory. If everyone on the jury bought our defense, then there'd be nothing to it. All they'd have to do is acquit. If not... someone might be holding out and that's good too." He stretched his neck, tensed his shoulders and released. He didn't have the patience to stand around. He mumbled something about a client he had to arrange a bond for in County Jail downtown and went back to the pay phone.

At 1:00 PM, I was pacing the corridor past the records department. Brian's voice came from behind. "Mom, the jury's in."

I looked at my watch. My limbs felt sapped of energy. Now that it was here, I couldn't move. I didn't want to know. "Four hours...is that good?" I asked, hoping for the right answer.

"Only if it's not guilty." Brian put his arm around me. "At least it's over."

He left me on the bench and went down to sit in front. Jerry was already seated at the defense table next to Louie. Judge Dowd instructed Jerry to stand and addressed the jury, "What say the court?"

The foreman stood, opened a slip of paper and, with only the slightest hesitation, read the verdict, "Guilty, Your Honor."

Wrong. He had to have read it wrong. I looked for someone to ask. But the defense table erupted in confusion. Suddenly, something was happening that I couldn't comprehend. Jerry was wedged between two massive policemen. Jerry's back was facing me. His arms formed a V behind him and sharp light glanced off handcuffs. Panic shot through my chest as if I had just witnessed myself in a car crash. Everything was speeding. And Jerry was being propelled through a door on the other side of the judge's bench.

My knees went watery. I crumpled forward onto the bench in front of me. Brian was suddenly at my side, gripping my arm, holding me up. I heard him saying things, but I couldn't make sense of it. Louie's law clerk was saying something to Brian, but I couldn't hear what it was. My mind had gone shallow, empty. Sweat leaked from my underarms. Confusion in the courtroom had increased to a wild pitch. Suits seemed to pile up. I needed someone to tell me what to do. Brian took my hand and then suddenly I was ahead of him. As I moved up the aisle, the crowd parted, creating a swath of isolation.

Brian steered me down a corridor past a window with lettering on it, 'Clerk of Court.' "What are they doing to him? What happened?" I asked, desperate to hear it was a formality of some kind. Some kind of momentary protocol.

"Dowd said since Reuben had escaped, he wasn't taking any chances with Dad."

Brian's eyes swam with tears. "Dowd is refusing him a bond, Mom. He's putting Dad in jail."

I started shaking. Tears ran down Brian's cheeks. He brushed them off with the back of his hand—my child, so vulnerable. We held each other. My crying came in two convulsive shudders, but I forced myself to stop. What had just happened registered. "Armed robbers are out on bail. How could Dowd do this?" I said, enraged.

Brian pulled out a handkerchief and wiped both our eyes. "He's the judge; he can do anything he wants. Listen, Mom, we're going to get him out. We'll get a hearing."

"Now?" My hope flew up to become elation.

"Well, not now. We'll have to draw it up…It'll take a couple of days."

I turned and started to walk away. "I'm going to see him. Where is he?"

Brian caught my sleeve. "You can't. Only his attorneys will be allowed. They're processing him now, fingerprinting him."

"Like a criminal." Jerry, having his fingers pressed on a pad of ink. "Where do they have him?" Brian pointed to the end of the corridor. I began to walk, obstinate, adamant, as fast as I could without running. "I'm going to see Dad."

The lettering on the frosted-glass window in the door read, 'Sheriff.' The waiting room was as small as a closet, dim and airless. An obese police officer came out of a door next to the reception window. His body was so close I smelled onions and cigarette smoke. He breathed with effort as he wrote in a notebook. Holsters hung from his waist with a gun on each side. I spoke into a microphone in the window where an officer was flipping through a blotter on the desk. "I have to see Jerry Kraig," I said to her day-glow orange hair.

She raised her eyes, black mascara clotted in her lashes. "Are you his attorney?"

I hesitated, stripped down to a child. I began to cry facing her straight on. Tears streamed down my face and snot ran from my nose. "His wife," I heaved.

"Only attorneys." She lowered her head down to her work.

"But I have to see him."

Her eyelids flipped back up. She sneered meanly. Lipstick marked her teeth. "Well, you can't."

At my back, the police officer shifted, ready for trouble. I remained standing there, silently refusing to leave, the policewoman staring at my streaming face.

I begged, "Please...we're supposed to go to New York." The policewoman sniggered. And I realized how outlandish that must have sounded.

Officers around a file cabinet were watching me, coolly curious, as if I were a minor spectacle. A male officer detached from them and came to the window. "We're not equipped for family visitation. This is only a holding facility. There'll be regular visiting hours when he's transferred to Lake County," he said, as if reciting from a manual.

"The jail?"

He said as he turned away from the window, "Yes, ma'am."

"Are you in charge? Help me, please!"

A woman officer approached and for a moment regarded the mess that was my face. She said to the flaming orange hair, "Give her five minutes." And then to me, "That's it, no more. Do you understand?"

"Yes! Yes, thank you. Thank you so much."

I wiped my face with the back of my hand as I walked past a line of desks. The woman officer opened a door and gestured toward what looked like the window of an exhibit at the Natural History Museum. "Don't even think of a minute more," she added.

Jerry stood behind the glass inside a glaringly lit enclosure only big enough for one chair. A caged husband, father, grandfather. His jacket was off. His shirt was surprisingly fresh looking, but his tie was gone. It was his face that I couldn't take. The Jerry twinkle was gone from his eyes. It was the most somber face in the world. He opened his arms in a gesture of surrender, his voice came from a microphone in the glass. "Honey, I'm so sorry for putting you through this.

"Please..." I couldn't get more words out. I just wanted to touch him. I choked down my urge to break down again.

"Gene, we only have a couple of minutes. Honey, I want you to go to your opening."

"My opening! No, my God."

"Gene, you have to. Please, don't let them take this away from us too."

"How could you even think I would leave you?"

"They told me you won't be allowed to visit tonight or tomorrow." His voice sounded almost normal. He was making plans, taking care of me. "And you'll come right back tomorrow and see me Sunday morning. Brian will be allowed to get in because he's an attorney of record. He'll call you in New York and that's all he'd be able to do even if you were home."

"I've already missed the flight. It's after two."

"Catch the next one! Honey, it's your opening. I want you to be with Karen."

Karen. Suddenly I was willing to walk to New York to get to my daughter. "Okay. I don't know how I'm going to do it, but okay."

Jerry's eyes misted as if I'd given him a special present. He put his hand up on the glass, and I matched mine to his. "Don't worry," he straightened his shoulders, "I'll be all right. I love you."

The officer touched my arm. "Time's up."

"I love you, too, honey."

CHAPTER EIGHT

OPENING

I left Jerry in custody of the penal system. He would be transported in a prison van with wire-mesh guard over slit windows to Lake County Jail, an hour-and-a-half trip east to Painsville, Ohio. His hands, cuffed in cold metal, loomed in my mind. The image was all the more distressing because Jerry's touch was so gentle. I could tell how he felt by his hands, flicking at seeds or crumbs on the table when he was disturbed, fluttering his fingers when he made a cute remark. We still held hands at the movies, and he drove with his left hand and held mine with his right. He kept his nails clipped short; his hands were always clean and neat. Mine were eaten up by solvents and abrasives of all kinds. My nails always retained a trace of paint no matter how often I soaked them in turpentine.

Brian sped to the Cleveland airport; his eyes focused straight ahead on the freeway. If he looked at me, he'd fall apart. He was taking care of me for his father and that was all he could manage. I felt a reliance on him I never experienced before. My son had become my strength and Jerry's and my connection. In thirty-two years of marriage we had never been apart without knowing we could get to each other. I rubbed Brian's shoulder affectionately. Ahead, the airport's 'Departing' sign swayed in the strong April wind.

"Mom, I almost forgot. When you were in the bathroom, I booked Karen a round trip from New York. She wants to see Dad with you on Sunday."

"Oh, that's good," I said, immensely grateful. "Thank you, Bri. Do you think Alex should come too?"

"He won't be on the list. Only two relatives are allowed to visit at Lake County. Then just for him to be with Karen, two last-minute tickets are a lot. None of us feel exactly flush right now." He sighed heavily.

"It's okay. I'm sure Alex will understand."

"But," Brian's eyes were burdened, "I don't want to hurt his feelings, either."

"Bri, you're not responsible for all of us. I hate leaving you. You look so...you've been through the ringer as much as me. In some ways more."

"I'm fine," he said, quickly. "Karen needs you more."

"I wish I could cut myself in two." He pulled up at the Continental terminal.

"Go, Ma, you'll miss the plane." He leaned over and kissed my cheek. I hugged and kissed him.

On the curb, I ducked my head back into the car, "I love you more than I could say."

"Me too."

~

I crawled over a man in the aisle seat as the flight attendant was demonstrating the inflatable life vest. As I shoved my carry-on bag under the seat, I remembered that Jerry's blood-pressure pills were still in his carry-on bag in the trunk of the car. A surge of panic made my temples throb. Somehow, Brian would have to get them to him. Jerry might have a stroke or heart attack without them, given the stress of these circumstances. Anything could happen; and it had. I buckled up and papered myself against the window, pressing my forehead against the cold pane as if it were an ice pack capable of anesthetizing my mind. I swallowed the sour aftertaste of a Coke Brian had pressed me to drink for the boost of caffeine before we left the courthouse.

The plane was picking up speed on the runway. I feared flying in the best of times. Knotting my fingers, I squeezed my eyes shut as we ascended. Tears ran down my cheeks. Up in the air the sky was chalk white. I hugged my purse like a security blanket. The pilot announced turbulence as the plane hit an air pocket and dropped, taking my stomach with it. Nausea was thick in my throat. I eyed the airsick bag, willing myself not to vomit.

"Hold on. Ten minutes and it'll be clear. Really, it's just a bit of a front. I'm a flight attendant," the man seated next to me said. He had a dusting of a champagne-colored moustache skimming his thin lips. "Are you afraid of flying?"

I nodded.

"As soon as we climb over the clouds, it'll smooth out." His face showed concern. "I know the crew," he said. "I can go back and get you some crackers. That might help settle your stomach." He offered me some tissues from his pocket. "They're clean, I promise."

"Thanks," I took them and dabbed my wet face. "I wish it was just that I'm afraid to fly," I said under my breath.

The attendant announced that the plane had reached cruising altitude and gave permission to move about the cabin, though, we were cautioned, more turbulence was expected later in the flight. "Great," I muttered and swallowed.

My seatmate unbuckled. "You look greener than green. I'm getting you some crackers."

The thought of putting anything in my mouth brought on another wave of nausea, but before I could stop him, he was halfway down the aisle. He came back with a handful of saltines and offered them to me with such compassion I wanted to hug him. I shook my head. "I don't think I can, but thanks."

He slid them into the net pouch on the seat in front of me, saying, "If you change your mind…." Then he asked, "Do you want to tell me what happened?"

His manner was so gentle, suddenly the need to talk was overwhelming. "I'm having a hard time believing what happened. I mean, here I am on a plane, and at two o'clock…" I paused, feeling the distress of the reality, "this afternoon a jury convicted my husband of conspiracy."

His eyes widened and he brushed at his moustache. "That's a terrible blow. No wonder you're so upset."

"I couldn't be more. It was one of those laws that a person can commit without premeditation, without intention." A bitter laugh came from behind my throat.

"Something like tax fraud?" he asked softly.

"Yes," I said, thrown by his acuity. "It had to do with my husband's client. Jerry was his attorney." I pictured Naomi Sturman on *Day One*, leaning lazily on her hand, admitting with her solicitous lips, how she offered sex to a male juror to vote in favor of an acquittal for Reuben. "It was very complicated. Finding my husband guilty was horrible but the worst part is the judge didn't let him out on bond. He was handcuffed and taken into custody." Shame inflamed my cheeks.

My seatmate's pale blue eyes remained on my face. As I was talking, I'd wound the strap of my purse around my fingers so tight puckers of flesh looked like tiny balloons ready to burst. "I think he's in a van now in transit to jail. I don't know. He was so positive he'd be on this plane with me." I pictured Jerry this morning slipping a Grisham novel into his carry-on bag next to the airline tickets. "We were supposed to be going to New York together. I have an opening in SoHo in an hour. My daughter's waiting for me, and I have to get to her. But I feel so guilty for leaving Jerry, even though I know I won't be allowed to visit him until Sunday. This is agony. I don't know how I got here." I unwound the strap from my fingers. Strap lines remained.

"You're going to see your daughter, right?"

"Yes, but it's crazy. We should have thought it out and bought a ticket for Karen to come to Cleveland. It was all such turmoil and rush. Jerry was so fixed on me going to my opening. It doesn't even matter now. And here I am. I can't believe I'm doing this."

"You've had a terrible shock. But it's not wrong for you to go to your daughter. Just try to accept that you're doing it."

"That's true." I smiled bleakly. "But...."

"No 'buts,' " he paused for so long I thought he was finished talking, then he said, "I don't know if this helps...but I understand because of my friend, Denny. He was in college and he's been put away for five years. Mandatory minimums, you know."

I nodded, though I didn't know.

The drink cart clattered to a stop at our row. Whatever boost the Coke provided had worn off. I asked for a black coffee. "Orange juice," my seatmate corrected, "coffee will just make you more anxious than you already are." He got juice instead.

I drank down the juice, realizing I was very thirsty. I thanked him and then admitted that I didn't know what mandatory minimums were.

"There's this Rockefeller drug law that says anyone who's found guilty of holding even the smallest amount of drugs must serve a mandatory prison term. They can't get probation or do community service instead. It's primarily for the 'war on drugs,' but it's for other offenses too."

"What was your friend convicted of?"

"Smoking marijuana at a party. A guy was dealing in the bedroom, and the party got raided. Denny got caught with a dime bag and he lost his scholarship to med school. Now, he'll never become a doctor. That's a pretty big price to pay."

"Jerry said he wouldn't serve time even if he was found guilty. He said a first time, nonviolent, white-collar offense with no direct evidence is a shoo-in for probation. But if that law, mandatory minimums, applies to Jerry...." My throat felt thick. I looked at my hand, remembering Jerry's assurance. It could have been him just placating my fears. "That means he'll have to serve time, too. There's going to be a sentencing hearing, but I don't know when." I shut my eyes, feeling dread for the future that at its core was doom. There wasn't anything redeeming. I could feel it. This was the beginning of an end. Negative. Jerry always said I was negative. This wasn't good. Tears leaked from the corners and I pressed my hands on them working to recover.

"Hey," my seatmate touched my arm, "I didn't mean to alarm you. Really, it's mostly for drugs." I blotted my eyes, grateful. He pursed his lips, regarding me as if I were a pot of boiling water he was waiting to see simmer down. "You've been through enough. Why don't you try to clear your mind for a little while."

The sky had turned charcoal gray. The overhead lights came on in the cabin.

I saw my seatmate reflected in the window and dozed off. I woke as the plane was skimming over Long Island Sound in a spattering rain. I turned to my seatmate. "I can't thank you enough. I don't know how I would have made it without you, and I just realized I don't even know your name."

"John Law."

"Seriously?"

"That's me. Funny, considering."

"Very."

Inside the terminal, John Law wished me luck, we hugged, and I rushed off to the taxi stand.

~

Disheveled and exhausted, I practically tumbled into the storefront gallery on Crosby Street at 7:45 PM with only fifteen minutes left until the end of my opening. My exhibit was in the back space. The large front space was packed with a black-clad crowd, still going strong. I worked my way around two black and white dogs on extended red leashes to avoid Nick, a painter, who also showed at the gallery and was the husband of Deirdre, the gallery director and owner. Nick had been testy, because I hadn't been in New York to install my art two weeks before the opening. When I had arrived late to do the installation, he and Dierdre had taken off for vacation. I had no choice but to do the work myself. In a frenzy, for two days I painted walls that turned out to be a botched job, because I couldn't find the twelve-foot ladder to reach the ceiling. I'd worked so hard to have this solo show and wanted so badly to belong there that I'd told Dierdre that there was going to be a trial only the week before the opening but that I was sure nothing was going to come of it.

Nick was the last person I wanted to talk to now, but he was waiting for me at the archway to the back gallery. "You finally made it! Your daughter and your friends have been asking about you every five minutes."

"I better tell them I'm..." I said, starting to move away.

Stopping me, he asked, pointedly, "What happened at the trial?"

I shoved my hands into the pockets of the same, now wrinkled jacket I'd worn to the trial. I hadn't had time to change into my new, black, opening clothes. My eyes were puffy slits; I was a walking wreck. "Guilty. He was found guilty," I said, suddenly so angry, I wanted to hit Nick for forcing me to say it.

A ripple of anger crossed Nick's face. "I thought you said that they didn't have a case against him?"

"They didn't," I floundered.

"Well, obviously, he must have done something...."

Before I could respond, Deirdre waved Nick over to the front desk near the window. He mumbled, "Collectors," and slipped between a group of art students. Confronted by the crowd in the back gallery, I felt so depleted I didn't have the energy to work my way in. Then arms wove around me. My friends and Debby's daughter, Alana, from New York, my Cleveland studio mates, Margaret and Layla. They already knew. They were sorry. So sorry. Anguish and sympathy as I had never experienced. All I could think was how I had to be with Karen. And suddenly, her blue, luminous, knowing eyes were there. She called out, "Mommy," and we clung to each other and cried as if Jerry had died. This was not an art opening. It was a wake. Alex hugged us and we made our own island of grief.

I asked for wine, drank it down, and had another. Then I remembered Jerry's pills. I asked Karen to call Brian, but she'd already spoken to him just before I arrived and Jerry remembered. He'd spoken to Brian on the phone before he was transferred. Brian had driven out to Lake County Jail and handed them off to the warden. Another good reason Brian was an attorney of record. He assumed Jerry had the pills by now. Why wasn't I relieved? The knowns and unknowns seemed to be stacking up around my mind as slippery, unfamiliar things.

Strangers congratulated me, artists talked about my work and about theirs. I heard them and nodded silently, but I wasn't absorbing what they were saying. My mouth felt frozen. Numbly, I repeated "guilty" and "jail" until they seemed pounded flat as old pain. I was too drained to encounter one more face or tell one more time what happened. I asked for another glass of wine.

Karen hugged me around my shoulders. She announced, "We have to go." She whisked the wine away. And she and Alex were guiding me through the dwindled crowd. I murmured something to Dierdre and we were on the street. The cobblestones glistened from the rain. Our ragtag entourage had left with us and we walked toward Broadway. I was between Karen and Alex and Margaret caught up to let me know she would meet me at my apartment after she picked up her suitcase from a loft in midtown where Layla was staying. I'd completely forgotten I'd invited her to be my guest for the weekend. The wine buzz was gone and I was suddenly terribly nauseous, clammy, and shaky. I didn't know how I would make it to my apartment, let alone talk to or host Margaret. "I really feel sick. I have to go home— now."

Realizing what kind of state I was in, Margaret checked with Layla and said she could stay on with her. The next thing I knew, Karen, Alex, and I were in a taxi and then inside my apartment, where I barely made it to the bathroom before vomiting. After, I stretched out on the small couch, my legs dangling over the armrest, my arm over my eyes. I was apprehensive about Karen and Alex leaving me alone, but I needed to sleep. I heard Karen open the refrigerator and then cupboards. Comforting sounds. She brought out cheeses, jelly, and crackers. "Mom, you haven't had anything all day, right?"

"I can't, but I'll sit with you."

Pouring tea into two mugs, she said, "You should have something."

Wrapped in a blanket, surrounded by pieces of art that hadn't made it into the show, we sat at the paint-smeared butcher block table that we'd had in our kitchen on Somerset. She'd sent Alex for ginger ale. My stomach was mercifully settling down and I nibbled at a cracker. It was four months since Lake Placid. Karen was thinner, older. She had Jerry's cheekbones and they stood out more prominently. Her hair was caramel brown and she had the complexion of a blond, but now her face looked almost colorless, transparent. Her eyes flashed cobalt. "Mom, I'm so angry with Dad that he didn't grab at the chance Dowd gave him to take the stand. How could he let this happen to us without putting up a fight? If he'd taken the stand, he would have won!"

"I'm not trying to defend him, Kare, but I don't think it mattered. No one could have won that trial. Who could have imagined the Oklahoma City bombing and the *Day One* exposé." I held my palms out as if to stop an onslaught. "There was too much stacked against us."

"Still, I'm talking about Dad taking control!"

"Don't you think I wanted him to take the stand? And Brian did, too. But when Dowd basically handed it to him, he couldn't do it."

"I just don't get it. Dad fought for every underdog in Cleveland and when it came to himself, he gave up! He was the rock in our family. He was who I've always counted on. Brian, too, more even. Dad was his hero."

"I know. You can still count on him. But he's fallible, Kare. How does anyone know what they'll do? I just cried, begging the police to let me see him with snot running down my face like a baby. He was locked in a glass cage. All I wanted was to smash it and let him out. "

"That's the other thing. I'm so angry with the judge I don't know what to do. It's horrible enough that Dad lost, but how could Dowd put him in jail? Dad should be here with us. I can't believe this has happened to him." She stood, scraping the metal chair legs on the concrete floor. She spilled out our cold tea and turned on the burner under the kettle.

"Dowd was punishing him," I said, incensed as my daughter, "punishing him for Reuben escaping! Believe it, Dowd watched *Day One*. What he did was unconscionable and none of it culpable. The judge is the God of the courtroom. He gets to go home scot-free. No matter what happens, Dad will have been an inmate of a county jail."

The kettle whistled and Karen refilled our mugs. "Waiting for you at the gallery was horrible. When it got to be 7:30, I went crazy, thinking you'd crashed. Why not? Everything else has! Your friends wanted me to tell them how it happened, over and over. It was as if Dad had died." Tears began slipping down Karen's cheeks. Thinking what Jerry and I had done to our children, a degrading powerlessness came over me. "Then," Karen's anger was still going full force, "Deirdre was wringing her hands about finally arranging for this collector to be there who she wanted you to meet but who couldn't wait any longer. I told her, if the collector wanted your art, what difference does it make if she talked to the artist or not? Deirdre huffed off. I'm sorry."

I went to her and kissed the side of her wet cheek. "I'm sorry too, Kare. So is Dad." I pictured Jerry pacing behind bars, having failed us and himself, his pride in being a lawyer shattered. Humpty Dumpty came to mind, the nursery rhyme Alison currently couldn't get enough of. I saw the egg wearing its respectable vest; an egg of honor and position who had it all, falling from that secure brick wall built to last forever. I squatted next to Karen and looked up into her distressed face. "I need to tell you something else I can't bear to think will happen."

"What?" Her body seemed to retreat into itself for protection.

"There's the possibility that Dowd could keep him in there until the sentencing. It could be months."

"God, why didn't you stop me from going off about the opening? I have to call Brian. Louie has to go to another court and get Dad out of there now."

"Brian said they're going to file petitions."

"Oh great, like all the other ones…that led Dad straight to jail!"

Alex buzzed from outside and Karen let him in. I answered the phone, relieved and apprehensive to hear Brian's voice. He said he'd finally gotten through to the sheriff at Lake County. Dad had arrived about an hour ago. He was going there first thing in the morning and he'd be at the airport to pick Karen and me up at noon.

Alex said to Karen, "I hate the thought of you going to see Jerry tomorrow without me. I wish I could see him to let him know I'm pulling for him as much as you."

"This feels like one more thing that's out of control. My father can't even see all of us. I can't believe he's in a cell with one of those disgusting toilets, like a criminal you see on TV." She stopped, then said with leveled sobriety, "You know, I've never worried about him before."

"He'll hold up," Alex said. "Of course what's happened to him is awful but your father has a lot of strength, Karen. I really admire him. I talked to him every night last week and though he was frustrated about the things that were happening he never whined or lost his perspective. That's the kind of strength I'm talking about, his character." Alex paused, arranging his thoughts as he spread cheese on a cracker. His thick dark brown hair fell over his brow. I focused on the cleft in his chin with the fleeting thought that their children might have it. Alex's handsome face was flushed. He shared Jerry's traits of kindness and tolerance. "He's going to win the appeal and the damage that *Day One* did will be exonerated by the appellate judges. There's no doubt this is rough, but he's going to come out of it okay."

I hugged him, "I'm going to hold you to that."

"We're all going to be okay," he repeated with even greater conviction. "We have to."

CHAPTER NINE

SHAVE ME

LAKE COUNTY JAIL

I cranked up the heat in the Blazer. Clearly irritated, Karen lowered her passenger window halfway and said, "What's with you and heat lately?" She forcefully commandeered stray hairs into her ponytail. I huddled into my coat, as a convoy of passing trucks whooshed by, letting in frigid wind. Let Karen freeze, if that's what she needed. I angled her heating vent toward me.

She spoke loudly over the traffic, her words barbed with anxiety, "Remember last night when Brian was telling us what Dad said?"

"Not really, what?" Karen streamed questions when she was nervous. I wasn't up for this.

"Dad told Brian that he was tired but all right considering...considering what?"

"You know Kare, Dad's not in the greatest place in the world," I said with finality. Her edginess was escalating mine. I concentrated on getting ahead of a semi barreling onto the ramp. "You'd think we'd be the only car on the road at seven on a Sunday morning," I grumbled.

"No, really," Karen wasn't letting the question go, "do you think Dad's in physical danger?"

"Well," I was trying to respect her fears while reigning in my own, "there's not much likelihood of any threat until they're done...." I paused, trying to remember what Jerry used to say happened to his clients. But I was pulling a blank. I either hadn't cared enough or he hadn't gone into the details.

"Done with what?" Karen persisted.

"Right now, he's in a holding cell that is basically solitary confinement. It probably means he's still being processed." I shuddered. Brian had said after they took Jerry away, "Dad's being processed now, Mom." I pictured raw meat with that purple transparent stamp on it.

"Do you think Dad has enough to eat? The food in that place has to be foul." Karen wrinkled her nose. "Mom?" Her voice was that of a plaintive child.

"I don't know, Kare. We'll find out if we're allowed to bring some in, ok?"

"What did Doris say when you talked to her last night?"

"I didn't think to ask her about that."

Doris Hall was my weekly housekeeper. Jerry was the attorney for all her four sons and grandson, among the contingent of Jerry's pro bono clients. Doris was distressed every time one of her boys got into trouble, nonviolent, petty thefts, always drug related. "I don't want you to even spit on the sidewalk," I'd hear Jerry warn whomever he'd just gotten out on bond. He cautioned that there were only so many times he could ask the judge to show leniency. Jerry was disturbed when one or the other 'caught 71,' a term for heading south on the freeway to the penitentiaries that housed Ohio's offenders: Lima State for the criminally insane, Mansfield Reformatory, and the Ohio Pen. Doris and her husband, David, raised decent sons, intelligent and good hearted. But their shabby rented house was in in the heart of Cleveland's east-side ghetto. It had made its claim on them and sent them into the turnstile existence of serving time, time out and back again, the accepted and expected way of life. The only thing prison taught young men, Jerry believed, was how to be better criminals. What they need was better opportunity for employment and drug treatment programs.

Doris's anguish each time one of her sons was behind bars was palpable. She baked and cooked for too many visits over the years and sent care packages for Christmas and their birthdays. David would drive her but always waited for hours in the car, refusing to see his sons locked up.

Last night when I told Doris where Jerry was she shrieked, "Not Mr. Kraig!"

Yes, Doris, I thought, I'm driving to see my husband just like you do to visit Robert.

She was a beautiful, strong woman. On Mondays, David dropped her off at my house early, on the way to his job. Doris and I took advantage of the extra time together over coffee. Many mornings she anguished over her sons but never expressed bitterness. I said I'd be plenty bitter if I were in her position. The frustration alone would drive me crazy. Their resources were few and they were up against crippling odds that offered little hope for betterment.

One morning, Doris told me how she sustained her spirit. It was rooted in the horror of what had happened to her father when she was a child in Cataula, Georgia. Julius Ward had been beaten by the Klan for refusing to give his best hunting dog to his boss, the white foreman at the saw mill. They'd taken him away and several nights later dumped his mangled, bloody body on the stoop.

Minnie Mae, Doris's mother, was a hump-backed woman only four feet, three inches tall. Her back had been broken by a white sharecropper when she was five years old, struck by a hoe in the field as a punishment because she wasn't working fast enough. Minnie Mae bathed her husband's wounds and nursed him through the night. The next morning, she sent Doris to bring back a bucket of water from the spring. Minnie Mae had made a long pan of corn bread. She stirred sorghum syrup into a big pitcher of the spring water. She cut a wedge of bread and poured the sweet water for each of her thirteen children, who were gathered around the table. As Julius moaned, out of his head in the other room, Minnie Mae instructed her children to raise their glasses and drink, saying, "You must always wash away the bitter with sweet water. The bread is from the earth to remind you to always bless the Lord for giving you this day on it."

But the foreman wasn't done with Julius Ward. Several months later, on a summer afternoon, after Julius had continued to refuse to part with his dog, the foreman told him to change the band under the saw. When Julius was under it, the foreman flipped on the switch. Doris was on her way to the mill with Pa's lunch pail. As she neared, a terrible confusion appeared ahead. A man stopped her, saying, "Chile', don't go any farther." But she pushed through the crowd and saw an incomprehensible horror. Her pa's head sat on a pile of saw dust next to the saw. His body was a distance away, thrown like a crumpled heap of rags. "What happened to Pa?" she screamed. She was only six years old.

After I graduated with a degree in journalism from Kent State University, I asked Doris if she wanted me to help her write her memoir. She said she thought it was important to tell of the things that try to tear you down and that you can't let them. You have to fight and stand tall. Without your dignity, you can't live.

We titled it *The Sweet Water Years*. For two years, I cleaned the house alongside Doris so we'd be done by noon. Then, we'd eat lunch and record her stories. She was a natural storyteller. Karen was ten, and she would come home from school and we'd go over what I'd written that day. She slid into the role of my astute daughter-critic. If she was home from school when Doris was recording, she would sit, listening with rapt attention.

Eventually, I went 'home' to Cataula, Georgia, with Doris to see where she had lived when the Klan came. We stayed with her niece Louise whom her mother had raised as a daughter, and I was welcomed into the family. I promised Doris that her story would be read. I got as far as winning an award for an excerpt, *"Surviving The Life,"* in the Whiskey Island Quarterly, Cleveland State University's literary magazine. I got representation with an agent in New York, but after a year of disappointing rejections, I shelved the manuscript. I was sorry to have let her down. I wasn't yet living in New York and didn't know what else I could do, but Doris was used to things not turning out. When Jerry went to work for Reuben, I stopped writing and began to make visual art.

Now, anguishing over my husband as Doris had over her sons: that they weren't eating enough or they'd been beaten up and anxiously driving, early on a

Sunday morning, to see them, I understood what it felt like to be swept under by the forces in power.

Karen had been somberly quiet. Then she piped up, "You know what terrifies me the most?"

I knew what she was going to say, the threat of Jerry being sexually assaulted. The side of my face prickled with fear. "I can't think about it."

"I'm scared."

I wished I could reassure her, but Lake County Jail didn't separate the men on drunk charges, rapists, petty thieves, or wife beaters. As a white-collar offender Jerry would be in the minority. My heart pounded in my ears. I let out a stream of breath trying to calm myself.

"Worrying is more exhausting than running a marathon." She closed the window and hunched into herself.

Twenty minutes later, an hour early, I pulled into a parking space at Painsville Lake County Jail, around the corner from an old town square. It was a fairly new building, where Jerry had often arranged bail for his clients. Karen and I exchanged weak smiles as we entered the empty waiting room. The immediate impression was of a bus station. Our voices glanced off hard industrial surfaces and the odor of disinfectant was overpowering. There was a window with a male officer behind it. We read posters for abused children and for a patrolman's fund-raising raffle. The prize was a Cadillac. Brass plaques along the wall near the bathroom praised the officers for exemplary performance. Karen and I took turns pacing, casting nervous looks at each other.

Finally, a half an hour late, the officer behind the window called my name. Slight and fidgety, he apologized, explaining that they were shorthanded this morning. I went through a weapons detector and another officer led me into a space that was shockingly bright. Then we went through another door, and it was like slamming into a wall of darkness. I bumped into the only chair and instantly, lights went on in front of me, revealing a cement-block cell behind thick green glass. An irrational fear gripped me that I was the subject of a double-blind experiment. Jerry appeared, his eyes widening at the sight of me, as if I were too good to be true. I realized I'd been holding my breath and exhaled loudly. I skittishly checked behind me, feeling an ominous presence. But I was alone.

Jerry was gaunt and unshaven, dressed in loose navy blue cotton pants with a drawstring waist and a matching V-neck pullover, the kind of uniform orderlies wear. He sat facing me at a narrow counter and looked around, at a loss. Then finding the phone on the wall next to the window, he grabbed for it. I patted around on the wall and found mine to my right, obscured by the dark. I had never been so happy to hear him breathing. His eyes were on me now, appreciating me. "How are you, hon?" His voice echoed in the receiver.

"Okay." I spoke at a careful distance, keeping my mouth from the phone. My hand was sweaty, and for a moment I had the sensation that the glass was liquid and I could swim through it to get to him. I pressed my hand over the loud pumping of my heart. "I'm worried about you."

"I'm okay," Jerry glanced sideways to make sure he was alone, "but I have to get out of here. I'm in a cell in solitary. There's a long row of them. They keep lights blazing twenty-four hours and there's twenty-four-hour camera surveillance: they said it's to make sure we don't do anything. I can't see anyone else, but the block must be filled, because the noise is constant. Yelling and screaming. One guy is howling, coming off drugs or crazy. I haven't eaten. I can't. Gene, what's happening to get me out?"

"Tomorrow Louie's filing the petition for a hearing with Dowd."

Jerry's upper body slumped. "That means I'll be here a minimum of two more nights."

I studied my hands, feeling his desperation. "Karen's here," I forced brightness into my voice.

His eyes lit up. "She is? She came back with you," he smiled, "that's nice."

"Do you know how long you'll be in solitary?"

"If I'm here on Tuesday, I'll be moved into population. Solitary's pretty hard to take. I haven't been able to sleep. I can't stop going over and over what I did wrong. I should have taken the stand. I know I should have. Brian said he wishes I plead out. But if I had to do it again, I'd still have gone to trial. But our time's almost up and I want to know about your opening? Did your art look good?"

"I guess the work was okay. I got there at the end and it was a blur really. Everyone was so shocked and upset. But I was glad I was with Karen, though."

"It's feeling pretty grim. I guess we have to get used to it."

"No, I refuse to give in. I was thinking about Doris on the way here. If there's anything I've learned from her, it's that we survive by keeping our dignity and fighting. We'll hire Messerman. We have to win back what we lost on appeal. You'll be home while its pending and we'll put it all behind us."

Jerry rubbed his eyes. "Right now, all I can think about is how I'm going to get out of here."

Simultaneously, a guard appeared in both of our booths. Time was up.

As I came out, Karen was going through the weapons detector and didn't see me. Fifteen minutes later, she was back out, relieved. "He was happy I came," she said. "I hated seeing him like that, but he's so strong. He said he's fine and there's nothing to worry about." She put on her jacket. "Just that he had it in him to be strong for me is good. I'm glad I came so he could do that for me. I feel much better." She scowled. "Do you think he's okay?"

The trapped look in Jerry's eyes came to mind. "He's beating himself up pretty hard. We've got to get him out of here."

~

Karen returned to New York late that afternoon and I went home. I stayed off the phone, hoping Jerry would call. The night stretched on and on. Rain spattered the bedroom windows. The woods looked etched black against a smoky purple sky.

Monday was more of the same. The only time I left the house was to pick Macabee up from the kennel. Cindy brought the kids over to cheer me up. They ran after the dog and whipped up a storm of toys. I was given exuberant hugs and slobbery kisses. Cindy said she was glad to get out of the house, where their phone was ringing off the hook. The concerned friends and relatives who didn't want to bother me were calling her. What was left unsaid was: "How long is this going to go on?" The future had become implausible.

I was so jittery I couldn't sit still. I cleaned the fridge, wiped counter tops, went after dust. Brian was going to see Jerry after work. I had that to hold on to. Brian had the petition for the hearing with Dowd. He was going to go over it with Jerry, which meant it had yet to be filed. The wheels of justice seemed to be stagnating, like the day.

Brian called from the car after seeing Jerry. The reason he hadn't called was because they were moving him up to population. I didn't understand why that prevented him from using the phone and Brian didn't get it either. But it didn't matter. We had Jerry fending for himself among criminals to worry about now.

The day wore on. Hundreds of daffodils swayed along the flagstone in the balmy April breeze. I watched them out the picture window and kept looking at my watch. The fireplace emitted damp smoke, which was not unpleasant but wrapped up in memories of all the previous New Year's Eves: the coffee table set with candles and champagne, snow transforming the woods, a fire dancing over logs, and Jerry jumping up to feed it. The year Andrew was born, we began the tradition of babysitting him so that Cindy and Brian could go out. This year, the indictment had been looming, but more as a feared bad dream than a nightmare. Andrew was old enough to understand we were having a celebration and I poured blue bubbly soda into his champagne glass. He excitedly "toasted" us through our dinner: his fried rice, our lobsters. Alison had been fed earlier and put to bed.

We'd stood over Andrew, his face deep into Stinky, his stuffed bear, tucked in his junior 'house' bed. Alison slept in her crib. Her double-fringed eyelashes innocently hovered over her cheekbones, and her curly hair spread out over her pillow as if she were swimming in a dream. She was dark and Andrew, fair. I recalled how my father had taken great pleasure in calling Karen and Brian his dividends. Alison suddenly stirred, flinging off the baby quilt that had been her brother's. She turned sideways and her petite leg dangled through the space between the bars.

Jerry and I had looked at each other. The Casper the Friendly Ghost night-light made Jerry's eyes appear hollow. "How," he whispered, "are we going to protect them if…?"

I'd been surprised by my sudden anger. "If things go wrong?" I said. "They already have."

"I guess they have," Jerry said.

I put my hand on his arm apologetically. "Let's get through the indictment," "I said, softly. "I don't care about waiting up till midnight. The kids are going to have us up at dawn. How about going to sleep?"

Jerry went downstairs, tamped out the fire, and closed up the house. My eyes were closed when he got into bed. I was enveloped in sadness. Feeling his lips on mine, I automatically kissed back. His mouth was gentle and sad. I'd turned and buried my face into the pillow, longing to feel normal again.

Lost in the memory, I jumped when the phone rang and tore into the kitchen to answer it.

"Hi, hon," Jerry said, "I'm so glad you're home."

"I've been glued here, waiting. How are you doing?"

"I'm so tired, I'm punchy." Jerry said, his voice sounded scraped. "But I can call you now that I'm up in population, and that's good. I'm in the common room. They play cards in here and eat meals brought up on trays. Wait a second, I have to put more quarters in the phone." There was a long pause.

"Jer, are you there?"

"Yeah, sorry. My change was in the other pocket."

"How much time do we have?"

"As long as no one is waiting in line I can talk as long as I have quarters."

"That's great! Is…anyone there?"

"We're in luck. Not right now. So we can keep talking, I hope."

"What is it like?"

"Well, pretty bizarre."

"Is it bad? Are you in danger?" Black clouds had rolled in and the kitchen window was being pelted by hail.

"There are a couple of guys in here who I'm going to avoid. They're very aggressive. They take seats away from people and are basically bullies. But I don't think…I don't feel like I'm in danger." He paused, "Wait a minute, a couple guys just came in. I don't want anyone to hear me."

"*Motherfucker! Motherfucker! Motherfuckers!*"

"What's going on?" I yelled over the screams, picturing the room under siege.

"I think it's okay," Jerry said, distractedly, "they're leaving. It was something about someone's hat. We're not allowed hats in here. Okay," he sighed. "Good, they're going with the c.o. to rec. Now, I can tell you. First of all, I'm in a pod that houses sixteen men. About two-thirds are white, one-third black, and a couple of Hispanics. There's only Dominic who's in for a white-collar like me. He's this wiry guy with a stringy moustache. He's been in thirty days and has the scoop on everything. It's like he's made it his mission to be my mother hen, so I'm very grateful for that. This was my commissary day but I missed it, because I got up here after they'd taken the guys down. I desperately needed to brush my teeth, and I needed soap. Dominic has this mini stockpile in his locker. He said it's to prevent having to ask anyone for anything. He wants to be the one they come to for things, which puts him in a position of power and respect. He lent me everything: a toothbrush, toothpaste, a comb, mouthwash, soap, paper and a pen, and a Snickers candy bar. I can't tell you how delicious that was.

When Brian was here, he left some money for me. So I've been going to the vending machine and I've eaten a lot of Snickers." He laughed, a self-conscious high laugh. "I decided to walk them off by circling the pod. I was on my second loop and a huge black guy, I mean a giant, with a bald head the size of a melon and this deep, booming voice called me. He was pointing at me saying, 'You, come here!' I didn't have any idea what he wanted from me, but I didn't want him to think I was being disrespectful, so I went.

"He held out a straight-edged razor. Honey, I was scared. I thought, 'He's crazy. He's going to cut me.' But, he bellowed, 'Shave me.' I was stunned. Then he turned around for me to shave the back of his head and neck with all these folds that looked like a shar-pei. My hands were shaking and I said, 'I've never done this before.' But he didn't budge. He was like this huge building. I began to scrape at his growth that was like coarse sandpaper. I was hoping my hands weren't shaking so badly that I'd cut him. He yelled, 'Harder!' I tried to do it but the blade was dull. He was getting mad and he yelled again, 'Harder!' His voice was like thunder. I said, 'I'm sorry, I'm not used to doing this.' He said, 'Aw, you all right. Never mind.' I wanted to cry I was so relieved. I'll never figure out why he picked me."

I started laughing, picturing Jerry scraping at that shar-pei neck. Jerry was laughing too; anxiety–relieving laughter that we needed so badly.

"All I could think of," Jerry was still chuckling, "was 'feed me,' from *Little Shop of Horrors*." We paused to catch our breaths. "Hey," his voice was still joking, "when I'm in the big house I could charge. I'll call myself the 'Barber of Cellville'." Then Jerry said a guy was behind him and he had to go. We hung up on that light note, despite everything. I wouldn't be seeing him again until Sunday, but he promised to call whenever he got a chance.

Dowd agreed to a hearing on Friday at 9 AM. Jerry had been in jail exactly seven days. I tried not to dwell on him being transported again in the police van, this time to court, where I was waiting for him to arrive. The bitter familiarity of my place on the same bench filled me with foreboding over what Dowd would or wouldn't do.

Our character witnesses were a bailiff, judge, sheriff, and one of Jerry's oldest friends who'd also grown up on 140th Street. In turn they were called to the stand and each expressed how appalled they were by Dowd's severe punishment and that they'd known Jerry throughout his career. They had never doubted the integrity of Jerry's work, including his work for Reuben. Jerry was one of the most trusted men of anyone they knew. I hoped Dowd heard their sincerity.

Judge Dowd had listened stoically. From his standpoint, these were witnesses no different from thousands of others pleading for a friend or loved one. What else were they going to say?

Now, Jerry took the stand. I was staggered to see the toll the last week had had on him. It was as if jail had diminished him. He looked beaten. Dark hollows appeared under his eyes, and he was deeply flushed, as if his blood pressure were high. A vein stood out on the side of his brow. "Your Honor," he said, "I come before you as a humbled man. In the seven days I've just spent in jail I've had a lot of time to think," he smiled, painfully. "My thoughts primarily centered around freedom. Many of my clients have been incarcerated and I have visited them. But I was always able to walk out the free man. Now I know what it's like not to have a choice over when I turn out the light to sleep or when I can eat or call my family. I beg the court to allow me those freedoms once more, until that time when I must serve my sentence."

Dowd took off his glasses and vigorously rubbed each lens as if they'd been responsible for clouding his vision. He granted Jerry the right to go home and go to work but he was not to travel out of the state until he began to serve his sentence. Dowd tapped his gavel and summoned his bailiff, impatient to get on with the next order of business.

My hand shook as I wrote the five-thousand-dollar check to the Clerk of Courts for Jerry's bond. Jerry was surrounded by his friends in the lobby when I came out. I thought of my friends at my art opening. He was smiling, but his eyes lacked luster. We'd had a victory but there was sadness inside it. I squeezed in and pressed close to feel Jerry's body next to mine. He hugged one arm around me and the other around Brian. "Thank you, son," he kissed him and pulled me closer. Jerry kissed me with the familiarity of a lifetime. He said, "What would I do without you, honey? God, it's so good to know I can go home."

"Let's get out of here," Brian said.

CHAPTER TEN

SENTENCING

JULY 1995

Jerry and I were retreating more and more into our own silence. The appeal wasn't going to happen overnight and the unknowns, what was going to happen to Jerry, my life, the practice, the kids, us, demanded concentration. Every so often I erupted, lashing out, pushing Jerry to rehash his complicity, his responsibility, his blindness, needing to purge mine. His admissions were a painful confusion of confession and denunciation: he saw now that after he quit Reuben he shouldn't have done anything more; he shouldn't have gone to Switzerland, "but…" he always said.

"No 'buts,' " I yelled at him, "you just don't get it."

"Get what? There are no grays for you."

Jerry stood firm, but with a broken back. I hated myself after the confrontations. This was consuming me, and eating him up. Jerry looked for comfort from me and I desperately needed it, too. But we'd become mirrors of each other's worst fears. For the first time, we couldn't find solace in each other's arms.

Though my show was still up at the gallery, it might never have opened. I was that removed from New York. At my studio, several pieces that hadn't made the cut lay on the floor like so much litter. I'd been so enthusiastic when I'd thought of doing these encaustic paintings on toasters. The old Sunbeams were my favorites. I'd prominently positioned the cords next to the toasters, each on its own Formica shelf, which I'd had installed at the gallery. The subject was about paying attention; if one wanted toast but didn't realize that the toaster was painted with wax, once plugged in, the painting melted and was destroyed. It couldn't be more of a metaphor for our lives right now. The thought gave me a sickly feeling as if the toasters were taunting me. I picked up a piece with light and dark cadmium orange dots, titled *Halloween Toaster*. The harsh fusion of oranges now brought to my mind the orange of a convict's jumpsuit.

The communal studio phone was ringing, an old rotary that had been my mother's. I ran down the hall where it sat on another spattered school desk next to the slop sink. Deirdre's voice lilted with good news. An art critic from the *New York Times* had just left the gallery. He'd spent a lot of time with my work and was going to review it in Friday's paper. Two Fridays ago, Jerry had been convicted and put in jail and I'd had my opening. Last Friday he was released, and this Friday my art was making the Times. Ecstatic, I called to tell Jerry at the office.

On Friday at 7 AM, Jerry and I were at a window table at the corner café watching for the truck that delivered the papers to the drugstore next door. After an hour drinking coffee, the Arts section was flung open across the table. Crossing my fingers for a favorable review, I read aloud the critic's praise of my toasters hearkening back to pop art with a conceptual edge. Jerry beamed, "It's great. You're on your way, hon. I want that for you." He kissed me. But it was now 8:30 and his time was running out at the office. He was impatient to get there.

I observed him as he went through the ritual pleasure he took letting down the top of the convertible, adjusting his cap snuggly, and tapping the rearview mirror back into place. The optimism of moments before suddenly extinguished. I turned back to the paper and reread my review, wanting to recapture the thrill, but all I could think was: "What good could there be for me to be on my way up when Jerry was plummeting?"

It had been three weeks and not even a rough draft of the appeal had been written. Jerry's sentencing hearing was set for July 21. No matter how the appeal was expedited, it wouldn't be filed and decided upon by the Supreme Court of Ohio in our favor before the hearing. Realistically, the best we could now hope for was for it to be won shortly after he began to serve his sentence. Then he would be free. No fine, no parole, readmission to the bar, and his law license reinstated. The blot would fade in the light of a future almost lost and which would then be revered more than ever.

Each day, I went to the studio and Jerry to the office as if we weren't in limbo, as if we were as ordinary a couple as we'd always been. The day he received notice in the mail that his law license had been revoked, and he was prohibited from practicing law, he left the letter, opened, on the dining room table as if it were a bill for something he'd already paid. He only said, flatly, "I'm not a lawyer." I didn't know how to react. We knew it was coming. We ate dinner and didn't talk about it further. This was happening with greater frequency. The more catastrophic the change, the less we could express.

Brian would inherit Jerry's case load and was in a near panic over how he would handle the avalanche of work and responsibility on top of his own full case load of clients. Jerry hunkered down to the task of writing a status report on each of his files, replete with instructions and recommendations.

The *Plain Dealer* covered Jerry's conviction. The headline was in the metro section. Jerry hadn't commented except to be grateful it hadn't been on the front page. I felt his humiliation as I heard him tear it out. He folded it carefully, like he was sealing an envelope and was afraid it would leak out. And he placed it in an unnamed file. I opened it later. There were also the clippings from the Jewish News and two others from the *Plain Dealer*: one about his indictment and a much earlier article that he'd been so proud of about him as a champion of the First Amendment with a smiling picture of him at his office in front of his law books. The grapevine had already been going strong, but after the article bugling his conviction, it spread with a vengeance. It seemed everyone Jerry had ever known was on the phone. The lines at the office were constantly flashing with well-wishing and appalled clients, as well as the clients alarmed about their cases. Friends and clients were dropping in to lend support, adding to the chaos.

Brian braced himself, anticipating that clients would fire him and take their cases to 'reputable' law firms. He steeled himself for the reality of possible bankruptcy and was feeling helpless about the bind he was in. Several years remained on their lease, and there was no tenant's escape clause due to incarceration. Until Brian knew how many clients would seek counsel elsewhere, he couldn't cut down on the overhead. If too many ditched, there'd be no choice but to fold up.

We agonized over what to do about the sentencing hearing. Messerman's fee was prohibitive. But we had already made too many mistakes that had cost more than money. Brian wanted to form a defense fund. Jail had been a degradation for Jerry and now his self-respect was lowered even further by his need to go to his friends with his hand out. He couldn't promise he'd ever be able to pay anyone back, but his friends wanted to help. Joe Sturman said, "Anything, Jer. Anything." Their outpouring of generosity buoyed Jerry's spirit. And he also took consolation in knowing that if the shoe had been on the other foot, he would have been the first to offer. Now, he could afford to go to Messerman.

~

Messerman reached his hand over his gleaming desk. The only two objects on it were a phone and a humidor with the lid open. He greeted Jerry, clipped and businesslike but shook his hand warmly. He shook mine quickly, almost as an afterthought. He was another Kinsman kid who'd done good. He had played doubles on the court next to Jerry's and mine for many years before I started commuting to New York. Jerry and Messerman had always enjoyed exchanging work related anecdotes, but I'd been aware of Jerry's slight deference to Messerman's success and reputation.

Messerman's office was corporate but homey. His desk sat on a subdued blue and red oriental area rug, surrounded by the deep richness of a mahogany wood floor. The chairs were comfortable and clubby. The view behind the desk intimidated. Like Gotham's monstrous teeth, concrete and steel skyscrapers jammed the wall of windows that wrapped around a corner.

Messerman tipped back in his executive leather chair and quickly ran his eyes over Jerry as if he were a doctor expecting to see a symptom he hadn't been told about. "You bring me a loser!" He kept his eyes on Jerry, waiting for the full impact to take effect. I felt the blow as if I'd been hit in the chest. I snatched a side glance at Jerry. He was staring straight at Messerman, like a child who would rather die than flinch in the face of a justified punishment. "All I can do for you," Messerman went on, "the best I can do, is damage control. I can promise that you're going to serve time." Messerman lifted his upper lip exposing oversized white teeth that made me flinch. He leaned forward. "I've seen this over and over and believe me, it's only a matter of how much time you're going to get. I want to make one thing absolutely clear, Jerry," Jerry's back was rigid, his jaw locked tight, "if you aren't prepared to take responsibility for your guilt and plead remorse for what you've done, I won't represent you."

Messerman's arrogance and confidence seemed absolute.

Jerry's face reddened. "I pled not guilty because I wasn't guilty. You're saying now that I've been found guilty, I have to admit to a crime I didn't commit and throw myself at the mercy of the court by showing remorse?" Jerry pulled himself up even straighter. "I can't. I can't do it."

"I don't care what you did or didn't do. A jury found you guilty." He sat upright. "Therefore in the eyes of the law and this country, you're guilty. And if you don't show the judge that you've taken full responsibility for the crime, and that you've learned remorse, he'll throw every book on the shelf at you." Messerman snapped the lid shut on the humidor. "Five to seven years."

"I can't do that," Jerry said, quietly.

For several seconds, Messerman looked at Jerry like a snake assessing a frog for the right spot to inject his venom. In this case, he was looking for Jerry's survival instincts. Jerry looked ready to leap. Messerman knew and I knew that it was too late. Jerry was going to have to do as he advised. Jerry had held onto his principles, but they couldn't save him.

"Jerry, the judge is bound to follow the sentencing guidelines and there are mandatory minimums." I felt a pang inside my chest; that's what John Law had talked about. "So Dowd, in this case, will allocate so many points against you for your guilt, so many for your role as the "point man" and so many for being an attorney who broke the law. Your admission of guilt will take points off. Showing remorse will take points off. So will the fact that you have no priors, no black marks in the legal community, etc."

"But we're going to win on appeal," I blurted out.

Messerman pressed his fingers on top of the humidor as if he didn't trust it to remain closed. "Your chances of winning on appeal are next to zero."

"But…"I began to argue.

"No 'buts.' " I straightened as if he'd put a gun in my back. "Do you know why Jerry lost the trial?"

"Because he didn't hire you."

Messerman laughed, appreciatively, "Well, yes. But no." He sunk his shoulders into the buttery leather. "It was because I wouldn't have let him go to trial. I would have pled him out as I told him to do when he came to me back in January. I could have gotten him a reasonable fine and a year, maybe two years probation. But do you know why I wouldn't have let him go to trial?" Again Messerman bared his expansive white teeth. "Because ninety-eight percent of all federal juries find the defendant guilty."

Jerry's jaw rippled. I felt the shock of what I had intuited but hadn't given credence to until this minute: that the trial had been a foregone conclusion and that was why neither Morford nor Wooley hadn't thrown anyone off during jury selection while Hirschorn had been jumping up and down, probing, objecting. A derisive laugh stuck in my throat. It hadn't mattered who'd filled the jury box, because the odds of the prosecution winning were almost one hundred percent.

"How long do you think I'll be gone?" Jerry's voice was muffled. His eyes cast down on the legal pad on his lap, which contained the notes he'd made.

"I'll talk to Morford. I think I can get him to agree to a couple years."

"Two years is outrageous. I figured with all of your experience you'd get it down to six months. It's going to be hell," I said.

"I told you. You brought me a loser. Two years is a good deal. You'll be lucky to get that," Messerman grinned.

"A two-year sentence is some luck," I mumbled, wanting to smack the smug smile off Messerman's face.

Messerman's eyes played. "Do you know what all the wives tell me?" he asked, conspiratorially. I had baited him and he was taking me out. "They tell me that they have more fun while their husbands are gone than when their husbands were home. They get a break from the grind. They travel. They get their freedom and they love it."

I stood abruptly and smacked my hand on his desk. "Well, you know what? I've already got my freedom. I don't need my husband to go to prison to liberate me."

"I'll bet you do," Messerman said. "Let me know what it's like after he's been gone a couple months."

Jerry stood. His fingers gripped my shoulder. "It's a good thing my marriage is in better shape than your serve, Mess. I'll let you know what we're going to do."

Jerry drove for a while in silence. I was still seething. It had become an ugly game. No referee, no rules, just the players who had no choice but to follow the leader. "You're going to do it, aren't you?" I asked, wanting Jerry to say both no and yes.

"I don't see what else I can do that would make sense at this point."

"I'm so glad you didn't give Messerman the satisfaction of telling him to his face."

"He knows anyway. What a blow, huh?"

I swallowed hard so I wouldn't cry, but tears burned my eyes.

"It's a wallop. I'm driving myself crazy, shoulda, woulda, coulda." Jerry half laughed. "If I went in a store right now, I wouldn't have the confidence that I'd buy the right-sized shoes."

~

After Jerry hired Messerman, he gave us the lowdown on the possible costs we should brace ourselves for. First was the fine and Jerry and I became obsessed with trying to figure out how we would come up with the worst case scenario of $250,000. Second was Jerry's payment for his incarceration— if we were placed in the wealthy category, we'd have to pay $35,000 for Jerry's room and board with the BOP (Bureau of Prisons). A five-year stay would make it $175,000. Paying for the pain was like being slapped on both sides of my face, trapped with nowhere to turn.

The penitentiary offered employment opportunity at a wage of twelve cents an hour. If Jerry was a prisoner of good standing, his last six months would be spent at a halfway house, and he'd only have to pay back to the BOP twenty-five percent of what he would earn working for Brian as a paralegal. The way I understood it, not only was the offender deprived of freedom but the wherewithal to reenter his life afterward. Some would say the offender deserves what he's brought onto himself, but did the offender's family deserve to be reamed, too?

I expected the government would determine our financial worth in a special audit. And they had. But they were too smart to judge based only on black and white numbers. We were given two days' notice that a presentencing assessor would be making a home inspection. He would then file a report on his findings to Dowd.

I went into a tailspin: dusting, polishing, arranging closets. Jerry said the guy wasn't coming to buy the house just to look it over. As I cleaned, I tried to imagine what among our things might be perceived as wealth. I assessed our neighborhood. Shaker Heights is known as one of the wealthiest communities in the country. But it is a diverse community, wealthy mansions around the lakes, where Reuben had lived, to low-income sections with multidwelling housing. This was the reason we had moved here, so that Brian and Karen would grow up mixing with all kinds of people from diverse backgrounds. And it had benefited them; they were open minded socially and in their careers. Our neighborhood was the middle of the middle class. We lived on a typical street of families with two and a half children, attached garages, and patios in the backyards. We were in walking distance of Thornton Park, shopping, and the rapid transit line to downtown. I woke up Jerry at 6 AM so that I could clean the bathroom again and make the bedroom as pristine as a four-star hotel.

At 9 AM, I'd decked the dining-room table with bagels, fresh fruit, cheeses, and an assortment of Danish. Coffee was ready. I was wracked with what ifs…if we have to pay half of the worst-case estimate, we would have to sell the house, our apartment in New York, and withdraw a major chunk out of Jerry's retirement fund.

Overweight and unkempt, Mr. Glatz gave the impression of someone who'd much rather be sitting in front of a TV than appraising our net worth. He surprised me by passing up the food with a dour expression that I took as a bad sign that he thought the breakfast spread was meant to butter him up. But he sat heavily at the head of the table as if he'd already exhausted himself, and agreed to have a cup of coffee. Jerry sat next to him. Glatz laconically told what I surmised was his standard war story: this one guy who cheated the government and how tough it was for him to pay the thirty grand for three years and said it was going to break him. Glatz clinked the spoon loudly while stirring in half-and-half. He took a slurpy gulp, satisfied by our chastened silence. His message was grinding in my stomach: he had the power to make us suffer, and he was enough of a government man to do it.

Jerry was too much of a lawyer to show he was thrown. With professional good sportsmanship, he meted out details of our finances, highlighting the fact that we lived well but weren't wealthy, and that we had spent most of our money on our children's education, had little savings, and our substantial money was in his retirement fund, but we couldn't access it without penalties. Glatz couldn't have been less interested. He shoved away his coffee and asked to see the rest of the house. Jerry remained at the table.

I led the way upstairs and Glatz stepped heavily behind me. I pointed out what had been the kids' bathroom, which was now Jerry's domain. It still had the original, forty-year-old chipped tile. The stall shower, I remarked, temperamentally leaked. Our master bathroom wasn't in any better shape. Glatz wasn't seeming to pay attention, but I persisted, opening closets, exposing the private us with nothing to hide. Not a fur coat, not a designer suit. See? Look. I went on and on about having converted Karen's old bedroom, small by today's standards, but it had been fine. Now it was just perfect for our grandchildren, Andrew and Alison. WE ARE GOOD, ORDINARY, LOVING PEOPLE.

Once downstairs, Glatz indicated that he was ready for a Danish, maybe two. But I couldn't stop. He hadn't seen the kitchen ceiling, rust stained, and cracked from where the shower leaked. Back in the living room, Glatz looked longingly at the food on the dining-room table. But I directed his attention to the art, lest he think we were 'collectors.' Nobody's but mine, nothing of value. A couple of framed prints, nothing of value. The den offered more of the same, a well-worn leather couch, once cream white and now yellowed as old teeth. A modest TV. Nothing. Another leak puckering the wall covering, which was hand-printed and verdant green. I hoped Glatz lacked an eye for this expensive splurge. I had never taken such pride in pointing out how much we'd let the house go and that it had to be worth less than market value.

Glatz gratefully settled back in his place at the head of the table and set to eating Danish, fruit, a fresh cup of coffee. Glatz, who had followed me through the house like a somnambulant, was fast on his feet when it came to the sidestep as Jerry adroitly fished for his evaluation. All we got from him was, "I knew what was up the minute I pulled up the drive. Your siding is faded, shutters peeling, trees and shrubs and grass are tended to but don't cry 'landscaped.' Rusted mail box, should be replaced." Victory swelled in my chest. Glatz knew what the BOP didn't: If we had contraband, we weren't going to put it on display.

Glatz asked Jerry who owned the house? "It's in Gene's name. It has been since I went into practice and so is the New York apartment." Glatz chomped away, rueful and disappointed.

On June 21, three days after our thirty-fourth anniversary, Jerry was sentenced to the FCI (Federal Correction Institution) in Morgantown, West Virginia. Dowd gave Jerry two years with six months off for good behavior, the last two months to be served at a halfway house, making the actual time served at FCI twenty months. He was to begin serving his sentence on August 21, the day after Jerry's fifty-eighth birthday.

Dowd had seen who Jerry was. He had listened to Brian and the other witnesses. He had read Glatz's report that showed us on the unglamorous side of middle class. We wouldn't have to pay for his incarceration and he only got a slap-on-the-wrist fine of ten thousand dollars, to be paid in five-hundred-dollar monthly installments after his release. He would be on parole for two years following his incarceration with an indefinite suspension of his license to practice law. After agonizing over the possibility of total ruin, this felt like something we could handle. We'd still have the retirement fund, and the fine would not bleed us to death. Despite Messerman's pessimism, we held on to what Louie still believed, that we could win the appeal.

In compliance, as ordered by Dowd, Jerry returned to his office the following Monday to notify all of his clients that he was a convicted felon. He was no longer an attorney and could no longer represent them. He said it was like writing his professional obituary. "I, Jerry B. Kraig, regret to inform you...." However, an indefinite suspension opened the door to getting his license back. After parole he would be eligible to petition the court and bar association for a reinstatement hearing. The process could take as long as five years, but we latched on to it as another ray of hope to reclaim our future.

CHAPTER ELEVEN

SURRENDER

The mood in our house was heavy and disorienting, as if we were fogged in. Dinners took on the significance of our last few, the food cottony in my mouth. Jerry enfolded me in his arms in bed and I cried as we made love, desperate for his presence but anticipating his absence. Helpless, we didn't talk about these changes. Repeatedly, I cheered we would make it to the other side, but my heart wasn't convinced it was true. Jerry was about to live in a prison for two years, but it might as well have been two hundred. We rolled over to our sides of the king-sized mattress, withdrawing into our defeat, inuring ourselves for August 21.

A week after sentencing, Jerry received instructions from the BOP in the mail: a photocopied list of what he would be required to bring with him when he surrendered.

I would have procrastinated shopping until the day before, but Jerry was eager to get it over with. On Sunday morning, we were in the parking lot waiting for May Company to open. Jerry wanted to be the first customer, to avoid running into someone who might guess that he was buying a two-year supply of prison wear.

At the bins of jockeys and boxer shorts, Jerry consulted the list that he'd studied before we left as if cramming for a test. "Seven sets of cotton underwear, white or gray, but no colors," he read. I grabbed two packages of Hanes jockeys. I was a careless shopper but this was a no-brainer. I felt as conspicuous as Jerry. I'd have us out in fifteen minutes. Jerry grabbed the packages from me. "We can't buy these," he said, as if he'd caught me red handed in the act of mutiny.

"What are you talking about? They're on the list," I thumped at the sticker, "size thirty-six, white." I raked my fingers through my hair as if it would move him along.

But Jerry rattled the paper in front of me and read, "All issue must be newly purchased, in its original packaging and in the exact quantities. Seven sets!" He threw the packages back in the bin. "These are sets of three." He eyed a salesman arranging ties, deliberated for a second, and decided not to ask for help. "We'll have to go somewhere else."

"Where? It's not like there's going to be different packaging in different stores." I snatched back up the three sets of size thirty-six. "Just buy these and tell them if they want packages of seven, they should sell them themselves! What are we supposed to do?"

Jerry angrily turned away from me and methodically thumbed through the bin, still hoping to find what he needed. Grudgingly, he took the packages of three. "I'll take these because we're here. And then I want to go to the Richmond Mall. There's a Penny's and a Sears. He headed down the aisle of socks as I tagged behind. We scrounged through the bins for white cotton, but none of those came in sets that would add up to seven, either. "Great," he said, "I'm accumulating enough black marks to put me in the hole before I even get into the joint. I wonder if I could send my appeal to Hanes," he laughed without humor, "I guess the joke's on me."

For some inexplicable reason, three-packs and two-packs of cotton T-shirts existed, all in the required light colors. Jerry took two V-neck blues, two V-neck grays, and three crew-neck whites. No problem with two, two packs of cotton gym shorts and two pairs of blue pajamas, though Jerry hadn't worn pajamas since he was a little boy. We hunted through the rack for a jogging suit in any color other than black, because black made it harder to see an escapee at night, and no logos because of gang affiliations. The only one that fit the bill was an all-weather, depressing army green. Bathrobes weren't packaged, either. We took a royal blue terry robe off the rack. The one Jerry already owned hung from a hook on the back of his bathroom door. In men's shoes, he was fitted with a pair of leather Adidas tennis shoes: the same ones lay strewn in the downstairs closet while his favorite Nikes were in his tennis bag.

At Sears and Penny's, we hunted through every variety of men's personal garments and still came up with noncompliant packaging. "I have no choice but to keep the three-packs," Jerry said, disgusted. Last was a pair of shower shoes that we finally found at the corner drugstore, an icky gel-like green plastic with gripper soles. The total cost to outfit Jerry for prison was $538.

I laid out all the purchases on what had been the guest twin bed in Brian's old bedroom. Everything had to have the inmate's name written prominently in permanent marker. There had been so many years of summers when Karen's and Brian's camp clothes had been laid out just like this awaiting my labeling them. Unless Jerry could pull off a magic trick he'd learned in an adult education class, I had no inkling of how to write his name on underwear that was supposed to be delivered unopened in its original packaging.

I heard Jerry on the phone in our bedroom accepting an invitation for dinner. I surmised it was Brian. Suddenly, a pain seared across my midsection. I guessed I'd just been bitten by a whopper of an insect.

It was only noon on a fresh, sunny July day, but all I wanted to do was go back to bed and sleep. I paused by Jerry's bathroom, where neatly lined up along the tiled counter stood his array of talc, deodorants, hair enhancers bought in his struggle to nourish and keep the sparse hair he had as well as foot powder, moisturizers, sunscreens, aftershave, and Stetson cologne: all products accounting for every part of Jerry's demands to feel dry, softened, and smell of what I had come to associate as his smells. These were small comforts that would be denied him; he wasn't allowed to bring toiletries of any kind, not even a comb or toothbrush, it said in italics. All personal items were to be purchased from the commissary. These expenditures, as well as his phone calls, would be deducted from an account that would be kept liquid by my mailing in money orders to FCI Morgantown. Opening the door to our bedroom, it felt like a deep freeze. Even the carpet was chilling under my bare feet. Jerry must have turned the air way up. I doubted that FCI Morgantown had air conditioning.

Jerry was stretched out on top of the comforter in his jockey shorts. His eyelids were squeezed shut so tightly, they looked sutured. Golf played soundlessly on TV. I laid down next to him. I reached for his hand, and without waking he twined his fingers with mine. We slept the escape sleep of the depressed until it was time to go to Brian's.

Cindy was in over her head with cranky kids. Brian was worn out and irritable, having spent this beautiful day holed up at the office catching up on a trial he'd just inherited from Jerry. Steaks, and a chicken breast for me, were still frozen on the counter. Jerry and I exchanged looks and told Brian to take Cindy out for dinner. We eagerly baby-sat Andrew and Alison, who were just as delighted for us to take them to the playground, dinner at the diner, and home for bedtime stories.

On the way home, Jerry said he had no intention of leaving Brian high and dry, that he'd keep up with his caseload and coach Brian by phone from prison. He sounded almost as confident as his old self, planning how he could still play a vital role at the office and help safeguard Brian's well-being and our future. My spirit brightened. The top was down on the convertible and we indulged like teenagers in Dairy Queen, Jerry had a mile-high super sundae and I went for a double-dipped cone.

The next morning, though it was only a little after eight when I arrived at the studio, it was stifling. I cranked open the industrial windows that only let in more hot air. My gallery in SoHo had scheduled a follow-up solo show in January, and I felt driven to make as much art as I could before I moved out of the studio at the end of September. Jerry's prison budget had pared my lifestyle down to the essentials, which meant the studio would go the way of his car and the tennis and golf club memberships. We would keep the house until spring, when the real estate market picked up. The first week in October I would be full-time in the New York apartment, make art there, and with only a twenty-five-minute walk up Hudson Street, I'd be at Karen and Alex's apartment.

The air was so hot and stagnant, it was like breathing through wool and the pain circling my midriff, where I believed I'd been stung, was reignited. I found a dusty bottle of aspirin in a box, among graphite sticks and pens, and took two with a swig of flat, warm Diet Coke. I'd built these studios. I was going to miss them and this historic building, prophetically named the Art Craft Building. Our floor was heady with the best smells in the world, the winy incense of turpentine, linseed, and stand oils. Ten studios of various disciplines jammed the hallways with art in progress and the now discarded. A patina of charcoal and sawdust assured that this was no legitimate business but offered us the place to submerge ourselves in the ways of artists for art's sake when we were here.

Out the window the view of Lake Erie appeared like dirty bath water on the horizon. Determined to work, I turned on the electric burner that glowed angry red as the wax in the pot melted. I stabbed a slab of beeswax and added it to the pot. Heat on top of heat. I must be out of my mind, I thought, as I dipped the fan-shaped brush into the pot of lemon yellow liquid and released a plump splotch onto the side of a Sunbeam coffee maker. Its stainless steel would be transformed into opaque and transparent dotted layers of pigmented wax. My head pounded and I had trouble concentrating on the developing pattern. The pain ran deep and hot up to my bra. I noted that it had been only a half an hour since I took the aspirin. I couldn't take more.

I hoped Margaret was in her studio, having come in from the freight elevator. The air in the hallway was gritty, and so many of her canvases were stacked along the wall, that it was like making my way through a culvert. The door to her studio was open. Two eight-foot stretched canvases were on the floor, primed and waiting for her to set to them with more rich layers of oil paint than any artist I knew. I loved Margaret's paintings. I let my eyes appreciate one that was hanging: a pileup of shoes with a bug climbing out, a plank for escape or hope, a brilliant vermilion sun in the sky—cartoonesque angst out of Dante. It was my dream to own one of these paintings one day.

Since Margaret had come to my opening in SoHo, we had drawn even closer. I had come to rely on her practical yet compassionate responses to the daily saga of problems I brought to her over morning coffee, standing by the slop sink outside her studio. I paced, wondering what was delaying her arrival at the studio.

No sooner was I back in mine, when the front lock clicked open and Margaret poked her head in. "Good morning, Gussie," she called out perkily. (We had given our-selves studio names one day. Mine was 'Gussie' for my mother's mother, who I'd never met and hers was Marvelous because she'd had a student with that name and wanted, she'd said self-consciously, to know such acclaim.) "It's a hot one. Probably good that I only have till two in this sweatbox before I have to go teach."

"Marvelous, I'm so glad you got here." I approached her, lifting my wax-flecked shirt. There was a touch of annoyance in her eyes, which I ignored. She shifted an armful of art materials from her chest to her hip as if it were an overly heavy baby. "Look at this," I said, "I think I was bitten by a tarantula."

"That's not a bite. It's shingles," she diagnosed, as clipped and fast as a doctor overloaded with patients in the emergency room. "You need to see your internist."

"Really?" The pain immediately seemed to get worse. "My mother had shingles and it was horrible. No wonder I feel so lousy. I don't know why I didn't think of it." Filled with self-pity, I continued on about shopping with Jerry for prison and all of the clothes that I had to label.

Margaret impatiently shifted her load to her other hip and said, "Gussie, you are the kind of person to turn lemons into lemonade." Then, Margaret mumbled something about it getting late and fled to her studio.

The sudden impact of such a cliche made me feel as if I'd been smacked across the face.

Alone again in my studio, I wove around the band saw, the worktable covered with plastic containers holding hardened pigments of leftover wax and supplies scat-tered on the floor as "lemons into lemonade" festered in my head. I felt it was as if I had told her that my legs had been amputated, and she'd told me not to worry because I'd win a beauty contest for the disabled.

I stormed up the hall, finding the hand truck stored in back next to the dump-ster near the ceramic studios. I clattered it back to my studio, and blind with adren-aline piled it high with boxes of scrap material and as much reclaimed junk as it could hold, rumbled back to the dumpster, and furiously pitched it all in. On my third trip, Margaret emerged from the back hall bathroom and caught me in the act of wrangling a large canvas onto the heap. "My studio could use a good cleaning too," she said, doubtfully approving.

Elbow deep in trash, I ignored her. I wanted the full impact of what her com-ment had caused me to do to hurt her as much as I was hurting. She would see soon enough that I wasn't cleaning out the old clutter to make room for the new. I was moving out.

I took several loads down to the Blazer and soon it was stuffed to the gills. Now, my studio was bare. I went back up one last time to sweep it out. Still fueled by anger,

I stirred up grime and dust, feeling sweaty from head to foot. The pain throbbed along what I knew now was my nerve line. Shingles came from inordinate stress, the doctor had explained to my mother. Suddenly the sun disappeared, and I saw waves churning on the lake. The sky was a milky gray, getting ready for a summer downpour.

Blocking the entrance to my studio was my last load of notebooks, sketchpads, and fragile works, piled sloppily on the hand truck, which I had saved for the passenger seat. Margaret stood beside it, like the unscathed survivor of a shipwreck, dressed in crisply ironed street clothes, off to teach. "But Gussie you don't have to move out until the end of September."

I didn't answer. I loved Margaret. Since January I'd been selfishly dumping my angst on her when she'd had her own problems. I realized she hadn't meant "lemons into lemonade" as I had taken it. She had meant that I had the tenacity of a survivor, like her. She'd suffered the worst loss of all, a six-year-old son hit by a truck, and she had survived for her family. I couldn't speak or I'd begin to cry and never stop. My eyes brimmed anyway. And so did hers. We both knew, regardless of what she'd said, how she had meant it, or how I had taken it, it was time for me to leave the studio.

Back at the house, I rushed to unload the Blazer before it stormed. I carried box after box down to the basement and I stacked the heaviest ones in the garage for Jerry to carry down later. The days of reliance on my husband would soon be over. A bleak feeling came over me, it was as if I were preparing to be a widow.

I sat in a lawn chair on the patio sipping a glass of water. Grit stuck to my face and arms like sandpaper. The sky was going dark as the wind picked up, swirling random leaves and the first drops of rainfall. I remembered my mother in the last year of her life, when she was bedridden. The only control she had left was over who came to visit her. She had been adamant about denying her most precious commodities of her time and energy to those friends and relatives with whom she had never really been close. Howie had said, "Mom is circling her wagons. She only wants the things in her life that have the most meaning." I now understood the profundity of what my mother had done. I was circling my wagons too.

Jerry's instructions ordered him to surrender on Monday at 8 AM. His birthday was the day before and Cindy and Brian threw him a brunch party. After, we would drive to Morgantown and stay overnight at a motel to lessen the tension of getting up in the middle of the night in order to arrive there on time.

The dining room was a heartbreaking circus of balloons. Hats, whistles, and confetti decked out the table like a birthday ticker-tape parade. Jerry hugged Cindy, visibly moved. The kids, high on the festivity and from dipping into the candy bowl, hung on Jerry's legs, begging to play 'catch me.' He lifted Ali high on his shoulder and took off after Andrew, squeals and shouts followed. Brian was taking a few moments to stretch back in the recliner. It hurt to see his eyes closed as tightly as Jerry's had been lately. Jerry's Aunt Faye and favorite Uncle Louie arrived. It was his birthday, too. Once strapping and handsome, Uncle Louie was frail and diminished from cancer. They hugged knowing of the finality, that Jerry wouldn't be there at the bedside at the end, that Jerry wouldn't mourn at his funeral. Facing another ending, I felt the fatigue of defeat and I thought of the lemonade. I wanted to scream, "What kind does one make of this?" Then Doris' voice answered, "Mama knew to make us taste the sweet water so that the bitter wouldn't harden our hearts."

We ate from a fish platter, the kind I couldn't help associating with the traditional one served after a funeral. We forced jokes with pasted-on smiles.

Brian went to the kitchen to get the coffee.

"Papa Jerry," Andrew asked, his upper lip smeared with cream cheese, "can I play at the playground with you when I visit you at camp?"

Quick on the uptake, Jerry said, "I don't know if there's a playground, Andrew. But if there is, sure you can."

"At my camp there's a playground," Andrew said.

Brian placed the coffee pot on a trivet. "This is a camp for grown-ups, Andrew," he said, abruptly.

"Oh," Andrew nodded, accepting, yet puzzled.

"Camp?" I said to Brian.

"Mother, don't start. Cindy and I decided it would be too hard to explain at this age."

"You won't have a choice when someone spills the beans. There've been four articles in the *Plain Dealer*, indictment, sentencing, and a profile piece and it was just in the *Jewish News*! It'd be hard to find someone who doesn't know and who isn't talking about us."

"No one's going to talk to a three-year-old," Brian said.

"You're being ridiculous." I looked at Jerry, imploring him to support me. But he had absorbed himself in spreading jelly on a piece of bagel for Alison, who was next to him, banging on her highchair tray.

"I could explain it," I said.

"You'd better not," Brian said.

I held his gaze.

"And it better not slip," Brian threatened.

"It's not about slipping. It's about not having secrets. But you don't have to worry. You're the parents," I said.

Cindy offered coffee. I held out my cup and had the feeling she would rather pour it on me.

"Hey, this is a birthday party," Jerry said to me, hugging around his uncle's shoulder, "How about some cake?"

~

The silence in the car was only interrupted by an occasional yip from Macabee. But after Jerry exited the turnpike at Cranberry, he said, "Hon, pay attention."

I startled, woken from dozing, and grumbled that he should let me sleep. Out the window I barely paid attention as we passed the strip of car agencies, fast-food restaurants, and service plazas.

"See, it's a ways until you'll get to the Route 79 cutoff," Jerry instructed, pointing to the sign and switching into the far right lane. I just want you to be aware that it's a little tricky when you do the trip yourself."

"I know how to drive," I said testily. My nerves had been on the brink since I left the studio. I teetered with fury that could flare up over anything, but Jerry suffered inwardly, his face so grim that sometimes I thought it would crack. I wanted it to. It felt imperative that he release what he was feeling. I found myself lashing out at him out of frustration and blame and I berated myself after. I was also being hard on Brian and Karen, Debby, and my brother. My kinder self seemed to be unmoored.

A couple weeks after I'd stormed out of the studio and the prescription from the doctor had pretty much abated my shingles, Marvelous and I met for lunch. "I didn't realize how bad a time you were having. You seemed so strong..." she said, groping tentatively, and that wasn't Marvelous. "But," she went on, "I understand now." I felt as if my anger was like an uncontrollable brushfire. It was the abnormal nature of what had happened to us. Jerry was the all-American man who everyone trusted, loved, and respected. He still believed in the justice system, which also made me furious. He was not a man who went to prison. I was making the ones I loved disappointed in themselves and disappointed in me.

I placed my hand on Jerry's thigh as if to steady us, and drifted off again into the sleep of the dead for the rest of the trip. I jolted awake when the car stopped at a light. "Where are we?"

"Morgantown," Jerry replied. The words 'University of West Virginia' swung in a light breeze on the green exit sign ahead.

It was 6 PM, on a very sunny Sunday evening. My curiosity was suddenly acute to know everything about this place at once. The ten-minute drive to the town limits was rural emptiness. Jerry touched my hand. Once he entered FCI, they would take away his driver's license. I would drive when he got a furlough, which we'd been told he would be eligible for in six months. I tasted the desire that I would feel when we would have those twelve hours together. I already missed him. I put my hand over Jerry's, wondering if he had these thoughts too, but I didn't ask. We had to pace the depths, repressing all that we wanted but would no longer have. He turned to me, smiled and sighed, "I'll make it up to you someday."

"You don't have anything to make up. Just love me."

He flashed his open, boyish smile. "I do." He removed his hand to navigate a sharp turn up a steep and winding road, wooded on both sides. "I thought we'd take a look at the joint before we check into the motel. I'm anxious to see it. Is that okay?"

"Yeah, I am too."

"Greenbag Road," Jerry noted. He was always pleased to have taken us from the spot on the map to the place we arrived. We passed a junkyard and a long stretch of trailer park.

"I should move into one of those and get a job at the prison, then we could sneak into storage closets," I said, carried away in the moment with the enthusiasm of a teenager, thinking it was a brilliant idea.

"I could just see you bossing around the guards. Telling the warden you don't like the color of the walls and that the place needed cleaning." He smiled at me, "I'd be very happy to have you tell me what to do." He reflected for a beat and asked, "But would you?"

"I wish I could." I felt ashamed, as if I'd built him up to let him down. I ran my finger along his jaw.

We reached chain-link fencing with a sign dangling from it that read, 'Do Not Trespass. Orders of the Bureau of Prisons.' Behind, a black-topped running track gleamed in the sun. A hard right and we were greeted by giant log legs displaying a rough-hewn wooden sign saying, 'FCI Morgantown,' in hand-carved lettering. Jerry followed the drive into a parking lot fenced in with more rough-hewn logs. "'Prison ranchero'," he said and let out a quick laugh. "So far so good, huh?"

"I don't see the prison," I said, peering into the sun, using my hand as a visor.

Jerry pulled into the first space near a path. "Let's have a look."

I latched on Macabee's leash and he hopped out, tugging, excited to be out of the car. The heat was more humid and intense than back in Ohio. I was surprised to be surrounded by trees and green hills. It looked as if it were false, like a backdrop in a Hollywood movie.

"There's a building over there." Jerry pointed ahead, at eleven o'clock.

Macabee was sniffing around for just the right place to go, leading me to a grassy area on the other side of a vacant guard house. "There's more security at my aunt's apartment," I said.

A young, wiry black inmate, dressed in khaki pants and shirt, approached us out of the blue. "Hey," he said, "if you're here to visit, you missed it by three hours." He chuckled and shook his head. "And when you come back, just so you know, you're not allowed to park in this lot. It's for staff. Visitor parking is up there." He pointed to concrete stairs that led to a lot on its own plateau.

"Where do the inmates live?" I asked.

The inmate's attention was drawn to Macabee, who was relieving himself. "Your dog is taking a shit on the pen's grass." The inmate chuckled, his eyes twinkling with pleasure. "The powers–that–be won't like that very much but it makes my day. Oh, you can't see the units from here."

"What's that building then?" Jerry nodded at the one on the other side of the guard house.

"That's the mess. But we're done eating for the day," he chuckled again, "if you could call it eating. It's more like feeding."

"So the food's not very good?" Jerry asked and then added, "I'm going to be feeding here for a couple years, starting tomorrow."

The inmate eyed Jerry skeptically. "You, man? You gotta be one of those white-collars. Not too many of them in here anymore."

"I'm afraid so," Jerry said.

The inmate held out his hand. "Otis Fields. I'm in Byrd. If I can ever help you out, just ask."

Jerry shook his hand, "Jerry. Jerry Kraig. Thanks."

"Yeah, well I shouldn't be out here. I just got a call out to see the doc. I gotta go before I get a shot." Jerry's eyebrows raised, questioning. "Oh," the inmate responded, "a shot is a write-up they give you, like a black mark. If you get so many, you can cop a solitary or you can lose your furlough, or you can even be shipped to a worse joint." He laughed sympathetically, "But you'll learn the ropes soon enough. You'll be okay, man." With a few strides he disappeared over a hill.

~

Jerry and I decided on a Traveler's Lodge off the highway, about five minutes from the prison. Two double beds was the only accommodation to be had. We hadn't thought we'd need a reservation, but orientation for new freshman and parents was going on at the university, so we were lucky to get the depressingly worn room that smelled of air freshener with a rust stained-sink. Macabee was happy and immediately snarfed down his kibble then proceeded to throw it up. Jerry and I laughed. "You can clean it up," I teased, going for a box of tissues.

"Just about sums it up. My stomach's not terribly settled, either." Jerry unzipped his bag and began to rummage around for antacid. "I guess we'll have to find a drugstore," he said.

We got back in the car on a quest for the quintessential West Virginian restaurant for dinner, a very Jerry-and me thing to do—find the best local food and then take pleasure in remembering it forever after. We took turns guessing what kind of food was West Virginian: grits, fried chicken, ham hocks, white bread, red-eye gravy and biscuits, pork roast with gravy—poor food. But it appeared Morgantowners had no appetite for West Virginian dining. Their satisfaction was clearly taken with Subway, McDonald's, Taco Bell, International House of Pancakes, Denny's, pizza to go, pizza to eat in, and pizza delivery. By the time Jerry pulled into a ragtag shopping plaza with a drugstore, he said his stomach was raw. We bought him Pepto Bismol, which he chugged out of the bottle. The sun was still high enough to be brutal. After the drugstore, across the lot, a homey looking Italian restaurant caught our attention. Tired of driving around, and not having really been in the mood for a food quest, the air conditioning sign drew us in.

It was small. Red and white checkered cloths and wine bottle candle holders on all the tables. Fake clusters of grapes vined along the top of partitions. We settled in a dim booth for our last supper. I became almost giddy as I read the prices on the menu. It was so reasonable I could afford to eat here when I came from New York and stayed overnight. I drank a glass of homemade red wine, then another because it was so cheap. Jerry abstained, knowing he'd be given a urine test in the morning.

We ate our homemade spaghetti from overflowing plates with prolonged and uncomfortable silences. Now that we were down to under twenty-four hours, I was doubting how I was going to handle two years of unknowns. His and mine. What I needed to talk about was how I was going to cope without him, but I sipped my wine. It would only make him feel more of a failure and me more miserable. I said instead, "I don't want you to worry about me. I'm going to be fine," and asked what he was thinking.

"You know, tomorrow. And I am worried about you. I've worried about you for thirty-four years," he smiled, flicking at some sesame seeds from a breadstick on the cloth. "And Brian. I'm leaving him with such a huge load to carry. But I also know he's really got what it takes. I'm so proud of him."

"Me, too. Both our kids." Changing the subject, I said, "Otis was nice," though we'd already covered meeting the inmate in the car on the way to the motel.

Jerry sopped up the last of his red sauce with a piece of Italian bread. "According to him, in a couple of weeks I'll be willing to escape to get this plate of spaghetti." He popped the chunk of red-stained bread in his mouth and chewed.

Watching him relish the taste of his food, I was overcome with disappointment. What I wanted him to say was that he'd be willing to escape to get to me in a couple of weeks.

After dinner, we got Jerry a large cone and he savored his last dessert as a free man. I wiped at my eyes, which he noticed with a flicker of irritation. "I know, honey, but we're here to get this over with."

"What do you mean?"

"My surrender tomorrow morning starts the clock. I have to get it ticking and keep it ticking to get to the end. That's my goal for the next two years."

In the room we watched TV like zombies, made our last love, watched more TV, slept in each other's arms, disengaged, woke and asked each other what time it was. Disoriented, we were unable to see the digital numbers on the clock. I got up and turned the clock toward us, 3 AM. I didn't want the night to end and I couldn't wait for it to be over. We fell back to sleep for a couple of hours and finally gave up at five. I watched Jerry shave at the sink outside the bathroom. He nicked himself in two places, applied septic pencil and winced. I winced, too. He saw me in the mirror and smiled. He screwed up his mouth and exaggerated a mime kiss to me. I smiled. I won't cry this morning, I said to myself.

Jerry slugged down more Pepto Bismol before we walked over to the motel's dining room. I urged him to have a huge last breakfast. He loved breakfast. But he only managed a couple bites of toast and scrambled eggs, a couple sips of coffee and pushed his cup away, saying he felt queasy. "They do a strip search on new inmates," he said, his eyes on his plate.

"You didn't tell me that before," I said, wondering what else he hadn't told me.

"I shouldn't have now. I don't want to make you feel worse. It just came out. I guess I'm really nervous."

"Well, you've just accomplished the opposite. The last thing I want is for you to keep anything from me when you're in there. It'll just make me go crazy imagining the worst." I skewered my eyes on his as I did with the kids when I wanted them to obey.

He looked away. "You got it. I promise."

Again, the hand-carved sign greeted, 'FCI Morgantown.' Jerry deliberated at the fork in the road. Up ahead was the visitor's lot, and to the right and below was the guard house where he decided would be the most logical place to turn himself in. He pulled up behind a Coke delivery truck. The driver's elbow rested casually on the frame of his cab's window. It was 7:45. "Maybe the shift begins at 8," Jerry speculated. He glanced at me.

"Uh huh." I found a nib of cuticle and, using my nails like a set of tweezers, painstakingly tore at it. I didn't have the nerves to drag this out.

Jerry slid his seat back from the wheel and stretched his legs. Then he opened the door and said as he got out, "I'll go see if someone knows what I'm supposed to do."

He peered into the vacant guard house window and said to the truck driver, "Are they usually here by now?"

"Nah, I'm early. Their shift begins at 8."

Jerry nodded, friendly, "That's what I thought, thanks."

At 8, the guard hadn't shown up. 8:15, still no one. Jerry worried he was at the wrong place and he'd be in trouble for surrendering late. I stared edgily out the window. "It's very frustrating," I muttered.

At 8:30, a stubby guard finally arrived at the guard house, fumbled with his keys, went inside and fiddled with a fan, adjusting it to blow on his face. It was overcast and very humid, the kind of weather that made clothes sticky. The driver of the Coke truck waved, and his head bobbed a couple of times. He put his truck in gear and it disappeared over the same hill that Otis had yesterday.

Jerry said to the guard through the window, "I'm here to surrender." The guard told him to get back in the car. Speaking into a microphone, we could hear him requesting a guard to come down from Admitting and Orientation.

Fifteen minutes later, a beefy guard, sweating profusely and holding a clipboard, told Jerry to get out of the car. I got out too. The guard asked Jerry, "Where's your issue?"

Jerry faltered.

"Your personal belongings," the guard shifted a candy from one side of his mouth to the other. I smelled cherry.

Jerry opened the trunk and brought out the large carton that held his new prison clothes.

"Okay, let's go," the guard said, leading off in the direction of the hill. Jerry caught up to him, and I caught up to Jerry.

The guard whipped his head around. "Hey, where do you think you're going, Mrs?"

"With my husband."

He sniggered, "This ain't no honeymoon. That'll have to wait for a while."

Jerry and I had only a moment to brush lips good-bye. Then, weighed down with the carton, his shoulders sagged in defeat as he hurried to catch up to the guard.

I watched him disappear over the hill, feeling a shiver of shock and got into our car. There was a line of traffic now backed up to the guard house. I detoured around them and drove so fast out of the lot that the tires screeched as I took a sharp left at the fork. I didn't want to think. I didn't want to remember. I wanted to hit the highway and speed into oblivion. But I had to pick up my dog and check out of the motel.

The sun was fighting through the cloud cover, its glare like splinters in my eyes. We'd left the motel room's drapes closed and I sat on the edge of the bed in the room void of light. Macabee begged to be petted, his nails scratching my knees. I had nothing to hold onto but this ten-pound dog.

CHAPTER TWELVE

BURNING SOUP

The voice in my head said, "I am a prisoner's wife." Not the way I wanted to wake up on my fifty-third birthday, plagued by a feeling of dread. At the kitchen table, my coffee untouched, I flipped through the *Plain Dealer*, puzzling over the monotone flatness of this voice, as if it were something I was trying to commit to memory for a test. The first time, it happened as I awoke, the morning after Jerry surrendered and it had persisted for the past five days, without regard for the time of day, how many times I tried to block it out, or how many aspirin I took, as if it were a headache.

I absentmindedly sipped the reheated coffee, which tasted of burnt charcoal, and came to Jerry's sports section, which he used to take along with him to read when he stopped for breakfast on the way to the office.I read the Indians' headline, wondering if he had also read it this morning, if the subscription Brian had arranged had begun yet. Before Jerry left, he'd restocked the wine rack, his extravagant insistence on life as usual. The corked heads seemed to chastise me for being alone in the house with all this wine and a nearly empty fridge, no laundry detergent, and only a short supply of kibble for Macabee.

I'd had to ask Doris to stop working for us. It was only temporary. Soon Mr. Kraig would be back, she'd promised.

"I thought nothing is given and nothing is promised. Isn't that what you've been quoting to me from the Bible for the past twenty years?"

Her eyes brimmed with tears but none fell. "Oh, Mrs. Kraig, I am going to pray for you hard. God will listen."

"I'm sorry, I wish I did, but I just don't have your confidence."

Her smile was forgiving. "Faith," she corrected softly.

I noticed a blob of Jerry's chocolate U-Bet syrup had hardened on the back of the counter. I wet a sponge, but as I went to wipe it off, the voice was saying, "I am a prisoner's wife." I shook my head as though I could shake it out and studiously wiped off the chocolate syrup.

Ten minutes later, like a somnambulist, I was in Jerry's stall shower, the water as hot as I could bear it, its needles full on my face, battering my closed eyelids and slightly opened mouth. I was so removed, it could have been a dream. I remained under the spray until the temperature dropped and then got out. My body felt boiled. My face, neck, and chest were lobster red. I laid on the bed naked, my skin seeking cool air, but there wasn't even a flutter of a breeze through the screens. I fell into a woozy sleep.

Waking at eleven, the blank day ahead seemed endless. My thoughts grabbed for Jerry, but I couldn't visualize where he was sleeping. He wouldn't be calling until the money order I sent had cleared and showed up in his commissary account. Then, his phone time would be deducted from it. He'd submitted a list of people he would be calling, including me, who had to be approved. That would take time, too. No one was allowed to call him. I figured the soonest I could hope to hear from him would be next Tuesday. The voice came again. I wanted to kill it like a mosquito. It was driving me mad. "Shut up," I yelled out loud and got up.

I hunched on the stoop of our house, impatiently squinting into a brutal noon sun for the mail carrier's truck. I was sure a birthday letter from Jerry would be in today's mail. He hadn't missed Valentine's Day, our anniversary, or my birthday since I was fifteen. He'd always sent roses that occupied center stage on the green glass vase on the living room coffee table for him to see when he came home from work. Jerry took sentimental pride in the burst of red buds that proclaimed yet another milestone. I suggested over the years when sometimes they drooped over night that he shouldn't get them anymore. But he hadn't listened. Expectation fluttered that he'd somehow arranged with Brian to send some today.

But mail and roses were too hard on my nerves to wait for. I retreated into the house and turned on the air conditioning as a present to myself. Then, struck with a craving for my vegetable soup, I decided to make a pot for my birthday. Yesterday, Brian had invited me over for dinner, but I'd declined, saying I'd already accepted an invite from Joan, an ex-studio mate, who I'd also declined, using Brian as my excuse. To go out and talk about art, summer vacations, and family togetherness seemed so removed from my life as to be intolerable. Angry and unhinged, I felt as if I had been sealed off out of bounds while everyone else's lives were proceeding forward. I had no energy for pretending to be an elephant with Andrew as Alison clambered for attention or to face my son, drained from overwork and worry, trying to give me a happy birthday, and my daughter-in-law going through the motions. Brian had said he was sorry that he hadn't gotten to me first, but he was glad I was going out, because it wasn't good for me to hole up in the house alone. I agreed to avoid further discussion, but I knew that going out wouldn't change my being alone. It was much better for everyone that I be miserable alone.

I scrounged through the refrigerator for soup ingredients and brought out a half package of limp carrots and a cabbage. Once rid of its rusty brown edges, both would be salvageable. The celery was edible and the onions were solid. I sautéed the vegetables, softening them slowly as I found a can of tomatoes. In the freezer behind the last of Jerry's chocolate marshmallow ice cream, I extracted two packages of frozen corn and lima beans. I liberally sprinkled in several kinds of dried herbs and spices and my soup was up and simmering. Why not have hot soup on one of the hottest days in August for a birthday lunch and dinner? I let out a derisive laugh at my developing lunacy. I'd already had two boiling showers this morning and the voice was turning off and on in my head like a tape player.

Again, I checked the mail box and I couldn't tell if the mail hadn't been delivered yet or I just hadn't gotten any. I slammed it shut as if it were harassing me. Sabotaged by my soup, I should have just sat on the stoop and waited. As hot as it was outside, I had to get away from the house. I jangled Macabee's leash, rousing him from the rug by the patio door, and he leapt on my legs. "Okay, buddy," I said as I latched it on, "wanna go for a walk?"

I let up the garage door and we were down the driveway to the grassy oval two houses from the end of Somerset, but I didn't have the patience to indulge Macabee's desire to lift his leg on every tree. Picking up the pace, I took block after block at a fast clip. No one else was out. The children must have all been squirreled away in camps or country club pools. As I walked, I went into a kind of automatic pilot, having given myself up to the isolation and was surprised to find myself at the rapid transit stop about two miles away. I'd gone much farther than I'd intended but felt better from the exertion.

Up the hill of our driveway, I noticed bare sections in the blacktop. We'd forgotten to have it seal-coated this year. In the winter, the plow would chew it up even more. I should have it done before I went to New York, but it wasn't in my after-Jerry-went-to-prison budget. I'd have to let it go and I wouldn't have it plowed this winter either. In October, I planned to drive once a month from New York to Morgantown, visit Jerry and spend the night, come here and see the kids, then swing back through Morgantown to see Jerry again, and return to New York. I would deal with a snowed-in driveway when it happened. I might be lucky. It could be a dry winter or maybe I'd miss the brunt of it.

Inside the garage, Macabee tugged to get into the house. I couldn't wait to get out of the heat either. But upon opening the door, I was horrified to confront a wall of black smoke that brought with it the noxious smell of burning plastic. Dropping Macabee's leash, I shielded my face with my arm and forged into the smoke. My eyes streamed as if bit by cinders. Choking and coughing, I blindly reached the stove, where my pot of soup was belching with the fury of a smokestack at the steel mill. I doused my head under the faucet for a second, wet a towel, covered my nose and mouth and turned off the burner. Then I raced to open the patio door, the front door, and all the windows in the house. My heart pumped wildly. "It's only smoke," I said, trying to calm myself. I pictured fire consuming everything. "Reprieve, reprieve, reprieve," I kept repeating as I took Macabee around to the patio and collapsed in a lawn chair. I was falling apart. My eyes stung terribly, but I was too upset with myself to cry.

The phone was ringing, but I made no move to answer it. I needed to talk to Jerry. I needed him to console me, tell me I would be okay and everything would be all right. But since it couldn't be him, I didn't want to talk to anyone else. Why I had refused both invitations suddenly came to me: because I didn't deserve to celebrate my birthday with Jerry locked up in prison. It would be disloyal to him. Brian had said that he had a very good bottle of champagne he'd been saving. I now vowed that I wasn't going to drink, either. I would abstain until Jerry got out. His denial was imposed.I was imposing denial on myself, but in that there was unity. A weight lifted. It was the right decision.

The pot was emitting a stench. I ran cold water over it, tied it up in a trash bag, and pitched it in the rubbish. After a couple of hours the smoke finally cleared. I showered for the fourth time. I had an early birthday dinner of subgum chow mein that I'd picked up from a nearby Chinese restaurant. I ate slowly out of the carton.

The phone rang as I was finishing. "Happy Birthday, Genie. How ya doing?" my brother Howie said.

I told him how close I'd come to burning down the house. He said quickly, "But you're okay." I read into it—don't make too much out of it. Howie was a professor of mechanical engineering and vice provost at Iowa State University. He had a healthy handle on factual reality. My sister-in-law, Lee, got on the phone next. She was a social worker in private practice. I repeated the event in need of sympathy, which she offered liberally, so I confessed about the voice.

"It's normal to be forgetful and get distracted."

"If this is normal…it's normal crazy."

"It's normal like post-traumatic shock," she said.

Something identifiable and real was happening to me. "Post-traumatic shock," I repeated, "how long do you think it'll last?"

Lee laughed, "You're just like your brother. Trauma today, and zap, it's gone tomorrow."

"I can't stand this. It's awful."

"Well, it can last. You have a lot to adjust to."

"Still," I wanted a time frame, "how long could it last?"

She hesitated, then said, "A long time. Like years."

"Lee!"

"You asked, so now you know. If it gets to be too much to handle, you could talk to someone and there's medication. But this is brand new. For the time being I suggest taking it day by day."

Howie and Lee asked if they should come to Cleveland, trying to sound upbeat about spending some time together. The thought of company seemed like an impossible task. I asked them instead to visit Jerry with me this winter after I got a handle on the routine.

~

The laundry room in the basement, one I never used because I had a utility room between the kitchen and the back hall, was as cramped as a closet. But I was so excited by the prospect of working on new art, I energetically swabbed away at a thicket of cobwebs, all but obliterating the pipes along the rafters. Gratified by how quickly the tiny space had come to order, I cranked up the hot plate and started feeding white transparent wax into a pot. Next, I squeezed in a sizable dollop of cadmium red pigment and turned the dial down to the lowest temperature. I envisioned a wax painting of a terrain where built-up areas created obstacles or blind spots on a small canvas. I'd never made a painting like this before, but I was excited by the fresh idea that just might develop into a fine solo show next spring.

Rummaging through the basement for the canvases I'd moved from the studio was like digging through rubble. The heavy, cumbersome boxes Jerry had brought down were strewn everywhere. It took a while to find them behind Jerry's golf clubs and an old plastic swimming pool and then took more time to select sizes.

But as I opened the door to the laundry room ready to begin, oily smoke engulfed me and through it, a flame shot up from the burning pot of wax. "No, no, no," I was whimpering like a trapped cat. I grabbed a damp rag I'd cleaned with and used it to grab the handle of the pot and fling it into the laundry tub. Beating the flame in fury and frustration, I screamed, "Stupid woman. Stupid."

~

Five nights later, I was in bed, finishing *The Gulag Archipelago*, when the phone rang.

"Hi, hon," Jerry said.

I clutched the phone to my ear, "My God, I can't believe it's you."

"Don't ask why, but the c.o. came up to me and said, 'Go on, fella', you've got phone privileges.' I jumped into line fast, before he could change his mind." Jerry laughed.

"You sound so good. Tell me, I want to know everything."

"Last night, I was in bad shape. I was missing you so much."

"Me too, awfully, " then with urgency, "I have lots to tell you, but you first. What's it like in there?"

"Well, I just went to my first nacho party," his voice rose enthusiastically. "But," he hesitated, "is everything all right?"

"Yeah, fine. But what do you mean nacho party? I've been picturing Midnight Express."

"Tonight was a little more like *Blazing Saddles*. This guy Marty, who's Brian's age, took me under his wing. I was lying in my bunk, and he came over and said I'd been too quiet, moping around. It felt good just to know someone was aware of my being alive. He said I needed a nacho fix. It's a tradition in my unit for some of the guys to throw a pig-out on Friday night. They buy most of the ingredients from commissary and borrow the rest from the mess. One of the guys is a cook, so he supplies onion and garlic," Jerry blew into the phone. "Smell that? Bet you're glad don't have to sleep with me tonight."

"Right now, I'd sleep with you if you ate rat knuckles."

"I'll have them for dinner the night before your visit. A week from tomorrow, I'm counting the minutes."

"Me too, and the seconds," I paused, luxuriating in feeling close. "So that was the party, eating nachos?"

"I know it doesn't sound like much, but it's the kind of situation where guys are trying to make fun out of the simplest things. I never laughed so hard, concocting this thing. Denny 'procured'— notice my new vocabulary—an industrial-sized garbage pail and lined it with two plastic bags. Always two, in case one tears. Cons are very picky about the cleanliness of their dinnerware. Then everyone took turns, layering their ingredients. First the chips went in. Then, the beans, and on top of them something like Cheese Whiz. Enough onions for an army, salsa, garlic, tomatoes, spices, and jalapeño peppers, until it was a foot deep. Since I was a last-minute invite, I supplied sodas from the machine. I won't have quarters to do my laundry tomorrow but, hey, when in prison, do as the prisoners do, right? Then we all made this circle around the garbage pail and dug in with our hands, up to our elbows in food. I can't tell you how silly we got. You can imagine the fart jokes. Like sixth graders at camp. I'm so full I could explode and my mouth is on fire."

"I'm glad you're finding the unexpected thrills of prison life. I can see why they call it 'Camp Fed', no pun intended." Jealousy barbed my voice.

"Yeah, but whatever they call it, these guys really picked me up. You sound like you need a nacho party. Tell me how you are."

I checked the clock. "I didn't quite have the fun with heat that you did, but I'm fine. I'll be fine. Our time's almost up. I'll go first the next time you call."

"Okay, as long as you're okay," his voice wavered. "By the way, did you get my birthday card?"

"Uh-uh, I thought you forgot."

"Oh honey, I mailed it on the twenty-second to be sure you'd get it on your birthday. Now I know the mail around here isn't worth a dime either. On your birthday, I laid in my bunk all day feeling so guilty, realizing how much I've let you down. Did you have a nice time at Brian's?"

"I didn't go. I just stayed home."

"Why?"

I stared stonily at the phone. "I was feeling too down to go anywhere."

"Gene, I want you to promise you'll go see the kids tomorrow. They love you so much. Take them to the park. They'll cheer you up."

I started to answer and the line went dead. Our electronically monitored call was over. Fifteen minutes on the dot—they weren't kidding. I rolled over on my back and wished I were the one in prison and that Jerry was the one left behind in the silent, empty house. I fell asleep feeling as rejected as if I'd been excluded from the nacho party.

In the mail the next day, there was Jerry's sweet and sappy birthday card. I read and reread his note on the back that said how much he missed and loved me. There was another envelope from him and I tore it open. Inside I was surprised to find a professional looking newsletter that I'd had no inkling he'd been working on. A note scribbled to me in the corner said, "Hon, I hope you like my first creative writing effort. Stacy did a great job putting it together and she did the mailing! I hope you give me a favorable critique. Love ya much, Jerry." It was the first issue of Jerry's *'Pen' Pals*, which he was sending to family and friends.

Stacy was Jerry's niece and the firm's paralegal. She and Brian had been cooking this up with Jerry and hadn't told me. I wished I'd known. I swallowed another moment of feeling lost and rejected. But then I started to read, and for the first time my heart opened to Jerry's plight, thinking only of him.

~

JERRY'S 'PEN' PALS
Issue No. 1   August 28, 1995

Well, the first week is out of the way and I am fine.

Let me describe the place to you. First of all, it is in a beautiful grassy, wooded area just south of Morgantown. There are six units within the complex and I am in Carlson. Each unit has a variety of rooming situations and you move through them in seniority. There are four wings in the units, two are dormitory style, one is single room (double occupancy at this time) or without toilet, and the senior wing is single room (still double occupancy) but with your very own toilet. So having been here just a week, I am in the dormitory, upper bunk.

The compound has numerous other buildings: health center, chapel, education facility, food services, etc. The grounds are really very pretty and extremely well kept.

There are two ball diamonds, two bocce courts, two horseshoe pits, one tennis court, and two handball courts. Behind every unit there is also a basketball court.

There is a gym and an indoor and outdoor weightlifting area.

Numerous wild ducks, turkey, and deer roam the grounds and many guys like to sneak out bread to feed them. I said "sneak out" because no food is allowed to leave the cafeteria, except a piece of fresh fruit.

This place is run by rules, rules and more rules. If you break a rule you could get a "shot." Too many shots and no furloughs or good behavior time.

The place is supposed to hold 770, but the count is almost 1,000 and growing.

There are doctors, lawyers, turnpike commissioners, stockbrokers, CPAs, businessmen and even a Kentucky coalminer who didn't keep the logbooks properly. But about 70% are drug offenders.

Out of the 1000 people here, not one had a good attorney, every prosecutor was a devil and every judge an asshole. The people are actually very decent. Everyone tries to help if you have problems and there has been no indication of any violence.

Most of the inmates just want to do their time and they all seem to want to remain healthy. Just about everyone walks, runs, lifts or plays baseball.

The food sucks, but there is plenty of it. The budget is $2.59 per person per day. However, the nutritionist seems intent on keeping it healthful. There is always a choice of low fat, low cal. selections for those who want it. Since I've been here, all I've eaten are fruit, veggies, and some rolls.

MY TYPICAL DAY

(Since I am new, I have not yet been assigned a work detail, but I have submitted an application to work in the law library. When that starts—in the next couple of weeks—my days will be different.)

At 6:15 am a horn goes off and the day begins *(a rule)*.

All workers must wear the uniform—khaki pants and shirt and steel-toed boots *(a rule)*. Only those who have a designated place to be may leave their unit *(a rule)*, unless you are going to the recreation area. Then you are free to go and dress as you please, except weight lifters must wear steel-toed shoes *(a rule)*.

Breakfast is from 6:30 am to 7:00 am *(a rule)* and you can only go to the cafeteria when your unit is called *(a rule)*.

After breakfast, work *(a rule)*.

At 11:00 am lunch is served and all who go must wear the uniform, shoes, and shirts must be tucked in *(a rule)*.

After lunch, back to work *(a rule)*.

At 4:00 pm every inmate must stand *(a rule)* by his bunk while the 'count' is taken *(a rule)*. When the 'count' is confirmed, mail is called (The rules about mail are too numerous to get involved in).

At 4:30 pm it is supper time and you can dress casually. You can also go to the commissary, but only on your designated days *(a rule)*.

The education classes are in the afternoons, but you must be registered for the classes to be inside the building *(a rule)*.

Every time you leave the unit, you must sign out and then sign back in upon return *(a rule)*.

Usually around 5:00 pm people go and watch the softball games or engage in their own sports. At our unit, there are two TV rooms, both with cable. You can apply to watch certain sport events (e.g. a boxing match on HBO) and the unit manager approves it *(a rule)*. Nothing else can be watched during that time *(a rule)*. Last Saturday, I watched my first NASCAR race.

There are two pool tables to be used after 4:00 pm *(a rule)* and a ping-pong table that is open day and night. At 10:00 pm there is another "count" *(a rule)* but you don't have to stand this time *(a rule)*. The last count is at midnight *(a rule)* and again it is freestyle.

By 10:00 pm most people are sleepy and hit the sack. But it now becomes 'quiet time' *(a rule)*.

On Wednesday night and Saturday morning, there is a movie.

There are no prison walls, no bars and each unit has 1 unarmed guard on detail at all times (he or she takes the count). Yes—'she.' There are female guards *(a rule)*.

Please write to me as follows *(a rule)*: Jerry Kraig, 52270-060 Carlson Unit, FCI Morgantown, Morgantown, WV 26507

I will keep you posted on my life and times.

Love to all,

Jerry

CHAPTER THIRTEEN

SECOND VISIT

I clipped the index card onto the visor. 'GOING' in bold red ink with directions to Morgantown underneath as clear as emergency evacuation instructions. This morning, I was not going to miss the Cranberry exit and wind up begging directions from a mocking, milky-eyed attendant at a one-pump gas station in Maryland. Jerry had tried to make light of it on the phone last night but he asked twice if I was sure I didn't want Brian to come with me.

I knew if I'd asked, he'd have been happy to come. I said, "He needs to work." But I knew I needed to prove to myself that I hadn't lost it entirely, and even more, I didn't want to share my precious time with Jerry, even with our son.

Backing out of the drive at 4:00 AM, excitement overrode my nervousness. I couldn't send Jerry presents and I couldn't call him, but I could surprise him by getting there when visiting hours began instead of our agreed-upon time of 10:30. He'd been insistent that I drive through the mountainous terrain of Pennsylvania when it was light. I figured that my arrival at 8 AM would preempt even one minute of him anxiously waiting. And then we'd have the entire time together. I pulled into the service plaza at the entrance to the freeway, gassed up, and got a large coffee. I scratched Macabee between his ears, which were perked happily alert for this unexpected adventure.

At 7:45, I pulled into the front row of the visitor's parking lot with a choice of shade trees to park under in view of the visiting-room window. I let the car windows down halfway and arranged a plastic container with water and another with kibble on the rubber mat. Macabee yelped as I got out. "Quiet, settle down, buddy, it's okay. I'll be back in a little while." But his yelping cranked up as I began to walk away and urgent barking followed me down the path to a short line, not counting kids, waiting outside the visiting center's door. In front, the pink lady was chattering away with a young woman behind her whose two boys under five chased around her legs. Taking my place at the end of the line, I screened myself from her between a shrub and a grisly man holding a toddler who was pawing at his face. I was wearing the same baggy pants I'd worn last week, the pockets straining with my 'allowed' essentials.

Though I'd committed Jerry's inmate number to memory, I'd also written it, my license plate number, and distance traveled on a paper tucked in my shirt pocket. I compulsively patted at it, reassuring myself each time that it hadn't slipped out somehow like a desperate bird through the tiniest opening of its cage. Precisely at 8 AM, the door opened and the line surged forward. I signed in at the first station, eagerly anticipating Jerry's unexpected thrill at hearing the loudspeaker call his name an hour and a half early. But the guard raised his eyebrows where I'd written the make of my car. "That's your red Blazer out there?" he pointed the same smoke-stained-finger that he had at my purse last week.

"Yes," I acknowledged, cautiously, instantly anxious.

He nodded as if I'd passed a lie detector test. "The one with the barking dog in it…well, pets aren't allowed."

"Of course," I laughed with camaraderie, relieved, "I'm not going to bring him in."

"Right, you're not. And you're not leaving the animal out there in your car, either." He hitched his thumbs into his belt and puffed out his cheeks, inflating himself with importance.

"I can't take him home. I live three and half hours away in Cleveland, Ohio.

He removed his right hand and flicked a finger at the form that I had been so prepared for, that I'd had every confidence a minute ago would be a cinch. "I can read, Mrs. Kraig."

"I realize I've made a big mistake." I clasped my shaking hands in front of me. "Perhaps you could make an exception this one time. I didn't know. I won't do it again."

"There are no exceptions." This would be the time in the movie when I'd offer my hand with a hundred dollar bill in it, saying I understand, and I'd waltz into the visiting room, no questions asked. Instead, I asked to talk to the supervisor. As the guard spoke into his walkie-talkie, he cast me a look that said, "Pushy broad, you won't win."

A short, sinewy guard with long sideburns swaggered up to me. "You have one choice and I'll only say it once. Get that animal off FCI Morgantown's premises."

My head felt as if a balloon was about to burst inside of it. Since the supervisor was my height, I faced him squarely. "I have nowhere to leave him."

"Well, call a kennel."

"Where am I supposed to find a kennel at 8:00 on a Saturday morning? Any reputable kennel will require medical records and since I'm not carrying a purse, I'm afraid I don't have my dog's records with me." His face reddened at my sarcasm. I wanted to congratulate myself. At the same time I realized I'd been out of bounds. My heart pounded in my ears.

"There's a trailer park across the road. Leave the dog in the car there."

"Do you have any pets?" I asked.

His eyes shifted and he pressed his lips tight before he muttered into his chest so quickly I almost didn't understand, "Ihaveadog."

I should have asked in the first place. "Then, of course you understand how irresponsible it would be for me to do that. Someone would be sure to steal him. Here, I can keep an eye on him and walk him, refill his water. Even under the shade it's already a hot day."

"Walk him?" He stamped his foot. "Dawg damn, it's a rule, you can't be going in and out of here like you live here!" He pressed his lips together again. Finally, he said, "All right, look. I can see you're new to the system. I'll grant a one-time exception. You can leave your dog in the car for two hours and you and your mutt are out of here. But try to pull this stunt again and you lose visiting privileges altogether, you hear?"

"Believe me, I won't do it again. Thank you."

Now, waiting at the end of a long line at the first sign-in station I thought how my stubborn pride had prevented me from asking Cindy to let Macabee out and just caused the penalty of losing most of the visiting day. As Stample punched in my ID, her eyes registered recognition but she handed back my license without saying a word. I thanked her. Because it was still early, only a few tables were occupied near the microwave, and I felt lucky to claim one with a view of my car. Macabee's head stretched as far out the window as it could and was yowling at a family passing by.

The supervisor had done me a big favor. I just hoped that Macabee's behavior wouldn't make him change his mind. A lanky woman with hair falling down over most of her face with a skinny girl, who was about eight took the table next to me. With a nearly empty room to choose from, why here? I prickled resentfully, feeling tethered to this table. The girl asked how much longer it would take to see her father. The mother answered, "You know, as long as it takes. Do you want something to eat? They have ham sandwiches. You like that." The mother, though, seemed to forget about it. I thought how much harder it was to raise a daughter who might not ever know what it was like to ask her dad for something as simple and taken for granted as to take her to the movies. There was no other situation where a child had a parent but the access to touch, see, smell, know, and love each other was so unnaturally monitored and restricted that it had to result in painful longing and deprivation. I smiled at the girl who smiled back shyly and quickly looked away.

The mother swung her hair back, looked at the clock, and unzipped a purse that I now saw occupied the center of the table. She pulled out a compact and applied coral lipstick. Then she brought out a soggy looking deck of playing cards and handed them to the girl who began to lay out a hand of solitaire without bothering to shuffle. I tried to make sense out of how this mother got to have a purse. They definitely weren't allowed and here was a purse, as chocked to the brim as I'd ever seen one. Maybe she had an in with the supervisor as the pink lady had with S. Stample?

The family who Macabee had just raised such a ruckus over entered: a heavily made up woman in her late forties, a withered old woman, and a boy and a girl in their teens, who now clambered into seats at the table on the other side of mine. I'd chosen the popular section. Three purses now occupied center stage on the tables. The boy fished around in one for a handful of quarters for the vending machines. Everybody couldn't be in cahoots in this place. Then, looking from one to the other, I understood that these weren't your ordinary bags but BOP accepted clear plastic bags. Prison purses. Well, next week I would ask Cindy to come over and take care of the damn dog, and next week I wouldn't be weighed down like a saddle horse, packing twenty dollars in quarters in my pants pockets. I would be fully accessorized with my own prison purse with a fresh deck of cards. I'd wondered how Jerry and I would do nothing but talk from eight in the morning to two-thirty in the afternoon.

Opposite Stample at the end of my row, the pink lady was already with her hubby. Stample must have waved her magic wand to get him up so fast. Wearing crisp lemon yellow today, she was grooming her mate like a chimpanzee, picking and extracting who knew what from her husband's beard. He was leering at her, as if in sexual bliss. I squirmed in my seat, ashamed for them. It seemed that the bottom of what was civil behavior had suddenly dropped away. Prisons, like mental wards and zoos, were all places of primal deviance. Jerry said they'd eaten out of a trash can up to their elbows in nachos. I wanted to give leeway but I couldn't help believing the cost was deep in lost human dignity.

I perked up at the sound of the loudspeaker's crackle. A male voice boomed out several inmate's names, calling them to the visiting room, but Jerry's wasn't among them. I tapped the table, thinking he wasn't going to be called, blaming the supervisor for getting back at me, blaming Stample for screwing up. But a few seconds later, the loudspeaker announced, "Kraig out of Carlson, please report to the visiting room."

Out in the corridor, there was Jerry, grinning as he entered from the compound. After his disappearance down the red carpet, we were kissing as if we hadn't seen each other in a year. He was thrilled by my still earlier than expected arrival and we walked into the visiting room with our arms around each other, feeling like it was a celebration. We filled our table with bagels, yogurts, and fresh fruit from the just-serviced full machines, and Jerry went to get his cappuccino. So this was the new us. I hadn't heard the voice in my head once this morning. Maybe this meant my sister-in-law was wrong about post-traumatic shock; maybe it was over.

Jerry ate as if he were afraid his food would be taken away and nervously glanced over every time another table was taken around ours. I asked if he was afraid of anyone. Surprised by the question, he said, "Uh uh. No, not at all." He pressed his hand over mine. "Maybe I have become a little nervous. Marty, my new friend who invited me to the nacho party, said he was going to watch my back. I could put my mind at rest; no one would mess with me. Then, I couldn't get it out of mind that my back needed watching. I guess since then I've been looking around to make sure."

"Do you know about others being threatened or sexually compromised?"

"I know that gang activity is rampant. But so far, and it hasn't been a month, I've only witnessed one fight and it was at a baseball game. Both guys were given ten days in the hole. They get pretty heated over sports in this place. I think I'm more nervous over how much there is to adjust to, like remembering to sign in and sign out every time I do anything. And how they keep changing the rules. That's enough to put anyone on edge. Last Sunday, it was okay to have plastic containers and the next thing we knew, on Monday, they're doing a shakedown, confiscating them. You'd think they were finding weapons or drugs. I mean they tore everything upside down. Everything was thrown out of our lockers. They went through every personal thing we owned. They even removed light fixtures and ceiling tiles. If anyone is caught with the contraband you get written up and that means a shot. You'd think by the way the guys complained that it was their drugs they'd have to do without. They love their plastic containers. It sounds ridiculous but they're used for everything around here, like for saving change and growing little plants but mostly for cooking in the microwave and using them as bowls. Everyone wants a break from the food in the mess. No containers, no cooking. If Strong hadn't warned me, I would have been written up for having four cottage cheese containers. These people are serious. They have to continually reinforce their power because that's all they have. They don't carry weapons and there are no walls to prevent escapes. So sudden changes in rules keeps us on our toes. Nobody even thinks to challenge their authority."

"But it's so unfair that they didn't even give you a chance to get rid of the containers. Like they didn't send me the visiting rules so I'd know not to bring in my purse."

"There was an announcement, the one Strong heard, but I was at med and it wasn't piped in there."

"I thought you finished with your medical workup during orientation?"

"There's a new situation."

"What?" Popcorn was popping in the microwave. I'd never get used to the smell of kernels smoking in oil. The room was now filled to capacity and tables filled with the day's snacks and meals; thinking ahead would pay off later when so many of the prime selections, like barbecue chicken wings, po' boys, and pizza were gone from the vending machines.

"They called me in to take my blood pressure again. I thought they were being conscientious."

"That's good."

"Not so good. The doctor was Indian and spoke so fast and with such a deep accent I had a hard time understanding him. He said that since I'd lost weight and was exercising regularly, my blood pressure medication was no longer necessary. I got so upset, my blood pressure must have gone through the roof. I said it seemed too risky. After all I'd only been here two weeks. Maybe after a couple of months? I really begged for more time. But he fixed this grin at me and said, "No, no. Perfectly fine. Come in two weeks and we'll check. No more pills."

My own pressure seemed to be skyrocketing. "That's malpractice."

"There's no such thing in the world of prison medicine."

"I know." I focused on him so intently he shifted his shoulders uncomfortably as if cornered. "I'll have your doctor order the prison to honor his prescription. Brian can file a petition. They're violating your civil rights."

"The prison has jurisdiction over my rights now, hon."

"You weren't given the death sentence. There must be something we can do."

"There's nothing we can do about it. And if you stir things up, it'll backfire. The last thing this doctor wants is trouble or having to exert one iota of energy more working one second harder than he has to. That's Prison Life 101."

The loudspeaker crackled, then, "Count, gentlemen. Count."

As if they were marionettes, all of the inmates were up on their feet and filing out of the visiting room. "It's the ten o'clock count," Jerry explained, "which means we all have to go into the holding room and be counted. It shouldn't take very long," he smiled apologetically. "If they count right, something I've learned not to count on," he grinned at his pun and pressed my shoulder before he caught up to a guy he knew and joined the line.

No sooner had the room cleared of inmates, then a guard was at my table. "It's ten o'clock, ma'am. I believe your time is up."

"I didn't say good-bye. My husband won't know that I've gone."

"He'll be told to go back to his unit, ma'am."

CHAPTER FOURTEEN

THANKSGIVING

The high-pitched swings of anxiety I'd experienced my first weeks home alone settled into a kind of low-grade fever once I got to New York. I was often asked if I was tired or if I had a headache. The hollows under my eyes were darker and deeper, and I'd acquired the habit of rubbing my forehead with the tips of my fingers.

The first morning I woke in my apartment's loft the pillows were thrown about like discarded inflated life vests. The burden of the day hovered over me with the weighted feeling of belonging nowhere. I took inventory of the niche I'd had built into the wall. I drew my finger through the dust on my books and the hardened film on the base of the gooseneck lamp. I laid my hand on the phone as if I Jerry were due to call.

Rolling to the edge of the mattress, I located Macabee, a black splotch curled on the couch under the front window. It was too early to take him out. Tribeca was dormant this time of day. The floodgates opened around 7:30 when parents escorted their children to school and people began to pour up from the subways, coming and going to work in the buildings fanning out from my street, blocks that housed New York Law School, the courts, and City Hall. That's when I joined the other dog walkers, plastic bags in hand.

A taxi passed too fast, jangling the early calm and I watched a man delivering bread to the Brown Derby across the street, in the Great Western Building. If Jerry hadn't worked at a Brown Derby, the likelihood was that he never would have become a lawyer or Reuben's First Amendment coordinator and would not now be shelving revised codes in FCI Morgantown's law library.

The second summer Jerry and I dated, he'd been near desperation. Day after day he was coming to my house late in the afternoon, tie loosened, forcing a tired smile. Time was running out. He didn't know how he was going to come up with college tuition in the fall. Over the years, he'd come to take it for granted that Reuben would always have a place for him, but Joe told him that his brother had already hired two guys with families who couldn't find other jobs. Jerry's pride prevented him from asking Reuben for straight-out charity. His commission-only job, selling encyclopedias door-to-door was barely paying for his gas. The boy who

I was mad for, a fearless, plucky college kid, going into his senior year surprised me by revealing the same aversion that I would have had calling on strangers. He said it sometimes took him fifteen minutes of pacing in front of a house before he summoned the courage to knock on doors that would more often than not slam in his face. I realized how much we were alike and it made me feel even closer to him.

At the end of June, Jerry's uncle Al, a manager at the Brown Derby, wrangled Jerry a job parking cars on weekends. The Brown Derby in Cleveland, a distant replica of the one across the street from me, had been within betting distance of Northfield Race Track, and Jerry was counting on celebrating gamblers as big tippers. I pictured him expertly jockeying the cars: every make and model, crunching gravel, braking on a dime under the Brown Derby canopy, jumping out, and running around to chivalrously hold open the door for a lady. But the high rollers turned out to be pensioners who palmed Jerry a reluctant quarter.

I could still recall my thighs sticking to the recently painted white seat of the kitchen chair. Jerry was across from me. His scalp showed through his crewcut as he bent over a stenographer's pad factoring in his best tip nights with his worst. At first, I settled my face into the grim attention that I'd seen my mother focus on my father when he stacked up the worn, stained cards of his 'deadbeat accounts.' But Jerry, in his absorption, seemed to have forgotten I was there. My hand clutched a glass of Coke with ice in it, and I took small sips, wishing he'd kiss me or suggest sitting on the couch where the pad would fall to the floor as we'd give ourselves over to making out.

We'd never been alone in the afternoon before. My parents were working as usual, but for once Howie had gone with a temple youth group to see a Cleveland Indians game. Finally, Jerry shoved the pad in front of me and morosely projected that he wouldn't make tuition.

I traced around the white lettering that spelled 'Coke' on the outside of the glass that Jerry had won for me at Geauga Lake Amusement Park, pondering the right way to voice my opinion. To me, the solution was perfectly obvious. "Maybe it's a matter of your being stubborn. Just ask Reuben. He said he'd always help you out. Maybe you're making a problem out of nothing."

"Maybe..." he said, indecisively.

"Okay, then what are you going to do?" I said, disappointed, feeling he was going to do nothing and never go back to college. I took my glass to the sink and distracted myself by watching the ice melt under hot water.

Jerry came up close behind me, sending heat through my body and an apology sprung to my lips. But before I could speak, he said softly, "It feels good to know you care so much." He kissed my cheek and said as he left the kitchen, "I'll call you later, hon." Hearing him say that word the first time, it was like a flash went off. But as the front screen door shut, I continued running the water, confused about whether that had been our first fight.

My parents didn't have the money to send me to college, either. What I made from teaching Hebrew and Sunday school would never pay my tuition. I'd be in the same position as Jerry if I decided to go. But in some ways I felt I had already surpassed college. I was too independent and required my own time too much to live with loutish kids hell-bent on playing pranks and getting drunk like those I'd come to know with Jerry when I went to fraternity parties at Kent State. My goal was set on teaching preschool after high school graduation.

I was preparing by studying books on early childhood education, and with my three years of volunteer experience at day care and teaching Hebrew and Sunday school I was confident I'd get a position.

The following Sunday, while the rest of my family was asleep, my mother lugged up the heavy wood window screens from the basement and leaned them against the siding on the front porch. After breakfast, as I was washing dishes, I overheard my mother in the living room ask my father to take down the storms and hang the screens. Because he resented his job, he slacked away from doing chores on his well-deserved day off. I knew by the graveled lethargy of his voice that he'd been half-asleep.

"After the game," he grumbled. My mother had been asking him to help her for the past three weeks. If he procrastinated another hour it was sure to rain and he'd have successfully gotten himself off the hook again. June had heated up fast that summer and another sweltering week was on its way. Great.

My mother walked past me heading for the basement stairs Taking a drag from her Camel, she said over her shoulder, "Don't forget to use Brillo on the pot from the oatmeal." The glutinous scrapings inside the pot looked like somebody had thrown up. "Howie," I screamed as loud as I could, "Come in here and dry." I hoped I'd woken my father, but I checked myself from marching into the living room and waging all-out war, as I was liable to do during any given dinner. I thought of him bellowing, "Who died and left you boss?" "No one, but it's summer!" I'd yell back, fearfully baiting.

I placed the pot in the drainer and left as my brother arrived and began to dry the pot. I walked into the living room and plopped down into my father's armchair. Angrily, I watched the rise and fall of my father's belly, which looked like a collapsing water balloon ready to spill off the edge of the couch. I glimpsed the corner of the stacked screens on the porch. "Dad?" I tested.

His eyelids fluttered and his eyes opened blearily. His body shifted unpleasantly for a second, and he grumbled, "Hmm?"

I swallowed and said, "You'd better get the screens hung before it rains."

"Wha?" For a second his eyes cleared, and I feared for my life. But his eyelids closed again and he fell back into his utter peace.

Marching down to the basement, I churned with the unfairness of it. The dryer was on the fritz. The last load of wash was heaped in the wicker basket by my mother's feet. She stretched my father's white, short-sleeved shirt along the clothesline, and took a clothespin from a pocket in her apron. "Dad's asleep," I said.

She deftly clipped the shoulder in place. Her hands were fast and roughened red. "I know," her eyes seemed to challenge me above the clothesline.

"Mom, he's not going to do it unless you make him."

"I can't make him do anything."

"Well, I'm not sweltering another night. I'll make him."

She stepped before me. "Let him sleep. He'll do it later."

"No he won't. You'll end up doing it like always, because you're such a martyr!"

With lightning speed my mother backhanded the side of my face so deftly and hard, my head reeled and my cheek screamed with pain. And, as if it were an afterimage of the act, her hand remained frozen in midair. I put mine on my scalding skin. Her eyes bored into mine. It took every ounce of will not to cry and all of my restraint to stop myself from retaliating, "I'll never marry a lazy man like Daddy. My husband's going to provide and take care of me and our children." I choked down the words, straightened my back, and marched up the stairs.

Jerry asked his uncle Al if he could work more hours at the Derby, maybe wait tables a couple nights, lunches, anything. Uncle Al was sorry. All the positions were filled. But he counseled Jerry about his future, saying Jerry was at the top of his class and with his leadership qualities, he had the makings of a successful attorney. Uncle Al's opinion meant a lot. Jerry was bowled over by his suggestion. An attorney. This was what Jerry had been searching for. The law was a goal worth sacrificing for.

Jerry's father was foreman of the construction site of the subdivision of bungalows, their skeleton frames baking under the sun on postage-stamp lots leveled of trees, where the Kraigs now lived. Theirs was in the first section built on E 305, a main road that vibrated as semitrailers whizzed by off the freeway, lending a feeling of dislocated transience to their house, as if it were a car on a train. Max pulled strings and Jerry, who'd never been mechanical or handy, began shingling roofs.

It seemed like every day he was sending boxes of nails flying off the roof. Not only did he have a threadbare butt at the end of the day but he was the butt of jokes on the entire construction site. He spread out his calloused hands for me and bent his head to show me his badly sunburned neck, egging me for sympathy. New squint crinkles were etched around his eyes. His face, so deeply tanned, was movie star swarthy, if it weren't for the expression in his eyes soliciting rescue as he continued the litany of his agonies. His legs (he stood and demonstrated) were too rubbery to stand straight. His rear end felt scraped down to the bone, and his hands, where they weren't calloused were too raw to hold a fork let alone bang a hammer the rest of the summer. He'd been thinking while he was up there like a fried cat on a hot tin roof—I smiled at how cute he thought I thought he was—that he could make better use of the summer now that he'd decided to become a lawyer.

I said ditching this high paying job for a job that he didn't even have and that would pay next to nothing would be the worst thing he could do. I was so aggravated I almost stamped my foot. He was lucky to be working at all.

Instead of turning on the worn heels of his new construction boots and going home to lick his wounds, Jerry smiled with recognition that I was more level headed than any of the college girls he'd dated. He said we made a great team. His eyes smiled, and he hugged me close.

Even though we had professed love and fantasized about getting married, it was in that moment in his arms, feeling his breath on my cheek, the summer smell of the peach that he'd just finished, that our future seemed real. Not only was I crazy about him but my newfound influence over him suffused me with a heady sense of power, it was as if I had already surpassed the drudgery of my mother's life.

I didn't quite understand what an attorney was, but I knew it was a profession. Professional people owned homes in the best neighborhoods and their kids went to camp, wore the latest clothes, and had lessons of all kinds, including the art lessons my parents couldn't afford for me. I was going to be Mrs. Jerry Kraig, an attorney's wife. Like kids drawing straws, trusting that we couldn't pick wrong, the biggest decisions of our lives were made that summer.

A man wearing a trench coat like Jerry's, which hung in the closet at home, came out of the Brown Derby carrying a briefcase and rounded the corner in the direction of the Common Pleas Court at Worth and Centre Streets. I'd brought transcripts of Jerry's hearings, letters from the courts, his humiliating disbarment letter, newspaper clippings, prison instructions, and the transcript I'd made of *Day One*. Why I had lugged all of this in a box with me from Cleveland I couldn't say, except it had felt necessary. I'd read all the documents, my heart aching and numb.

I reached for a pillow and buried my face in it, waiting for the voice. It was still occurring shortly after I woke up. I perversely missed it when it didn't happen. The showers had become less frequent, too. Just as Jerry was acclimating to his life in prison, I attributed the voice's silence to my acclimation as well, another disturbing sign that the fibers of our normal lives had been torn. New York was out there. I needed to go to the gallery. I fell back to sleep and an hour later, as I was waking, I heard, "I am a prisoner's wife." Disturbing and reassuring. I got up and took a shower. Karen called. She and Alex were coming for dinner. She wanted to go over the transcript of the trial. Normal, abnormal, I didn't know myself anymore.

~

The weather was crisp and dry as Alex drove my Blazer over the steep and winding hills of the Appalachians. Disorienting vistas over the guardrail turned my stomach as I felt the sensation of flying. Through a stretch of torrential rain followed by opaque fog, I projected what this torturous drive would be like when I made my first trip alone from New York on Thanksgiving. Even Karen, who was an easy traveler, was relieved to arrive at FCI in one piece. Surprised pleasure lit Alex's face at the natural beauty surrounding the compound. Even the parking lot, he exclaimed, had been scenically carved out of the mountainside. "It's like a resort." Karen agreed and shot me a skeptical look, as if I had misled her and all my complaints had been negative exaggeration. I wondered if she was right.

We waltzed through the sign-ins and in a flash we were before Stample, who Karen couldn't wait to see. It seemed as if someone had replaced the surly guard with a kinder, friendlier replica. Smiling and accommodating, she jumped on the computer, saying, "I'll have Jerry up in two shakes, Gene."

Karen poked me, mocking sarcastically under her breath "'Jerry,' huh? 'Gene'? She's quite the brute, Mom."

"Okay, she's a doll. Why don't you get Alex nabbed by the Feds so he can live here?" I picked up a handout about visiting hours for Thanksgiving.

"Stop being so touchy. I'm just relieved it doesn't seem so bad," Karen said to my lowered eyes. "I couldn't help but think of it being as awful as Lake County Jail." I started to protest as she made a waving motion. "You didn't say it was."

Alex stepped between us. "It's better than I imagined too, but I can see how that can make it harder, because it means Jerry has to enforce his own imprisonment. It appears anyone can just walk out the door and go off for a hike up the side of the mountain." Alex swept back his hair and took Karen's hand. I led them to the window in the corridor. Their expression sobered as we waited among the other inmates' families. A backdrop of a Hawaiian beach had been hung and an inmate with one arm around a teenage girl and the other around an older woman were having their picture taken. Karen pointed to the scene, "Well, you can't say that FCI doesn't have a sense of humor."

Jerry came up from the compound almost instantly. He was back from his search almost as fast. He was kissing and hugging Karen and then Alex. I was last, and after we kissed quickly, he protectively cupped my face. His eyes said, this is hard. The four of us crowded into a table in a section across the room from Stample. I didn't have a view of the parking lot, but I wasn't worried today that my car might be stolen.

I nudged Karen's arm, "Look, it's the face picker." I pointed at the woman in mint green two tables in front of us, who was unabashedly plucking fast and furiously at her husband's thicket of beard, as if it were infested with gnats.

Karen made a disgusted face at Jerry, "What's with them?"

Jerry answered in mock befuddlement, "This is normal for FCI." And he went on like a docent in a living history museum, answering Karen's stream of questions: Who this or that inmate was; what was this one in for? Alex asked about a skinny guy with long, straggly hair who barely looked old enough to drive. "A friend," Jerry said, "set him up, then squealed on him so he could cut a deal. The poor kid got seven years. He's got such a hot temper that they call him Chili. Everyone assumes we're winning the war on drugs because most of the two million behind bars were indirectly or directly involved in drug-related crimes. But the shame is, most of the guys are like Chili. There are lots of two-bit dealers in here and the kingpins and drug czars are out there doing business as usual." Jerry pondered for a second and rubbed each eye as if he-d just woken up. "The government is so busy pulling the wool over our eyes while the lambs are being skinned alive."

Karen, half teasing, wanted to know if he was going to make me keep kosher when he got out, now that he was going to Friday night prayers, studying Torah with the rabbi, and celebrating Jewish holidays. Jerry said, "Of course," and we laughed a little harder than was called for. Then having run out of levity there were a couple seconds of uncomfortable silence. "You realize we'll never be the same," Karen said fixing her gaze on Jerry. "Mom hearing a voice and you're," she paused, "you're in here."

"We'll always be your parents, Kare."

"I know, Dad. It's just so outrageous that it got this far. What I mean is, what I can't understand…Mom and I have been going over all the testimony, and I still don't get why you didn't tes—"

"Karen," Alex said sharply, and pressed his lips together as if by example it would prevent his wife from going further. She was so like me, my daughter. I saw how important it was for her to have this out with her father. I caught Jerry's eye and he seemed to get what I was thinking, that our family was bleeding at the seams and he was the one who could cauterize.

"I'm here now and I want to hear it from him," Karen said to Alex, quickly cocking her head as if breaking it loose from a tight grip.

Jerry spread out his hands and pressed them down on the table as if he were drawing strength from it. "Kare, if I had an answer that would satisfy me, it would be easier to live with myself. I've gone over it a thousand times and all I can say is, I was so afraid of saying the wrong thing I froze. I'm just as angry and disappointed in myself for giving up as you are." He turned his hands over and splayed his fingers, forming wings that wouldn't take flight, and added "More."

"That's the thing. Going over it is so frustrating. Like the trial. It was so bungled, Louie got Garfield to say 'point man,' for God's sake. And Louie's decision that you not take the stand…If you were going to lose, fine, well, not fine, but if ultimately there was nothing you could do about it, but I still believe it was critical that you should have showed the jury and the judge that you weren't like Sturman. The jury saw the slime on Day One. No one could convince me they didn't watch. And now, all I'm hearing is you're working with Louie on the appeal. It's crazy. I think you should hire Messerman to do it."

"Karen, I made bad judgments, terrible judgments. But I still know the law and I know what I'm doing," Jerry's tone deepened defensively. "Louie has an excellent record in appellate court and he's nailed down all the issues. My appeal is ready to be filed."

"All right…" she said skeptically and then more generously, "That's good. At least it's done. This place is better than I expected, but bars or not, you're still locked up. I have to be home at 7:45 on Wednesday night to talk to my father on the phone. I just want you out of here."

"I do, too." He stood and smoothed his shirt over his leaner, stronger body. Then he said, smiling sadly, "My prison-improved self." His eyes showed tenacious intelligence. "We're going to be better for this. Don't ask me how. But we will be. You'll see. I promise."

We ate good junk and bad junk, talked less seriously, and had coffee.

The brutality of parting was upon us. In the corridor, Karen buried her head on Jerry's shoulder and he stroked her hair as protectively as he had when she was a little girl. "I love you, honey," he said, tenderly apologetic.

~

The Wednesday before Thanksgiving, I pulled into the Holiday Inn about two miles down the mountain from FCI just as it was turning dark. I took a first-floor room to accommodate Macabee. The wall covering was peeling and the room's musty overuse was evident in everything from the nicked dresser to the dented lampshade, but the rate was cheap. I spread my own sheets over the stained, pimpled blanket, excited to be so near Jerry. Tomorrow, I would tumble out of bed, drive just five minutes, and whoever was manning the computer would know who I was, and Jerry would be called up to the visiting room without delay. I should be thankful for God's small favors.

The bed was clammy and I was cold all night. Truckers roared in, motors ground to a halt, heavy steel doors slammed. In my sleep, the trucks were driving through the walls into the room. I was awakened by headlights shining through a crack in the drapes and it was like being a kid again when a lamp became a hulking monster, sending a shot of fear in my heart. I forced my eyes shut and tried to clear my mind. Macabee jumped up on the mattress, bringing me back to reality with his wet cold nose nudging my arm. It was only 2 AM. The only way to make it through the night was to sleep. But I was so wide awake it took all of my will to stay in bed. I drifted in and out of fitful sleep. When I finally gave up and got out of bed at 5:30, I felt as if those trucks had ridden over me.

But the early-morning crispness was rejuvenating. The air was laced with smoke and pine as I took Macabee up the wooded road. Now familiar with this walk, Macabee strained the leash anticipating just which clump of turf he wanted to water. There was no zoning in West Virginia. We passed shacks, ranches with lean-tos, a multiple dwelling with torn shades that reminded me of a frat house. A colonial with a couple of frostbitten bikes surrendered on the frosty grass. Lonely sights. No lights on. No one baking bread or pies so early. Store-bought would be the West Virginian way, in their see-through boxes, naked pumpkin topped with Cool Whip, awaiting the end of the dinner on the counter next to the microwave.

Having left Macabee back in the motel room, I was in the FCI parking lot at 7 AM. My coffee in hand and a book in my lap. I slid back the seat, happy to be early. Then, like crisscrossing shadows, I watched the changing of the guards out the windshield as the morning shift dawdled in, calling out to one another, waving to the night shift hurrying to their cars in the lower lot. Suddenly, like a preying bug on my windshield, a guard blotted out my view and leaned in my half-opened window, "You a visitor?"

"Yes."

"Who ya here for?"

"Jerry Kraig, out of Carlson."

"Oh, Jerry. I know him," he smiled. "Well, you're not supposed to be in the lot earlier than a half hour before."

"I didn't know." I reached for the ignition.

"You can stay this time. I just wanted to inform you." He nodded his head, a gesture of pride to serve.

"Thanks," I smiled. He wasn't much older than a high school kid. Morgantown, West Virginia, offered two career paths to the under educated: coal miner or prison guard. I watched to see if he was headed into the compound or was leaving. He bound with the agility of a jackrabbit across the lot toward the mess. He wouldn't have the authority to clear me if I got busted by another guard. I weighed whether I should leave for the half hour. Why hadn't I found out his name?

I sipped my coffee, feeling shaky. Lately, I could never tell how I would react to anything. Big things slipped by me without a dent and then a small encounter of no real consequence would set off anxiety that I could feel in my toes.

I took my shakiness as a sign that I should drive somewhere else to wait. But like male robots parading off an assembly line, the inmates began filing out of the units and snailing toward a path that led into the mess. I'd never seen the men out before and the sight was mesmerizing. There was a stark order and the silence of a death march, as if the men were walking to their last breakfast. Jerry was somewhere among them.

I entered at exactly eight o'clock, one of the first in the visiting room. The mostly empty plastic-topped tables glared under the fluorescents. And a mother's voice bounced from a table at the other end, "What do you think you're doing?" She badgered an obese inmate hunched into himself as if he were trying to disappear. Then I saw her reach into her coat pocket and bring out something wrapped in tin foil. The inmate snatched it up with amazing speed for someone with such humongous arms and hid it under the table. The mother smiled slyly as he stuffed a hunk of whatever it was into his mouth, chomped, and before he swallowed she slipped him another package.

Later, I overheard her in the bathroom saying she'd just come off losing her visiting privileges for six weeks for smuggling in food. Her son had been a heavy-weight wrestler and he couldn't keep his weight up on the food they fed him. She needed to help him. She threatened to sue those "BOP assholes" if they caught her again and tried to revoke her visiting privileges permanently. She'd win, she boasted. She'd talked to a lawyer.

After Jerry and I settled in with our food, he filled me in. The fat guy was a regular in the law library. Every day he pored over the law books, working on one suit after another against the BOP's mistreatment. He couldn't accept that the BOP had absolute rule over the inmates and couldn't be sued. A grievance could be made in writing, but all that accomplished was red flagging the inmate as a troublemaker, and if he thought he had a problem with the BOP before, he'd most certainly have many more after.

"Speaking of food," Jerry said, sheepishly, "Ralph, one of my Friday pig-out friends, is pulling two shifts working in the mess. He's a baker now. The cooks are going all out for Thanksgiving with real turkey, real mashed potatoes, and pumpkin pie." Jerry's eyes lit. "Ralph's putting in extra spices for me. There's going to be two seatings, at one and two. But," he took my hand," we have until five today and I want to be with you."

I thought of the inmates winding down the path to the mess for their morning coffee, watered down and cut with chicory. The oatmeal floated in starchy liquid. The raisin bran shared resemblance to wood chips.

I wanted to please him; he deserved the dinner. He'd begun eating a concoction of commissary staples, mixing together a two-ounce can of mackerel or chicken, a can of beans, and a bag of microwave instant rice, liberally seasoned with garlic powder and red pepper flakes for most of his evening meals. For breakfast and lunch, he contended with the noise, complaints, rules, his table with its fixed seats and guards monitoring, the unrelenting reminder of how low he'd sunk. "Honey, you're going to the first seating," I said adamantly. Jerry turned my hand over and we laced our fingers together, invincible.

"But what about you?"

"I'll read. Pick something up. I'll be fine."

Out the door, six wives bunched together blocking the path, happily debating what each would contribute to their Thanksgiving dinner at the bone-thin blonde's trailer. I circled the fringe, suddenly dreading leaving the compound to find somewhere to eat alone. I took a step closer, hoping one of the wives would rescue me and invite me to join them. But the blonde spotted me and brought the prison purse she'd been loosely holding in her hand up to her chest as if I were about to snatch it away from her. Feeling an irrational rejection, I took off for the steps to the parking lot.

I headed for the highway of fast food near the university. Taco Bell, a grilled McChicken, it made no difference. One after the other was closed. I took a chance at the Italian restaurant where Jerry and I had eaten the night before he surrendered hoping it might offer a special holiday meal, though I didn't relish sitting alone with turkey and trimmings in a restaurant of rejoicing families. But there wasn't a car in the lot. I had no other options but to hunker in at the Holiday Inn and feast on candy bars. I was suddenly so hungry I could plough through the whole damn vending machine. I entered the lobby, remembering the machines were near the pay phones. The unmistakable aroma of turkey made me giddy. "Are you serving Thanksgiving dinner here?" I asked the lethargic college student working the reception desk.

"Upstairs," she pointed to several ceramic tiled steps. I had never thought to eat here. I had brought in a pizza, tacos, and made a sloppy salad from the salad bar at the Giant Super Market, eating in my room. Not knowing anyone in Morgantown made me feel uncomfortably conspicuous, as if the upstanding townspeople and students would know I was one of the convict's wives because I was alone and I'd taken on a drabness. My face had a collapsed quality as if what had been its interior hope had drained out, and my eyes had become glossy and hard, but something bruised was there, too. That's what I felt most self-conscious about.

The lids were off of the stainless steel steamers and no uniform-clad server was to be seen. Thanksgiving was over. The white-draped buffet tables showed a variety of gravy stains, some stray green beans, and a smear of mashed potatoes. The plate atop the help yourself stack was streaked with grease and sported a depressing wobble of orange Jello mold. But my stomach churned with an overwhelming emptiness. My mouth watered as I extracted a clean plate and began to glob together the remnants of turkey.

"Can I help you?" a skinny, pimply faced boy said too loudly, as if I were a thief he'd caught in the act and wanted to scare me away.

"I was just taking dinner," I stammered, realizing how desperate I must appear, perhaps someone homeless who'd been reduced to scavenging these dregs. "Don't worry, I'll pay," I rushed to assure him.

He flushed with pity. "I'll see if I can get you a discount seeing that the buffet's over."

"No. Really, it's okay. I just want to take a plate to my room."

He removed the lid from the only steamer that had one. "Well, there's some stuffing here." His brown eyes encouraged, as if placating a child. "Then, it'll be eleven dollars." I sensed he'd pulled the amount out of the air.

I rested the plate on the edge of the table. Fake autumn leaves skimmed the rim like oversized garnish. I rummaged in my prison purse for money and withdrew a ten and a five. "Keep the change," I said hurriedly, before he could respond.

"Okay, thanks!" He happily pocketed the money. "Help yourself to as much as you want. I'll wait to break everything down."

To my dismay, he stayed, leaning against the wall. But his eyes were cast down and I set to the steamers, trying to forget him. Ravenous for carbohydrates, I scraped every last hardened spoonful of mashed potatoes, the remains of the stuffing, and blobbed cold gravy over them. Then I harvested from a watery puddle of sweet potatoes. There was plenty of three-bean salad. No more pie, the boy apologized, but a piece of chocolate layer cake was left in the kitchen. I soared with delight.

I could hardly wait to cover the blanket with three bath towels, setting myself up to eat on the bed. As I dug in, Macabee jumped on the side of the mattress, whining for his share. I ate as fast as a starving person along with my dog, forking in Thanksgiving food, too cold to retain any flavor. Even the chocolate cake had a metallic aftertaste and the frosting left a film on the roof of my mouth. I washed the plates in the cup-sized sink under sputtering water with bar soap. Enviously, I pictured Jerry enjoying a hot Thanksgiving meal that he'd had eaten with friends, which made my desolation complete.

I removed the towels, turned on the TV, deciding on the channel with the least static, and got under the cover fully clothed. It was just turning dark outside, and I should walk my pup. I closed my eyes to the time blinking on the digital clock and tears, cold as ice, slipped down my cheeks. I drifted off to sleep and when I woke it was in the pitch dark. Macabee had waited. I took him out, shivering under the bluish white moonlight, hurrying him along. Still dressed, I went back to bed. The digital clock glowed ten. Would Thanksgiving never end?

CHAPTER FIFTEEN
'PEN' PALS

JERRY'S 'PEN' PALS
Issue No. 2   November 1, 1995

Well, here it is, the beginning of November and I am still adjusting. Many have asked me about my fellow inmates, so here are the facts as I know them:

Population
About 950-1000. At this time we are crowded. The institution got a large grant for a drug program and we are getting new guests every week to participate in the program.

Race
About 50% black, 40% white, 10% mixed, but heavily Hispanic.

Sex
Supposed to be all males. But there are two guys here who have breasts. No one knows what to call them (i.e. 'he' or 'she'); but most of us call them 'Lucky'.

Professions
Mostly drug dealers. Some very successful. Some small time. About 8–10 lawyers. About 50 doctors. About 100 CPAs. About 30 stockbrokers. At least two coal miners and maybe 20 pharmacists.

Famous People
None, but we do have a retired Cleveland Brown, the former producer of TV's *America's Most Wanted*, a former turnpike commissioner, and a person whose case appeared on *60 Minutes*.

The Jewish Inmates
There are eight. The other is from Cleveland and ironically, about 20 years ago, I represented him in a rear end automobile accident. One other attorney, and four businessmen— one charged with arson to his yacht.

Locations
Detroit, Cleveland, D.C., Pittsburgh and Virginia. Haven't met one guy from West Virginia.

Age
The 'Old Timers' baseball league is for 33 and over. I am one of the older inmates. There is one guy 87 years old. A doctor. He has nine more years to serve.

Interesting Facts

Tattoos
About 60%. Most common: a full-sized python being stabbed in the head by a

full-sized sword with the word 'Mom' spelled out by the dripping blood.

Teeth

Percentage of those who have all: 1%. Percentage of those who have both their upper fronts: 30%.

Hair

Everything and anything goes. There is a guy here who has made a braided ponytail from his beard. When he wears his hat backwards you can't tell if he's coming or going. I have let my beard grow. I'm starting to look like Sean Connery.

Muscles

What they say about prisons is true. The guys spend a lot of time lifting weights and working out. There are some really big, muscled guys here. At the visiting room, most inmates look good. The family visitors look overweight.

Language

Most common word: "m_____f_____." Second most common: "Chump." Most common subject: food (Surprised it's not sex?) We get bad food here, so we all complain. Second most common: sports. At all times, you must talk loudly (some sort of a rule).

The O.J. Verdict

50% felt he was not guilty; 40% felt he was guilty; 10% didn't care *(note—see 'Race' above)*.

Things I Have Learned

Etiquette—How to Eat Meat

1. Take fork in left hand and place into the piece of meat.
2. Grab the portion of the meat extending past the fork with your right hand.
3. Rip meat away from fork.
4. Eat the piece in your right hand.
5. Repeat.

Etiquette—How to Eat Mashed Potatoes

1. See 'How to Eat Meat' above except substitute 'spoon' for 'fork'.

You won't believe what they do with Jello. I have also learned to eat a half chicken with a spoon.

Electricity

I asked a black roomie about how long I could expect my radio batteries to last. He said, "I can't say about yours because I like to play mine real loud and you people don't."

Work

I am a full-time employee of the Morgantown FCI Law Library. I enjoy the work and the chance to help people. The other attorneys are good guys. We are really busy and that helps the time fly. My wages: 12 cents an hour, but lots of benefits.

My Unit

I have learned to sleep through the constant barrage of noises that emanate from the human body. The guy next to me is a world-champion snorer. Not only that, but he suffers from sleep apnea, so just as he gets into the rhythm of the snore, he stops, there is a long pause, and then a loud, gasping snore that wakes everyone else up. There is also a guy who blows his nose all the time. He blows so hard that it sounds like someone starting a weed whacker. There is another guy who is always clearing his throat, except he must think that his phlegm is located in his feet. He pulls up so hard I'm surprised he has toenails.

A new guy just moved in, and he's undoubtedly the ugliest man alive. How ugly?

1. He's the model for pirate flags.

2. When he was a baby his mother fed him with a slingshot.

3.They had to tie a pork chop around his neck just to get the dog to play with him.

He's ugly, and he talks in his sleep. He usually just yells out loud in a long moan, but last week he yelled, "It's not as shiny as I thought it would be, but I'll still give you $20,000." We don't know what was supposed to be so shiny, but we're pretty sure it's not a mirror.

Sports

My partner and I played the 4th of July winners in tennis. We won the first set 6–0 and they quit. Finally lost a set 7–5. (was up 5–3). I also got wiped out in singles against an 'A' player 6–1. He's teaching me his big topspin forehand.

On Saturdays and Sundays we walk 10 miles. Average time: about 2 hours 10 min. I now do about 35–40 miles a week, plus tennis every day Plans: to go to the weight room and work on my pecs.

Religion

The prison built a sukkah next to the chapel for Sukkot. We were pleased when it didn't fall in on us.

Keep those card and letters coming. They really help.

Love always,

Jerry

CHAPTER SIXTEEN

CROSSROADS

T he Friday after my non-Thanksgiving with Jerry, as I drove back to Cleveland, I recalled his intensity as he'd described the Chanukah play he'd written and had begun rehearsing with a handful of Jewish inmates. "It's important," he'd said, "to represent what Jews celebrate this time of year."

I felt the uncomfortable expression on my face when I asked him if he couldn't come up with something that would make a real difference. I'd been reading about imprisonment in our country. So much was wrong with it. I'd been thinking how counter to life it was to have people locked away who could better make restitution by bettering themselves on the outside. Look what was lost by putting Jerry in the pen. He should be working and paying taxes instead of costing tax payers thirty-thousand dollars a year, a double loss there. He should have been given a hefty fine. And he should be performing community service, such as pro bono legal counseling, working with troubled boys, teaching. Instead we'd been destroyed financially and we were being ripped apart emotionally. We'd pay with these wounds as long as we lived. I came to the conclusion that first-time nonviolent offenders should never serve time at all.

"Look, Gene, I'm not going to get the BOP. to accommodate the one hundred or more guys waiting to take the computer course on the twenty computer relics still running DOS. And I'm not going to convince them to provide us with even minimally competent health care, but I've experienced something that's opened my eyes. I'm a double minority in here: I'm white and Jewish. No, actually, throw in lawyer, and I'm a triple minority. Many of the guys, including the c.o.'s, still believe Jews have horns. In the food line, one guy asked me if I could loan him twenty dollars. I said, 'I don't even know your name. Why should I give you money?' And he said, 'You Jews are too rich. My friends and I think you should spread it around.' I said, 'When I get out and get a job and pay off my fine, then call me and I'll see what I can do to spread my money around.' For some reason, he liked my answer. He said, 'Aw right. You're cool.' But it was pretty dicey for a few minutes."

Jerry half smiled and placed his palm face up on the table. I met his hand with mine and we clasped tightly. "That's why I think showing the guys that we have pride in our holiday may lead to more respect for us. And it's not only for the inmates. The prison says it's throwing the Christmas party but really it's us, the inmates, who get presents together and do the entertaining that goes on all afternoon Christmas day for the disadvantaged children in town. It won't hurt them to know there's such a holiday as Chanukah either."

My mind wrapped around the irony of the Morgantown kids whose parents were so down on their luck they'd bring them to the prison for Christmas cheer from inmates who'd cobbled together gifts and reenacted the miracles of the everlasting light and the birth of Jesus. Jerry had also steeped himself in research to prepare a 'Great Trials in History' course he hoped the warden would approve for him to teach to the inmates. He'd always wanted to teach, and it would be stimulating for him. So many of the guys who visited the law library fancied themselves superior to the lawyers who'd lost their trials. He was certain the class would be full if he got the OK.

The changes in Jerry were uplifting and touching but also sad. It reminded me of Doris' selflessness. There was the time she'd been so beaten after a visit with her son in Mansfield Reformatory, but that night she'd shopped and cooked for a wake. She was always scraping her precious little money together for the sake of others. 'The meek shall inherit the earth' and 'giving is receiving' were her double sources of strength. Her sixth sense was belief. I missed our Monday mornings over coffee and toast, struggling with these things. Her spirit never flagged but mine was more like heat emanating from a sidewalk, cold after the sun went down. Jerry's focus was not only his own survival but his fellow inmates.

I pulled up for gas at the service plaza just over the Pennsylvania border in Ohio. I'd become a veteran at this trip now, a long way from my first visit, I noted wryly. If they gave prison report cards, Jerry would be magna cum laude when he was released. My 'sentence' had to account for something, too. I needed to do some kind of work that would make a difference. I was still pondering what it could be and how to go about it as I cut the ignition in front of Brian's house.

We ate Thanksgiving leftovers and I asked Brian what was going on at the office. "It's in a state of chaos, Mom. What can I say? Dad took on too many cases that will never see a dollar. I can't dump them because no other lawyer will take 'em. It boils down to panic control."

"It has to get better," I said.

Brian scowled. "Really? Who says?"

"Well, it can't get worse, right?"

"The only things that will save us are *A*—Dad wins the appeal. *B*—Dad gets out and is reinstated to the bar. Neither of the odds are in our favor." He cut another wedge of pumpkin pie. "Dad's favorite. He told me how guilty he felt leaving you on your own on Thanksgiving. Were you upset?"

"Let's just say I wouldn't want to do it again. I'd feel better if he said it was worth it to enjoy his dinner with his buddies."

The phone rang and he made a face. One of Jerry's old clients was in jail and had somehow got hold of Brian's unlisted number. I handed him his pie and he alternated taking bites and jotting notes on a legal pad. He promised to call the guy's wife and a bondsman. Andrew, having been bathed and in his pajamas, yelled for me to come upstairs to tell him an installment of my 'Tiny the Elephant' story.

Ali laid curled against me on Andrew's bed like a soft snail and Andrew sat upright, hugging Stinky, and chiming in. Andrew, still believing Jerry was at camp, proudly brought out a bright orange box from under his bed and counted the number of Papa Jerry's stories he now had in his collection. Every week he sent Ali and Andrew stories that he'd written when he wasn't busy in the law library. He illustrated them with pictures cut out of old magazines. The children pointed out their favorite images and we made up silly things until Cindy said it was way past bedtime. I kissed them good night from Papa Jerry and then from me. Andrew asked why I wasn't in my house anymore so they could sleep over? I said they could when Papa Jerry comes home from camp. But it won't be for a while yet. Accepting my explanation, he cuddled under his blanket and adjusted Stinky like a pillow against his thumb in his mouth. I kissed the top of his forehead and whispered, "I love you infinity. And Poppy does, too."

Driving from Brian's, passing through the familiar streets, a gray-stoned house seemed as cozily inviting as a fairy tale and the Borders at the upscale mall, where I used to spend a couple hours browsing and drinking coffee, along with Karen's red-brick elementary school, as solidly respectful as Shaker Heights itself, almost embraced me, welcoming me back into the fold. I needed to be in our house again.

The grass had become matted with brown patches and the house looked forsaken as I pulled into the garage. Eight weeks of must assaulted my nose as I entered the back hall, another sign of our absence. I dropped my bag next to Jerry's worn moccasin slippers. Above them, his Cleveland Indians' cap hung off the post of the molded plastic coat rack. I hadn't made it easy to come home, but I'd needed his things in place, superstitious that if they were out of sight, he'd never come back to them.

Out the picture window in the den, the branches of the huge old oak in the front yard slapped at the upper panes like wild hair. I slumped into the lounge chair, tapping my feet on the ottoman as if they'd conjure something good. The silence of the house took on the property of darkness. I considered what a relief it would be to be absorbed into it. My black mood was suddenly overtaken by a compulsion to make art that was just as suddenly dashed, remembering I'd moved all of my art materials to New York. They were piled up in boxes blocking all but a narrow path in the entry hall of my apartment.

Like my mother when she went off in a frenzy in search of a cigarette, I rummaged through shelves and dug through drawers hoping to find ink, a box of pastels, anything to draw with. Then, in the cupboard over the washing machine, under a pile of screwdrivers and a hammer, I scored markers that I kept for the children. And not knowing what I'd do with them, I snatched up a half-roll of glossy black electrical tape, a bland roll of tan masking tape, duct tape, a black cloth, and an old half-roll of white bandage. Feeling lucky, I checked in the cabinet, under the TV, and there was the red, rubbery edge of a watercolor block under an old candy tin filled with family photos that I told myself not to open. It would be another thing that would wait for Jerry, all of those happier times when we smiled effortlessly.

I put on an old Bob Dylan CD and set all the materials on the table next to the lounge chair, settled into it, knifed out a sheet of paper, glad it was a heavy-weight, and began to rip off pieces of tape, sticking them along the edge of the table. I affixed the first, a piece of masking tape across the top of the paper without any idea what I was doing. Next, a strip of the thin, black cloth, alternating them down to the bottom of the sheet. The metaphor came to me: tan represented Jerry's khaki prison uniform and the thin black lines represented the disruption of our lives. Impulsively, I began to write '52270-060,' Jerry's prison number, in fine permanent black marker and continued to repeat it, the numbers appeared to be running along the khaki spaces. The last line was black. I was glad it had worked out that way.

Once finished, I knifed out another sheet of paper and taped down a different sequence, vertical this time. Prison bars were the obvious metaphor, but because it was abstract, it evoked more associations. One was heavily layered with patches of Jerry's prison number, legible and blurred, just how I read our lives. At 2 AM, I'd created seven new works. The way they seemed to have composed themselves on the wood floor reminded me of prison windows. I dragged myself upstairs to bed, tired but satisfied, but not because I'd made some art. I still had no idea what the pieces were except a tangible expression of a me that words could not express, the confusion of who I was now or where I belonged.

Back in New York, Karen was so taken with these prison tape pieces, I mustered courage and carted twelve to the gallery to show Deirdre, hoping she would offer to show them. When I arrived, she was already engaged with two women, talking about the new show of large, colorful abstract paintings that had just been installed. I deposited myself on the window ledge, battling the temptation to leave, but the women moved off, examining the largest of the abstracts, and Deirdre said to me with a perky bounce, "Gene, what's up?"

I picked up the bag with the pieces as I stood and laughed self-consciously, "Nothing, really," I paused, "I just wanted to show you these new pieces."

Deirdre eyed the women as if they were going to get beyond her reach. "Okay, I can look for a minute."

"Maybe I should make an appointment." I said, giving her a way out and now wanting out myself.

"No, let me see what you have."

I pulled out a 5"x 7" canvas, banded with orange electrical tape and crowded with tan and black swaths. I displayed it in front of me, aware of bungling the presentation. Deirdre blinked as if it made her dizzy. Knowing I should probably stop, I continued to bring them out as if I'd finally made it to the stage and, by golly, I had to finish my act. Flushed, I wished for the applause that would not happen. Deirdre smiled weakly. "I might have another sale for the green and white toaster. An artist came in who really loves it. She's trying to see if she can afford it," she said, as if she'd completely forgotten the twelve pieces of art I'd just shown her. A wave of humiliation came over me. My tape pieces hadn't made it, and Deirdre had made it clear that if I was going to continue with this art I wouldn't be showing it at this gallery I'd worked so hard to get into. I told Karen on the phone later, "Maybe it's just my personal angst and of no value to anybody else, but my need to express imprisonment visually is too great for me to stop."

Karen teased, "Reference intended: you always turn lemons into lemonade, somehow, Mom."

"Thanks, my darling daughter. I just hope I don't wind up with the lemonade and no pitcher."

JERRY'S 'PEN' PALS
Issue No. 3   December 13, 1995

Law Library

Some people question the fact that I work in the law library here. They say, "How can it be that after only a few weeks he's already obtained such a prestigious position?" For those who doubt, I have this picture of me doing research in the law library. As you can see, we have a rather impressive collection of law books. Unfortunately, all of the books are the same edition, *Vol. 31, Federal Reporter*. We have 460 of these, but they look good on the shelf!

Typical Questions and Problems:

1. "Can they do this to me?" *"Yes!"*

2. "Hey man, I want to file a paternity action against my wife. Do you know anything about that?" *"No I don't."*

3. "Hey man, I've been convicted of the crime of foreseeability. Do you know anything about that?" *"No I don't."*

4. "Hey man, since I've been here I gotten tuberculosis and I want to file a claim against the government (cough, cough). Do you know anything about that?" *"No I don't and please leave!"*

5. "Hey man, do you know anything about Texas divorce law?" *"No. I don't."*

6. "Hey man, I want to sue the warden. Do you have any of those 'forms prosper-

ous'?" *"Yes I do, but don't tell the warden where you got them from!"*

As you can see, I'm worth that 12 cents an hour!

Food

It continues to be bad. Everything I eat has been provided by the lowest bidder.

I was curious as to why they serve beans, cabbage, sauerkraut and cauliflower. I found out why. It seems that if you escape, it makes it easier to track you.

I am enclosing a copy of our commissary order form so that you can see what's available.

I am having a contest. Using only the items on the form, send me one recipe that I can use to prepare a decent meal. Remember, all I have available is a microwave oven and mustache scissors, so don't get too exotic. First prize is an autographed picture of me. Second prize is two autographed pictures of me. Oh, and neatness counts!

I must tell you of my banana-pudding pie night. My buddies Bruce and Benny decided to prepare a special treat for dessert one night because of a fortuitous event that had provided Bruce with 15 bananas. As a result, it was decided that we would make a banana-pudding pie.

When I returned from work that night, they were ready to go. Now a basic essential to fine dining is ambiance. With this in mind, I sat down in my underwear and my plastic spoon poised for the attack. Bruce produced three plastic bowls and a coffee mug. He signaled the 'ready' to Benny. Benny disappears into the storeroom that holds the mopping equipment, where he has hidden our feast.

Another basic essential to fine dinning is presentation. Benny rolls a mop bucket over to where Bruce and I await. With the flair of the headwaiter at Lutèce, Benny removes the garbage bag lid from the bucket, where we behold a plastic rubbish pail embedded in a bed of ice. Inside the pail is a clear plastic bag tied in a neat knot, within which lies our ambrosia. Benny undoes the knot, and inside, on a pillow of vanilla wafers, is a delicately blended elixir of vanilla pudding, chocolate pudding, and fifteen bananas. On the top floats thinly sliced portions of a 16th banana. The odor of banana mixed with Ajax is exhilarating and soon a crowd gathers, at first just curious but soon begging for our favors. Hah—no chance for them!

With an ever so delicate motion, Bruce plunges the coffee mug into the mixture and withdraws a cup of the ambrosia. (He also managed to get pudding all over his knuckles, wrist and the back of his hand.) Bruce deposits the contents of the mug into one of the plastic bowls. Before he continues, he licks his knuckles clean and announces a culinary triumph, but not in those words. He scoops and scoops until the plastic bag is empty and then we dine. I wash it down with a Diet Pepsi, 1995. It was wonderful. However, the next day I had a horrible stomachache and an urge to climb a tree. For copies of our secret recipe, send $.25 and a picture of Carmen Miranda to '*Benny, Bruce and Jerry's Banana Puddings R Us*', c/o FCI Morgantown.

Fights

With 1,000 'nonviolent' men living together, fights do happen. Some make sense—a fight on the tennis court over a line call, a fight between the basketball coach and one of his players. These things happen. Some make a little sense—a fight in the food line over a request for a clean bowl. Some make no sense—a fight during Christian Choir practice. What in the world can there be to get into a fight over during Christian Choir practice? All combatants to the hole. The aggressor is shipped out to another institution of higher security.

Sex

Remember in my last newsletter I mentioned two inmates have breasts? Well, they were caught in the mens' room having sex. (Oh boy, what a violation of the rules that is!) They are both gone. But think about it, sending them to a facility where they'll be locked up with other men is like sending a hungry man to a smorgasbord!

Well, that's it for December, 1995. Keep those cards and letters coming.

Love always,

Jerry

~

JERRY'S 'PEN' PALS
Issue No. 3   February 2, 1996

The holidays are long gone. There was no joy here. December 25th and January 1st were just Mondays. For Christmas, the food service served us 'game hens.' I don't know what games those hens played, but I do know we didn't get the winners.

Need to answer some mail:

1. Norm in South Butte, Virginia, wants to know what items can bought.

YES

Paperback books

Magazines

Photographs

NO

Hardbound books (unless sent by a book store)

Food

Guns

Dynamite

Knives

TV sets

Automobiles

Cellular phones

Greeting cards

Body parts

2. Sally from East Los Angeles, Maine, wants to know if this place is really 'Club Fed.'

Of course not. There is no golf course or swimming pool and the track is only ¼ mile long.

Christmas

Of the Jewish congregation, all eight of us (there are nine, but one guy only shows up if there is food) volunteered to participate in the Christmas program the institution has for the needy children of Morgantown.

This is an annual program here in the institution. This year the inmates raised $3,800 (mostly from drug sales) to buy gifts for the kids.

Since I volunteered our group, I took charge and wrote a script explaining the Jewish holiday of Hanukkah. I also had puppets made so the kids could watch as the story was told.

The emphasis of the play was how Judah Maccabee defeated the Philistines, so they named our group the Maccabees.

After recruiting three others, we had our first rehearsal. Needless to say, you get four Jews in a room and arguments ensued. I was sure the play would not go on. We finally agreed to a script and a production that pleased everyone.

On December 20, 1995, the Maccabees debuted at Morgantown FCI. The room was filled with 'needy kids' and their parents. Although a coat room was available, the parents clutched their coats tightly to their bodies, refusing to hang them up and let them get out of their sight. I can't imagine why they didn't trust us.

It was great fun and many of the inmates still talk about how much they enjoyed our performance. We also got a nice write-up in the local newspaper.

The Warden was so pleased with our skit that he personally came over and congratulated me. He insisted that I take a picture with him and extended his thanks for a job well done. (However, no additional time off.)

We also lit Hanukkah candles every night during the holiday. No problem there. Three of the Jewish inmates are in here for arson. So when we needed someone to light the candles, there were plenty of volunteers.

Medical

This is no place to get sick. The prime concern is budget, not the inmate's health.

My woes began one morning when I woke up with enormous pain in my lower back. I couldn't move without pain. Off I go to Health Services. There is one doctor (from Egypt) and four physician assistants (from Hell).

I get one of the PAs and we talk:

PA: *What is your problem?*

Me: *I woke up this morning and my back is out. I have a lot of pain and I can't move. If I sit, my back locks up.*

PA: *Oh, I have the same problem. What are you doing for it?*

So I insisted on seeing the doctor. After examining me, he prescribed the latest invention from medical science for relief of back pain—a hot water bottle. He had to write up a special order for this and they allow you to have a hot water bottle for two weeks max.

It seems that after 10 or 12 days, the inmates develop romantic attachments with the device, so it must be returned. What nonsense. However, I really hated to see Wanda go back. It took me six weeks to get better.

I also came down with the flu. For the flu, they again dig deep into the budget and give the inmate the latest in modern medicine. I received a prescription that I took to the pharmacy to fill. When my name was called, I was handed a small plastic bag with white crystals in it. The instructions read, 'Mix 1 tablespoon into warm water and gargle 3 X day.' It was salt. I still cough.

Sports

The badminton season has arrived. My team is 7–3 and we are in 5th place. However, there is no chance we can beat the #1 and #2 teams, so third place would be great. The last time I played badminton on a marked-off court was in 1958. It is really a fun game and I get a lot of exercise from it. I have also started weight lifting. (I guess that officially makes me a convict.) The attached picture was taken as I tried to lift 250 pounds. I couldn't quite do it, and I am now two inches shorter!

Food

First, the 'Commissary List Recipe Contest'.

First prize goes to Angela F. from Seattle, Washington. Her recipe for gefilte fish was outstanding. Even substituting the sardines in mustard for the white fish, it still made a wonderful treat. Thanks Angie, and the pictures are on their way.

Second prize goes to Abraham G. in New York City. Abe's recipe for 'Triple Mustard Chicken Dijon' was wonderful. Even substituting the sardines in mustard for the chicken, it still made a wonderful treat. Thanks, Abe. Your prize is on the way.

To the other 37 entrants, thanks for trying and better luck next time. I honestly did not realize how many recipes there are that you can substitute sardines in mustard with.

Just how bad is the food? Let me give you some more examples:

Apples. How can they ruin an apple?

Remember when you were a kid and in art class you had to draw an apple? Well, you made the apple firm and plump. It was rosy red with the shiny skin and maybe a green leaf still attached to the stem. Yum-yum. Now imagine the apple Charles Manson drew. That's the kind we get.

We also get military surplus. For example, at Christmas, they passed out little bags of candy to us that had been designated for the troops in 'Desert Storm'.

I usually enjoy a bowl of bran cereal in the mornings. The bran cereal here is so hard and so tasteless that nobody can eat more than one spoonful. I couldn't understand how cereal could get to be so bad until one morning I noticed the huge container that it came in. On the side was printed the message, 'Good Luck General Custer.'

They made special cake just for Christmas, but I couldn't eat it—too many bones!

Well, that does it for another edition. Keep those cards and letters coming. I miss you all.

Love always,

Jerry

A couple weeks into the new year, an acquaintance mentioned Crossroads, an alternative-to-prison program for women that was just a short subway ride away.

I made an appointment with Taylor Harris, a slight, young social worker, fresh out of Vassar. I launched into where Jerry was and why, expecting an empathetic response, but she met my eyes with the same stony dismissal Deirdre had shown toward my prison art. "So, you feel your husband's a victim of the system?" she asked, more of a statement than a question.

"Yes." I met her eyes. "The government spent twenty million dollars to get Reuben Sturman and those connected to him. I'm concerned that my husband is one of two million people incarcerated in this country, more than any other country in the world."

"Russia has more," she corrected.

"My husband, guilty or not, would never have been thrown in the slammer five years ago. As a nonviolent, first-time offender, he would have been out on probation and paying for his crime with a sizable fine and by giving his considerable wealth of expertise to his community. Don't you think we're just a little lock-em-up crazy?"

Taylor put out her palm, stop-sign fashion. "Hey, our program is about getting the women here to take responsibility for their behavior. It just may be that you're too involved in your own situation to fit in."

Suddenly, I was fighting for this volunteer job. "I think I can be an objective leader, and my empathy and understanding will make me more effective."

"Okay," she said as she scrolled down her computer screen. "We'll give it a try. There's one group that needs to work on self-esteem that you'd be right for. But," she cautioned, "if you work here, I highly suggest you don't reveal anything about your personal life, like where you live, and especially that your husband is in prison. You're supposed to be a role model, someone they can emulate. And believe me, they are very quick to take advantage. Don't get taken in."

I hoped I wasn't heading into a tougher situation than I was prepared for.

Taylor set me up with a group of twelve women, and on Friday afternoons I was to lead a creative self-expression workshop. She sat in on the first session as if she were the prison warden, bored yet also on the alert. I sensed her disapproval of my informality as I introduced myself to each woman, asking questions and making comments to set a tone of openness and acceptance. The women spanned the ages of twenty to mid-thirties and were vibrant and full of individuality. They had all been drug abusers and involved in petty crimes.

I brought in a dozen magazines, scissors, glue sticks, markers, and paper that made a river of materials down the center of a large table. I'd been thinking how Jerry's image of himself had changed from lawyer to his new identity as a felon. It would be stamped on his passport. The felons who'd founded Australia had become outlawed. And upon arrival in Las Vegas, felons were required to register. The image came to my mind of Jerry's new, shameful identity continuing to drag behind him like a dirty tail. I'd remarked one day how defeated he was sounding, but he'd tossed his head as if to flick me away—what was done was over.

I introduced the concept of self-image to the women, dying to risk sharing with them how Jerry's and mine had changed since his incarceration, needing to engage in mutual understanding, and wanting them to know my insights weren't coming from an outsider of privilege but from someone who was like them. Glancing at Taylor, I muzzled the impulse. A couple of younger, warm, and talkative women vied for who had the worst self-image. Two stared through me. Another belligerently demanded to know how some 'bullshit art class' was going to get her a job. I said it might not, but that we use language and images to communicate, and that it couldn't hurt her to sharpen her abilities. She was so thin, she seemed to collapse into herself with exhaustion. I asked them to cut words and images they could identify with from the magazines spread out on the table and make two name tags, one with their given name and the other with a name that would best describe how they saw themselves.

One woman was afraid of getting glue on her new jacket. Another didn't want to mess up her long, curved nails, polished grape black with sparkles. I suggested that her nails were like a name tag. What, I asked, could we tell about Rhonda from them? This cracked their reserve as they called out, "She's tough, strong, but wanting to shine." She joined in, revealing how her nails were her pride, something unique to her, but she still didn't want to mess them up. They laughed. This was what my class was about. If anyone had a problem, they could sit it out or walk around and observe what the others were doing. I didn't believe in forced creativity, but I hoped they'd give it a try. I promised that they'd learn something about themselves. Taylor piped up that they were here to participate or they would be marked absent. Rhonda's eyes flashed angrily as she accepted the magazine I handed to her.

On the subway, going home, I thought about the incredible tags the women had made, from flowers to tears to shapes like jagged shards. They renamed themselves Moth, Angel, Heart, Twilight, Star, Hope, Courage, Mama (because she was hoping to get back custody of her daughter), Onyx, Pearl, Diamond, and Desire. I was excited by the success.

Taylor stayed on for all eight sessions. After the last class ended, she called me into her office to tell me she'd talked with the women and they didn't think they got much out of playing like kids in school. Her eyes glinted with triumph.

My disappointment was as sharp as if I'd been fired from a paid position. "What did you think?" I asked.

"Oh!" her shoulders jerked up. "I agree."

Packing up the materials I'd stored in her office, I was embarrassed to think I had been fired from a volunteer job. It was a brisk but sunny day in March. Though the two bags were heavy and cumbersome, I continued past the Seventh Avenue subway to walk and think through what I had done to make Taylor so hostile. Near

Houston, I ducked into a seedy coffee shop I wouldn't have thought to walk in before. Warming my hand around the cup of coffee, I realized why Taylor had let me go. She'd heard that my husband had a law practice with our son as his partner. We'd had the American dream and we'd lost it. She'd made up her mind at the interview that I was not a worthy role model for the women in her charge at Crossroads.

Doubt bit into my confidence. My gallery had rejected my art and Crossroads had rejected my teaching in the last few weeks. Now as I trudged home down Varrick Street, I questioned if I should go forward with my new art consulting business. I'd gotten the idea after I'd recommended a New York gallery to Margaret that I thought would show her paintings. We were thrilled when she got accepted and she suggested that I do this for a couple other Cleveland artists. I'd been successful with them too. I kicked it around with Karen, and she got excited. Thousands of artists were looking for galleries and it could generate much needed-income. We came up with the moniker, 'IAM', for 'Individual Artist Marketing'. Karen had come over for dinner the past couple weeks and we worked on the ads for local and national art magazines. Jerry believed I'd hit upon an idea that had a lot of promise, too. And I heard relief in his encouragement, as if he'd been waiting for me to step up to the plate.

I reached my block, and as the light changed to green a bus blocked the intersection. Walking around it, the handles of the bag cut into my palm and I thought, I'm definitely at my own crossroads.

CHAPTER SEVENTEEN
COOPER'S ROCK

JERRY'S 'PEN' PALS
Issue No. 5   April 4, 1996

It has been a long, horrible winter and boredom has set in. I hope spring will bring a new time of joy, but I doubt it.

The first order of business is mail. From Norm in Austin, Texas, comes this letter:

Dear Jerry: How do you spend your days?

Well, Norm, my days usually begin at 5:45 am My cubicle is located about 8 feet from the bathroom entrance, but I can't see inside from my bunk. The bathroom is cinder block so all sounds are amplified and echo. Although I can't see it, here is how each day begins:

At 5:45 am or so, a farmer from nearby brings his horse into the bathroom to pee in the urinal (at least it sounds like a horse, but it could be a bull).

At 6:00 am, a tribe of cough-spitters arrives in the bathroom. Each member is determined to purge all the phlegm from his body with huge, heaving coughs and then spitting—at who knows what.

So, by the time the 6:15 am horn is sounded, I'm already pissed off and in a bad mood.

I'm usually at breakfast by 6:45 am We have a little coffee group that meets to complain each day, and then I'm off to computer class (Monday to Friday). I go at 7:30 am The class lasts until lunch time, about 11:15 pm

On Saturdays there is a movie (video) in the auditorium at 7:30 am, or I will play badminton, tennis, or jog. Sundays I jog.

Next edition I will discuss the rest of the day.

Nicknames

Guy from Butte, Montana: 'Montana'
Guy from Houston, Texas: 'Tex'
Guy from Lexington, Kentucky: 'Kentucky'
Guy from Richmond, Virginia: 'Bud'

There's a new guy in the cube next to mine. He's bald except for a scraggly frame of hair around the sides. He has a bushy, ugly, unkempt beard and surgical scars on his head from brain surgery to remove tumors. He has only one eye—lost the other in a motorcycle accident. He has one upper tooth in the front and no teeth on the entire left side of his face. He lost his teeth in a fight. His cheeks are caved in from lack of teeth. He wears a bag because he lost his colon to cancer. He's missing three fingers—lost them in an accident at work. He walks with a limp—broken leg and shattered hip from an accident with a truck.

Me: What do they call you?

Him: Lucky

Law Library

We recently received word that one of my colleagues at the law library had his conviction reversed. The Circuit Court of Appeals granted him a full acquittal. Our group is rather unique. Ron is from Detroit and is not a lawyer. He is very Germanic and looks a lot like Adolph Hitler. We call him 'Herr' and joke with him a lot . He's really a lot of fun and takes the ribbing well. He's an expert on plant life, but not all plants.

Len is probably one of the smartest people I have ever met. Aside from being an attorney, he's studied ancient religions, Greek and Roman architecture, ancient poetry, and is prepared to start graduate school in archeology this fall. While in prison, he has taught himself to speak French. He also speaks Spanish and Latin. He was born Italian Catholic but has converted to Judaism. Len was in a segment on *60 Minutes* that dealt with his trial.

Tony, the one acquitted, practiced law in Pittsburgh and represented many sports celebrities. He was captain of a small-town basketball team that won the Pennsylvania state championship in the early 50s. A Broadway play and a movie have been made about the team and their championship season.

'Little Jerry' is from Detroit and a real expert on criminal law.

That was our crew. When Tony left, he was replaced by Bernie. Bernie, age 67, is a Polish parish priest purportedly from Pittsburgh, Pennsylvania, who was presumably prosecuted for purloining pennies from parishioners in order to purchase property in the panhandle portion of Florida, in the proximity of Pensacola. His pitifully proclaimed plea of proof prevented him from prevailing. His promised punishment was a period of prison.

The real tragedy is the number of prisoners who 'work' the library. Accountants, scientists, doctors and assorted jerks sit here all day and do 'legal' work. The inmates come to them for their legal work. And they do prepare and file all sorts of papers for the inmates. Their limited knowledge of law (learned here in prison) allows them to flood the courts with worthless appeals.

The reason I say 'tragedy' is because this indicates the great lack of trust and confidence that exists regarding lawyers. Inmates would rather trust a non lawyer inmate with their legal matters than an attorney. It is really sad.

There is one guy who sends away for everything regarding drug laws that exists in the market. A few weeks ago he showed me a package of legal briefs he received from the Erwin Rommel School of Law. (I kid you not.) He paid $180 for the package and thinks that by sending in the school's proposed motions, he'll be out in a few weeks. The only 'out' he'll be is $180!

Sports

Badminton is over. My team came in 3rd. However, in the championship round, we beat the #2 team. Then we lost to the champions in the finals.

Got in one or two days of tennis in March. My doubles partner and I remained undefeated. He is now home back in the Cleveland area.

We have some new tennis players, so the courts will be crowded.

I've started to jog. I'm up to five miles. I hope to be able to enter a marathon by the time I get out.

Law Library

Pretty good. My blood pressure is still borderline (without medication), but my cholesterol is down to 163. As I write this, my weight is down to 183. I haven't been that low since the Browns won their last championship. This is no place to get sick. Got to stay healthy.

That's it for number six. Please keep those cards, letters and magazines coming. I miss you all.

Love always,

Jerry

~

From the day Jerry surrendered, we'd pinned our salvation on the appeal's blessing of exoneration, the reclamation of our normal past, and the reinstatement of our future. There would be no parole or fine. No shame, pity, and scorn. No permanent damage. As important for Jerry as breathing was the resumption of his identity as a lawyer and to once again become the provider. Restored, we'd wholly resume to being the Kraigs.

I could see Jerry in his office, tipping back in his oxblood leather chair, laughing into the phone as he signed papers, every so often glancing out the window at the view of Public Square, the BP building, checking traffic, speculating on the weather, if he'd need his coat when he went to a deposition. With powerful binoculars he could see all the way up to 26th and Superior where I could once again have a studio.

Margaret had offered to clear walls for me anytime I wanted to come back. I said, "I hope you don't regret being so generous. I just might be knocking on your wall sooner than you think when Jerry wins his appeal."

The more Jerry had researched the basis of precedents for his appeal, the more confident he was that it would be granted. He wrote up the salient issues, and mailed them off to Brian and Louie. Despite his assurance to Karen that the appeal was practically done, after Thanksgiving Louie admitted it still hadn't been filed and we couldn't get a definitive answer that it was finished. During Karen and Jerry's weekly Wednesday call, she kept asking, "What is holding it up?" None of us wanted another Thanksgiving without him.

"I don't want that either," he said. "But the process takes time. We don't want any argument to be left out. Be patient, just a little longer."

Karen and I become true believers that the objectivity of the higher court would see through what we called the mockery of the Sixteenth Circuit. Brian, who always gave his on-the-other-hand speech, was almost as convinced we'd win. He was also praying for his father to resume his load at the practice.

The appeal was finally filed after the new year and Jerry didn't pay attention to the possibility of a furlough, because he was that certain he would be released before the nine months were up when he would become eligible for one. But as March came upon us and there still had been no date set in court to argue it, he became consumed by being free on furlough, even though it wasn't really free and even if it was only for twenty-four hours. He said he'd be thrilled to have the twenty-four, but if he was lucky, and some guys were, he could possibly get forty-eight. "Bliss," when he said it, his voice filled with hope.

Following procedure, Jerry made the rounds to acquire all of the department supervisors' signatures, waiting for hours and when they didn't show up, going through the bureaucratic red tape again. Exactly six weeks before, as required, he submitted his application. When he didn't hear by the beginning of April, he worried over the likelihood that his application was sitting under a pile on a c.o.'s desk. Then he worried after he checked on its status, that the c.o. had had a short fuse or was a control freak and hadn't taken kindly to being hassled. His application could have been permanently 'misfiled.' By the time he'd applied a second time and gone through the rigmarole all over again, the delay could take months. It happened all the time. Jerry anxiously waited and reminded me not to count on it, though I was.

I couldn't stop daydreaming of privacy: we could say whatever we wanted without fear that a c.o. might overhear something we'd said out of context and Jerry would be written up. I fantasized about our thighs touching as we sat next to each other. Lying alone in the twin bed at the Holiday Inn, I imagined us in a king, our skin and smells enveloping the expanse of white sheets, as if I were lusting for a great luxury. But what I ached most for was to be home, making love in our bed. After, I would make us breakfast and we would eat in our kitchen, Jerry remembering his apple butter that we bought every year at the farmer's market, getting up to hunt for it in the fridge. No urgency to cram in talk about the appeal, the kids, Brian's ongoing mess at the office, missing each other, loneliness, or the storm abating for my drive to Cleveland or to New York. Just eating and being ourselves in our kitchen. But home was a dream that wouldn't come true until after Jerry's release. Inmates on furlough weren't allowed to cross the state line. "Even if I get approved," Jerry said on the phone, "we still can't count on it until the day I have the confirmation in my hand. Yesterday, a c.o. had it in for a guy across from my bunk and stuck it to him in his report. He picked fights with everyone because his furlough was denied. And now he's spending his furlough in the hole. His wife didn't know until she walked into the visiting center to pick him up. The c.o. said he'd tried to contact her." I was mortified to think of driving six hours to face that kind of disappointment.

The c.o.s' reports from all of the departments came through. He received the highest scores from all of them. The weightiest was his supervisor at the law library. The BOP smiled on inmates who took their work seriously. Occupied men caused fewer problems. Occupied men ran the facility. "Now I'm sure to get the furlough, and these reports are like evidence for my approval for halfway house." His voice was as elated as a kid who just made honor role for the first time. FCI loses too many papers, so he mailed copies of the reports to me for safekeeping.

"Why are you thinking about halfway house? You're winning your appeal!"

On April 18, Jerry called, beside himself with the good news: he got his furlough with three days' notice. "If there's a lockdown at the last minute, I don't know what I'll do."

I was to pick him up at the visitor's center, April 21 at 8 AM.

The drive from New York to Morgantown went so smoothly I felt charmed. There were fewer trucks than usual, and no opaque fog to terrify me as I took the hairpin curves of the Appalachians. Dew sparkled on the grass. The trees fluttered their new spring leaves.

Jerry was eagerly waiting in the visiting room as I walked through the door. Grinning ear to ear, he pulled me to him, his face a cleanshaven surprise. "Let's get out of here," he said urgently, as if we were making a getaway. We practically ran out of the visitor's center and up the concrete steps to the parking lot.

He buckled himself into the passenger's seat and said, "Hon, you won't believe what just happened!" He laughed, waving a form like a rescue flag. "The BOP goofed in my favor for a change. I can't believe it. They gave me a five-day furlough! I'm shaking. I don't know how it happened."

Excitement and skepticism collided in my stomach. "It's too good to be true.

Are you sure?" I took the form from him. "Where does it say it?"

"Right here," he thumped at the box where a five had been written in red ink.

I honked the horn triumphantly. "Maybe this is a sign our luck has turned. You're definitely going to win your appeal."

"Hey, that wouldn't be luck, it would be justice. But right now all I want is to make crazy wild love to you."

"Here we go, Holiday Inn."

Macabee raced around Jerry's legs, yelping and sniffing before Jerry could get inside the room. He stooped down and scratched Macabee between the ears. "You missed me, boy, huh?"

Seeing the message button flashing on the phone, I said, "Please, no bad news," and I picked up the receiver.

"Mom, call when you get in," Brian said.

In two strides, Jerry was at the nightstand taking the receiver from me.

"We can call him back later," I said, the euphoria of a second ago gone.

"He probably just wants to make sure I got out okay." Jerry said as he punched in Brian's number.

Then, smiling into the phone, he said, "Hi Andrew, it's Papa Jerry. What are you doing? Yes, you are talking to me." He laughed. "Can you get Daddy?"

I began to unpack the plastic bag with Jerry's few toiletries and underwear and saw that he'd only brought enough for the one day. Later, we'd go to K-Mart and buy a couple more changes of clothes. My excitement returned as I thought of the two of us on a shopping excursion.

"Bri, guess what happened?" Jerry paced as far as the cord would allow. "I'm out for five days. They made a mistake." He motioned for me to come to him and I pressed my head against his heart, loving his life under his chest. Jerry was smiling as he listened and said, excited, "Okay, we will. Sure, if we both leave now…Mom and I will meet you in Pittsburgh at the Hilton by 1:30. Love you, son."

Jerry kissed me. "This is great. We're going to meet them for the afternoon in Pittsburgh."

I struggled out of his arms as he resisted letting me go. "Jerry, what are you thinking? You're not allowed to leave the state of West Virginia, remember? Tell them to come here."

"They can't. Brian has a trial in the morning. The trip is too long for them to come here."

"Then what do you think you're doing? If anything happens, you'll really be sent up the river. It's crazy."

"Nothing's going to happen."

"Call him back. I'm not going."

"But Gene, I don't have my driver's license."

"But you'll cross the state line?" A burst of recrimination filled my head. This is why you're in prison, I wanted to yell at my husband. You don't know right from wrong. Then I felt sick by my severe judgment. I was the boundary pushers of pushers. This is what happens when someone is a felon, he becomes guilty the rest of his life of mishandling everything. I stood there wavering, wanting to say no and wanting to say OK.

"Do this for me. I need to be with Andrew and Alison as a free grandfather. Can you imagine what I go through when they visit? They want me to take them outside to play and I have to tell them no. Andrew asked if he could stay at my camp and have a sleep over. I had to tell him next year when I'm home. His eyes were so big. A year, he said, for my birthday, when I'm four? I lied and said yes. Please don't be disappointed, Gene. We'll have four whole days after this one. We'll be together every minute and it will be wonderful. I promise."

∼

"Welcome to Pennsylvania." I read the sign as we crossed the state line. "Welcome to get in an accident or get a ticket and our kids can visit both of us in the Big House. Me for aiding and abetting a fugitive, and you for being a fugitive." My foot had been so tense on the gas pedal that pain shot up my arch.

"Hon, just drive," Jerry gave a nervous laugh and then relaxed in the seat, looking out the window and calling my attention to a carpet of daffodils on the median strip. "Nice. I forgot how much I missed being in a car. This is something."

He directed me through Pittsburgh's city limits as if he had a map in his head, right to the Hilton near the Carnegie Tech campus. Animated, Jerry remembered when he used to visit a friend there during his Kent State years. We had gotten to the hotel early and at one o'clock we started to anticipate the kids' arrival. We circled the lobby, bought Diet Cokes, and peered up the street. "He knows where we are. He'll call the desk and we'll get the message. Stop, you're making me nervous," Jerry said and went to buy a newspaper. It felt for a second as if time had reversed and prison was a figment of another lifetime.

At 2:30, I said, "Why can't anything happen without our having to go through fire to get there?" And then they were spilling out of the revolving door and into the lobby. Andrew ran into Jerry's arms for a huge hug and kiss. Ali was groping for her turn and Jerry soon had both of them in his arms. He was telling Alison how pretty she was and she was hugging around his neck with all of her two-year-old strength. Brian beamed. Cindy smiled, looking tired. Just before they had left, Ali had felt feverish. She had an ear infection and they had been delayed trying to get a prescription filled before they got on the road.

Jerry announced that he'd taken a room for the day. Up the elevator and we were the free Kraigs doing our Kraig thing. Jerry with the two grandkids hanging and jumping on him. Books, toys, hide and seek, and Ali playing with water in the bathroom sink. Brian went out for the works at a Jewish deli. Soon, corned beef sandwiches, cole slaw, and coconut bars sat open in their white-paper wrappers, an armada of delicacies for Jerry, who ate with the relish of a shipwrecked sailor. Andrew was pasted to Jerry's arm, taking bites of his food. Brian had brought a couple of files for Jerry to go over and they put their heads together as they drank coffee. Suddenly, it was 5 PM. We forced cheerfulness for the kids' sake as we headed to our respective cars.

"That was the best present you could have given to me," Jerry said, as we crossed the state line into West Virginia. I sighed with relief.

"It was great," I agreed.

~

The next day we were back in the car. It was a chilly overcast morning. We were happy as kids. Jerry pointed as we traveled over the bridge at the blue, serene water on both sides. Then a sign said, "Cheat Lake." "Just to keep the prison theme going, huh?" he chuckled.

In the backseat a shoe box concealed Jerry's worn, ill-fitting Nikes that he'd purchased from the prison commissary. On his feet were new Nikes we'd just bought from a sporting-goods store between a dusty looking jeweler and a country clothier on Main Street in Morgantown. Several of Jerry's fellow cons on work release were on litter patrol. They clapped him on the back, wishing us a great furlough.

"Seems like you hit the mother of jackpots, Jerry, five days, huh?" a guy from his unit said. He tapped the sporting-goods bag. "Good shopping?" He winked.

Jerry clapped him on the shoulder, "You know wives...." "You know husbands," I countered. We were on our way to scuff and work mud and dust into the soles and leather and laces. Upon his return, when Jerry would be searched, he would hold his breath until after his shoes passed as his old beaters and he was on his way up the hill to his unit.

"We're becoming regular Bonnie and Clydes," I said, feeling the satisfaction of pulling the wool over the BOP's eyes. Several miles later we came to the entrance to the state park that had been recommended to Jerry by an inmate for its mountain overlooks and variety of hiking trails. The sun cracked though the clouds and soon we were tramping into the forest on the moderate blue trail. The towering pines infused the air with a turpentine sappiness, so pungent I wouldn't have been surprised to come upon an artist painting in oils. We clasped hands as if at any moment we were going to be separated, until the path, rutted with roots, narrowed and pitched downward, then we had no choice but to pick our way single file. Jerry led, pausing every so often to rub the side of his shoe on a damp clump of earth, scuffle through some matted leaves, and tromp on what looked like plain old soot. "This is coal mining country." He delighted in the discovery as if it were gold.

At the base of a steep slope we found ourselves in what felt like the ruins of nature's living room. Underfoot, the ground was carpeted with layers of pine needles. The surrounding trees felt as protective as a house. There was a long, high brick wall with remnants of what looked to be a hearth, mostly intact, and a boulder before it that offered the hospitality of a seat. I climbed up to rest on the cold smooth stone. "What a perfect, peaceful hideaway. It feels like no one has ever been here but us." I wished that Jerry would join me and talk, suddenly lonely for him. But he just continued whistling behind me, as he had when he'd come home from work. He was himself now, exploring the relic of wall as if it were a Roman ruin. Leave him alone, I told myself.

"Well, guess what you're sitting on?" Jerry said, regarding a plaque. "According to this, it's Cooper's Rock. It seems we've found the legendary hideaway of a cooper, a barrel maker, who escaped from prison over a hundred years ago and lived here. I guess I'm like the divining rod of inmates. You can take me out, but I'll find a fellow con, even in a forest."

"It is weird. I'm glad he didn't get captured."

"It's making me nervous. Maybe it's a sign that I should go back in wearing my old shoes."

Thoughts of the con known as Cooper stayed with me as we followed the blue dots guiding us to a promontory, a ledge that could have been the end of the world, with a steep drop and a sprawling panorama. An eagle's majestic wingspan swooped over us. We tipped back our heads to watch it perform glides and dives with the force of freedom only the truly innocent can know.

Three days later, Jerry handed himself back to the C.O. at the guardhouse wearing his new sneakers, which carried the patina of the five-day furlough we shouldn't have had. Rumor ran rampant among the cons and the c.o.s that Jerry had snitched to get the five day. He was asked for several weeks, "Who do you know, Kraig?"

~

JERRY'S 'PEN' PALS
Issue No. 6   May 30, 1996

Well, here it is, supposed to be spring, but the weather has been absolute garbage. It seems to rain every day. Just another reason to hate this place.

Letters

Continuing on with my response to the letter in Issue No. 6 regarding how my days are spent, I'll move on to my day after noon.

I work just two afternoon shifts at the law library, Sunday and Monday, and the rest of my afternoons are free. I mostly try to jog or play tennis. I've also gotten into the routine of taking an hour nap about 2:30 each day.

I work three evening shifts, Sunday, Monday and Tuesday, so I am free the rest of the week. On Wednesday evenings there is a movie in the auditorium and I usually go to that. On Thursday evenings I teach my class on constitutional law. I have the entire day off on Saturday but I have Jewish studies from 1:30 to 3:00 so that breaks up the day. I keep very busy. I hate Saturday nights because there is nothing to do. I usually just read.

Passover

Passover turned out to be rather interesting this year. After a lot of whining, we were able to get the institution to give us the officers' mess hall for two days so we could hold our Seder. We also got some special food sent in, matzo, gefilte fish, horseradish, kosher chicken and about a half pound of veal for the eight of us. There were also supposed to be two boxes of macaroons for each guy, but the kitchen staff stole those before they got to us.

On the first night, the table was set and two of our guys prepared a wonderful meal for us.

We started the Seder with "Doc" reading in Hebrew. In the meantime, it turns out that the officers' mess hall is also the place where the Muslims who work in food service are allowed to pray each day at sunset. So right in the middle of the Seder, in come two Muslims with their prayer mats. They plop down on the floor and go into their prayer ritual.

Well, there are eight of us and two of them so we start praying louder. The Muslims will not be out prayed and they pick up the volume. Soon the prayers and chants are taking on a threatening quality. Even the Jews who don't speak Hebrew are chanting away in a strange gurgling sound trying to sound like Hebrew.

The Jews realize that all this is futile so we resort to other means. We uncover our food trays and start eating. The odor of chicken soup, baked chicken, horseradish, veal and even grape juice permeates the room.

Instead of Hebrew prayers, the sounds of chewing, chomping, sucking, slurping and "Oy, is this good!" now dominate our side of the room.

The Muslims, who have been on a Ramadan fast, are starting to weaken. They peek up from their mats to see what we are eating, their nostrils flare wide to inhale the smells of our food, and soon they surrender. They roll up their mats and leave with a final chant, "m_____ f_____s."

There is no time for us to celebrate our victory because we just keep eating. For us Jews, eating beats celebrating any day.

The Great Shakedown

As I have previously indicated, there are many, many rules that govern our life here. One that deals with personal property is that we are allowed to have ONLY $20 in coins. No paper money is allowed and anything over $20 is a violation. Every Wednesday we can buy the coins at the commissary.

We are also restricted regarding electronic devices. Only radios with earphones and a small fan are allowed. Nothing else electronic is allowed, not even an electric shaver, and cellular phones are absolutely a no-no.

A few weeks back, my housing unit was subjected to 'The Great Shake Down.' This was an all-out search of the unit looking for contraband. Drug sniffing dogs were brought in and every inch of the unit was searched. Every fixture was removed from the wall or ceiling and completely inspected. Every ceiling tile was pulled down. Every room, cubicle, locker and bed was torn apart.

In a far corner of my unit lived the leader of the institution's Nation of Islam group. He was a tall black man who never smiled and never said "Hello" to anyone white. In his room they uncovered currency amounting to $51,000 (that's right, FIFTY ONE THOUSAND DOLLARS!) and two cellular phones. They tore up every inch of that room, even pulling the tile squares up from the floor. He was taken to the hole and who knows where he'll go from there.

In another room (where a food-service worker lived), they found 40 chickens and $500. He and his roommate were taken off to the hole.

All in all, seven guys in my unit were taken to the hole for serious violations.

The only thing taken from me was a box of Kleenex that was legally purchased from the commissary. I have no idea as to why it was taken.I filed a protest.

Rooms

Speaking of rooms, I finally got one. I have been moved from the dorm area into a room. Keep in mind that this facility was built as a youth center. Each room was constructed to hold one youth. Now we have two adults living in each room.

The room is about six feet wide and ten feet long. The wall to the right has a sink, a shelf and a toilet that takes up about two feet of width. The bed on the left takes up another two feet of width. That leaves about two feet of space as an aisle in the room. This creates a real problem for me because my roommate is two feet, three inches wide.

Frankie is an Italian guy from New Jersey who is probably the only adult in America shorter that Danny DeVito. He's under five feet, but is about 200 pounds of muscle. The two of us cannot be in the room at the same time unless we are in the bunk (I have the top). He's really a good guy and he's a wonderful cook. Pasta every night.

A Sound

"Joe Smith, report to the back door of R&D." Whenever anyone is released from here (and it happens just about every day), the PA announcer makes the announcement for that person to "report to the back door of R&D" and they are processed out. Once they are gone, you probably never see them again.

Recently, Jeremy left. He is 27 years old and has spent the last 6½ years in prison. His crime: drugs. Jeremy is a great kid. He is very handsome, very bright and a terrific athlete. Although he is Catholic, he liked to attend the Jewish studies, "just to learn." He did so many drugs that to this day, he still shakes when he lifts his fork to his mouth.

What a wasted life. His entire adult life has been spent in prison. As I heard his call to R&D, I silently wished him well and hoped that someday the Federal Government will come up with some realistic approach to their 'War on Drugs' besides "let's just punish the shit out of them."

I can't wait to hear, "Jerry Kraig, report to the back door of R&D."

Appeal

My appeal is being argued on June 3, 1996, however, we won't know anything for at least a month or two. Keep something crossed for me.

Keep those cards and letters coming. I miss you all.

Love always,

Jerry

~

JERRY'S 'PEN' PALS
Issue No. 7   July 11, 1996

This issue will cover the period of time from Memorial Day to the 4th of July. Like other holidays, just another day, both days. However, they do try to make the days special by offering 'special' food for the holiday. For Memorial Day they had 'One-half of Chicken.' Unfortunately, it turned out to be the bottom half. For the 4th of July, they had 'T Bone Steak.' The "T" here stood for "tail bone." Needless to say, I passed on both meals.

One of the things they like to do is to make the holidays seem special. They always have contests and festivities for the occasion. Things like the 100-yard dash; 3-mile run; baseball throw; egg throwing contest, and even Boccie Ball tournaments. I entered the Boccie Ball contest and enjoyed it. We lost in the first round, but then won two matches in the losers bracket before being eliminated.

From the Mailbag

Mr. Jim Fixx writes: "Keep up the good work with your jogging. How do you keep from getting bored while you run?"

Jogging can be very boring, especially if you run around a track all of the time, so there are a couple of things I do to keep occupied. I wear my radio so that the music keeps my mind off the boredom. There is a problem with this, however, the only station around here that doesn't play 'Country and Western' music is WDUM-FM. This is a very weak station that promotes itself as 'Covering the southern portion of Morgantown.' You can pick up the station during the day but at night, if they turn on the lights at the station, the power is greatly reduced. So as I run, the station wafts in and out and smacking on my radio keeps me occupied.

Another thing you can do here is to read the tattoos on the other guys who are also jogging or walking. There is one guy who walks a lot and he has an entire Louie L'Amour novel tattooed on his back. I'm on Chapter 4 of the book *Cowboy Courage* and hope to finish it before he goes home in August.

Food

It continues to be horrible. I never eat any meat that is offered here. As a result, all I usually eat are the potatoes and a salad. I've eaten so many potatoes that I'm starting to think in Russian. The real problem is that everything comes from the "lowest bidder." For example, we get ice in every unit. But, because it comes from the lowest bidder, it is warm ice. Your drinks never get cold, they just get warmer. We also get some unusual brands that you have never seen in the supermarkets. We get a mouthwash from the commissary that leaves a bad taste in your mouth.

Religion

We got a new Jew on the compound. He is from New York and studied for 20 years at the yeshiva. He is a religious genius. But, he doesn't look like a rabbinical student, he looks like a 'biker.' Long hair that he keeps up in a ponytail. A full beard. He's 5 feet, 6 inches and weighs about 250 pounds. His hands are so large and thick that that fact alone would disqualify him from being a urologist. But despite his appearance, he is indeed a very gentle and very intelligent man. He will be fun to know and to learn from.

Health

Good news, I had no allergies this June. The first time since 1957. Bad news, my blood pressure has been up. Because I am concerned, I try to keep tabs on my blood pressure. However, here, where all of the doctors and physicians' assistants are graduates of Kevorkian Medical School, I am a bother. The last time I went in to get it checked, one of the PAs seemed rather annoyed by my request. So after she took my reading she said, "You're OK." I asked, "What is it?" She replied, "I'm not going to tell you." And some people think this place is a country club. I continue to lose weight. I was down to 180 this week. My goal is 178.

Good Reading

The most popular book here at this time (the Dennis Rodman book is not here yet) is *Green Gold*. This book makes a case for marijuana saying it is a religious matter. They say that everywhere in the Bible they refer to 'incense' they are actually referring to marijuana. Now all these guys want to appeal their convictions on the basis of freedom of religion. I wish them well.

Well, that's it for now. This Independence Day has not been one for me. But hopefully, next year will be better and I'll be at my family picnic. Keep those cards and letters coming. I miss you all.

Love always,

Jerry

~

JERRY'S 'PEN' PALS
Issue No. 8   August 15, 1996
One Year Anniversary Special Souvenir Edition

Well, August 21st marks my one-year anniversary in prison. So here I go with more information about what I've learned in this last year.

There are two types of security personnel on the compound. Those who do general security (like guards) and operate out of the 'Lieutenants' Office' and those who stay in the units during their shift. None are armed.

Each unit is occupied by an officer who watches over that unit during his shift. He has one basic responsibility, to conduct a count of those inmates in the unit. During the week, this is done at 4 pm and 10 pm. On weekends, 10 am, 4 pm and 10 pm Each guard is provided with an assistant who also counts to confirm the result. They each walk through the unit and count each inmate, then compare results. When both have the same number, they call it in to control.

Since a unit has between 95 and 110 inmates, this requires great skill and supreme intelligence. Finding people who can perform this difficult mathematical feat must be a real challenge for the Bureau of Prisons.

The name that the inmates have attached to these geniuses is 'HACK.'

Most HACKS put on their polyester gray slacks, come to work, lock themselves in their little office and wait for the day they can retire and get their pension. The count to them is as difficult as if they had to dig the Panama Canal with a soup spoon. They finish the count and fall exhausted in their chairs to complain about how overworked they are.

However, other HACKS take the job rather seriously. They are determined that no injustice shall be committed in the unit during their watch. I will tell you about two of them.

There are things that are not allowed to be brought back to the units from the mess hall. But every day guys take broccoli and cauliflower from the salad bar and smuggle it back to the unit to cook with rice, pasta or fish later that night.

This is a job for SuperHack. She (the government is an equal-opportunity employer) has a mission in life and that is to rid the unit of broccoli and cauliflower.

First of all, you should see this prize (but not too soon after eating). She's just under 5 feet tall and weighs about 160 pounds. She has a face that looks like she ran into a 500-pound iron frying pan. Her face is so flat that her glasses are always at the tip of her nose, held there only because the frame curves around her ears.

Can you imagine what she must feel like knowing that she has full authority and power over 95 to 110 men each day? What power the BOP has bestowed upon her.

So every night she goes on her patrol, searching lockers, beds, clothing, containers, etc. for that dreaded broccoli. The booty of her search makes life worthwhile for her.

Another item considered contraband is used containers. When you get goods from the commissary, once the container is empty, you must throw it away. Even though the cost of the article includes the container, once empty, the BOP considers it contraband.

Every year at Christmas, the BOP passes out candy and caramel corn in neat plastic containers to all the inmates. These make excellent bowls to cook in or to mix and hold your salads. However, by the rules, once empty, you are supposed to throw away these perfectly good containers. Many inmates can't afford to spend the $3 charged for an official, BOP approved container at the commissary so they keep their present for as long as they can.

But, this is a job for Container Cop. This HACK is notorious for his love of confiscating containers. He is also notorious for being a prick. He was recently assigned to our unit and the first night, as soon as we left for dinner, he searched an entire wing gathering up many, many containers, especially of the Christmas genre. But to prove what a prick he is, he dumped one guy's coffee out of the contraband container onto the guy's clothes. He must have enjoyed it because he did it to a few other guys.

Then he loaded his sack and took the contents down to the Lieutenants' Office to brag about his prowess.

While he was gone, some of the inmates, angered by this, went to each office that belonged to HACKS or counselors and somehow managed to plug up the locks so that no one could get into their office, including this HACK.

A locksmith had to be called out and 7 or 8 locks had to be replaced. The lieutenant in charge that evening called for a conference, and after spending an hour with the HACK, declared to our unit that there would now be 'peace.' It seems to have worked.

You hear me complain about the ridiculous rules here, but let me give you a test.

SITUATION: An inmate in his mid 50's has fallen to the ground clutching his chest and has turned blue. You are the HACK who, (after finishing your cigarette and coffee) rushes to the inmate. You check for a pulse and there is none. You:

A. Start immediate resuscitation.

B. Beat the shit out of the inmate.

C. Call for an emergency squad.

D. Call for medical assistance.

E. Put handcuffs on the deceased inmate.

Pursuant to BOP policy, the correct answer is 'E.' Yep, the first thing you do if an inmate dies is handcuff him. The thinking is that this death may just be a clever trick to escape.

Food

I know that some of you think I complain too much about the food. After all, this is not a Holiday Inn. At great expense to *'Pen' Pals*, I have retained the services of ace reporter Jimmy Olsen, who investigated my claims about the quality of the food here. Mr. Olsen managed to photograph the government buyer of meat as he inspected a prospective purchase. The photo is attached. He did happen to get a very good price for this 'side' of beef.

Last week we had cheesecake. First time I have ever had cheesecake made from Velveeta.

Roommate

My new roommate has found numerous ways to offend my senses.

He has some money so he has hired two other inmates to work for him. One does his laundry, makes his bed, sweeps and cleans the room, and polishes and waxes the floor. The other cooks for him and procures his extra food needs.

My room is a constant hubbub of noise, activity and food being served. In the middle of the night he'll open his container to eat and the room fills with the odor of his food (broccoli, cauliflower, onions, peppers and fish). A few hours later he passes the chemical reaction this food has created in his system. This guy is the Ethel Merman of farting.

He leaves for work at 5:30 am so he's up before me. I've never known anyone who makes as much noise as he does just getting dressed. He actually makes noise buttoning his shirt.

But aside from the noise and the smells, he's really a good guy. Very kind and very generous.

Anniversary

Well, since I've been here one whole year, Warden Willie W. Wilson personally visited me to congratulate me on being such a good prisoner.

He holds me in high esteem. He brought along Sir Frederick Waugh, the director of torture at the Tower of London in London, England. Sir Frederick was on a tour of the U.S. prisons at the time and I enjoyed meeting him.

I told him about my roommate's habits and he is thinking of installing such tactics into his repertoire.

Well, that's it for the year. Keep those cards and letters coming.

Love you all,

Jerry

~

JERRY'S 'PEN' PALS
Issue No. 9   August 1, 1996

Well, here we go with another edition of Jerry's 'Pen' Pals.

A lot of people want to know what is going on with my appeal. Nothing to report at this time. I remain extremely anxious. It was argued on June 3, 1996.

Food

Once again the commissary has come up with an inferior product for sale. In an effort to battle the flu bug, I decided to take vitamins. But because the commissary gets what other institutions throw out, all I could get was Vitamin C minus. It doesn't help much.

I know I complain a lot about the food, but you have to realize that the system is very, very structured. For example, we have recently had some serious problems with the food service. We used to get toast at breakfast a couple of times a week. However, we haven't had any in a few months, so I inquired with the manager as to what the problem was. He informed me that they lost the recipe and that a new one has been ordered from Washington. I'll keep you posted (or toasted) on this.

They have also been offering pepper in packets and the tables no longer have a pepper shaker on them, just salt. I inquired about this also and was advised that the inmate whose job it was to fill the pepper shaker has been released. They are trying to train some new inmates to fill the job (and the shakers) but it is taking longer than anticipated. Usually, you have to spend at least 18 months on salt before you are qualified to be upped to pepper, so it will be a while before we see full pepper shakers on our tables again.

I know I dwell on the food, but it is very important. For the most part, our life is rather humdrum and boring. Complaining about the food gives us something to do.

Also, because we usually eat between 4:30 and 5 pm, it means going until 6:15 am the next day before you can get something to eat. Most of us do not go 14 hours between meals. Therefore, the snack at about 8 pm takes on great importance and significance. You can acquire a number of good snacks from the commissary, but nothing beats the works of man's imagination.

Preparation begins at breakfast. Those who arrive early bring various types of containers (plastic jars, garbage and trash bags, coffee mugs, etc.) concealed in their clothing. The first to go is the sugar. Containers are taken from the tabletop and held below the table. With a deft hand, the top is removed and the contents emptied into the 'take out' container. If you get to the mess hall 5 minutes after it opens, you will not have any sugar. Next is milk. Again, all sorts of makeshift containers are filled and then secreted away in clothing to be removed to the housing units.

As one eats he sees cereal being poured into pockets, fruit dropped into jacket sleeves and rolls or bread stashed under sweatshirts. Especially valuable is the broccoli and cauliflower because it mixes with so many other foods. But boy does it smell. This goes on at every meal.

You also have to understand that this is a federal institution. A certain amount of 'skimming' is expected.

For example: Let's suppose 3,000 pieces of chicken have been purchased for the compound. The chicken is delivered by the supplier and unloaded from the truck to the warehouse. Now there are 2,700 pieces of chicken. Two days before the chicken is to be served, it is brought from the warehouse to the kitchen. The cooks now have 2,200 pieces of chicken to prepare. After the chicken is prepared by the kitchen staff, the remaining 1,600 pieces are then cooked and made ready to be served. Those 1,200 pieces have to serve the 900 inmates. From the time they leave the kitchen to the time they are served, there are 800 pieces left. That usually covers it as there are about 100 vegetarians who get special meals. That night in the units there will be a special on chicken parts. The men who work in food service will be hawking their goods, 'chicken, 3 pieces for a dollar.'

Others will have 10 lb. bags of cereal, or pasta, or large cans of tomato sauce, or fruit cocktail, or even, 'kiwis, 4 for a dollar.' By 9 pm, food of all sorts is being prepared all over the compound and everyone seems happy. Somehow, the system works. The funny thing is the guys who 'take' in the summertime. The temperature will be 95 degrees and the worker shows up with his winter coat on. As he leaves the mess hall you can see him carrying his coat in his arms like a precious bundle of cloth being strained by the weight of his booty. So though we complain, the food situation does make life interesting.

Zimmer Bill

A new law is now in effect that will change the institution. Congress passed the

Zimmer Bill, which is designed to make prison life tougher.

The new rules include: no weight equipment that develops upper-body strength; no more HBO; no more movies that are rated above PG (we'll be seeing *The Sound of Music* a lot); no clothing that is red, blue, black, brown, etc., only white, gray and the issued tan or green. (This is supposedly because the reds, blues, etc. are gang colors and they want to prohibit any gang-type displays) They also have prohibited pajamas (I guess there was a notorious pajama gang and that should put an end to that).

It also means no more photographs for my 'Pen' Pals. Warden Wilson stopped by to tell me how sorry he was about that because he's been getting nice letters from people across the country telling him how good he looks in my newsletters.

So life here will be just a little more miserable.

Sports

I did not do well in the tennis tournament this year. Got to the 3rd round and lost. Badminton has started early this year and I hope to do well. I played last year's best player five times already and I've beaten him once (15–9) and gone to 18–16 in a loss. So, I should do well this year because he is a great player.

I continue to jog and recently set my record for six miles. I did it in 52 minutes and 58 seconds. Not bad for an old fart.

I'm teaching a class in Everyday Law this year. So far it has been a lot of work, but a lot of fun also. There are a number of other classes being offered at this time: Bridge, Creative Writing, Small Business Administration, Banking, Racquet Ball, Quit Smoking, Vegetarian Health, Basketball Refereeing, Sign Language, Spanish and Volleyball, to mention a few.

A Sight

Ever have the problem where you're about to sneeze but can't get to your hankie fast enough? Well, I saw an inmate handle this in an ingenious manner recently. As the sneeze began to well, he grabbed the collar of his sweatshirt and pulled it outward. Then he pulled the shirt up over his nose and sneezed away. When he finished, he took a napkin and cleaned the inside of the shirt. Try it next time you have to sneeze. This could put the hankie business into bankruptcy if it catches on.

Well, that's it for now. Keep those cards and letters coming.

Love you all,

Jerry

~

'PEN' PALS bulletin
November 8, 1996

At press time, the staff here at 'Pen' Pals Publishing was hit with extremely disappointing news. Jerry's appeal was denied today by the United States Circuit Court of Appeals. The good news is the government's appeal was also denied. The minimum sentence that Jerry was given by the lower court will stand and he will be released in April of 1997. Jerry is very disappointed but he is glad to be able to 'see the light at the end of the tunnel'. He will continue to keep in touch through the 'Pen' Pals newsletters. Thank you for all your friendship, kindness and support.

Brian and Stacy

~

JERRY'S 'PEN' PALS
Issue No. 10   January 6, 1997
Special Holiday Souvenir Edition

Happy New Year everyone. 1996 is finally gone. My year was the same as the Cleveland Browns: lost, wasted, nothing, etc., but 1997 looks promising.

First I have to extend a formal apology to Warden Willie W. Wilson. I understand that my son, Brian, added a note to my last 'Pen' Pals explaining that my appeal had not been allowed. He also added, however, that I could 'see the light at the end of the tunnel,' referring to the fact that I'll be out in April.

Well, a few days after that issue was released, I returned to my room to find it crawling with guards and HACKS wearing those miner's hats, sniff dogs and FBI agents. Everything had been torn apart. Warden Wilson put his arm around me and we had the following conversation:

WW   Alright Kraig, where's the tunnel? We've searched your room, the entire wing and most of the unit. We can't find the tunnel."

JK   There is no tunnel

WW   But your newsletter mentions the tunnel, and that you've dug enough to see the light at the end.

JK   But that's just an expression, a metaphor.

WW   What's a meta for?

JK   No, it's not what a metaphor is for.

WW   Oh, a meta four by four, one of those Jap vehicles. So, you had   that   waiting for you at the end of your tunnel.

JK   No, no, that's just an expression of speech. Haven't you ever heard someone say, "I'm so hungry I could eat a horse"?

WW   Oh, oh, you've been talking to the cook. You're not supposed to know where we get our meat. I'm going to have to talk to that cook.

JK   No, no, I've never talked to the cook. Look, you were born and raised in West Virginia and you're a big follower of West Virginia football aren't you?

WW   Sure.

JK   Haven't you ever heard the expression, "A tie game is like loving your sister"?

WW   Hmmmmmm. Look Kraig, you keep that quiet and I'll forget about your tunnel. Just promise not to use it.

JK   You've got a deal.

So I want to apologize to the Warden for any anxiety or apprehensions these newsletters may have caused him.

Roommate

Well, I have a new roommate. I just couldn't take much more of old Odie, so I switched.

Let me give you an idea of what life with Odie was all about. He went on a diet so he would not eat meals at the chow hall. Instead, he had this Jamaican guy cook for him each night.

So now I have another roommate to contend with. The Jamaican spent a lot of time each day in Odie's locker and in the room preparing the evening meal.

His specialty (he made it every single night) was rice, mackerel, sardines, octopus, onions, green peppers, garlic, garlic powder, red peppers and lots of jalapenos. Jamaica would whip up two big bowls of this for Odie every night. He'd eat the first bowl between 8 and 9 pm, and then leave the other one next to his bed.

Odie would fall asleep around 10:30 or 11 pm and all the lights would go out. At about 1 am, his snoring would start and I'd be awakened. At 2 am, he would wake up and pop the lid on that second bowl. The smell from that concoction would fill the room and I would start to gag. Then I would hear, "GLUMP, GLUMP, GLUMP" as he shoveled large spoonfuls of that crap into his mouth. Some more "GLUMP, GLUMP, GLUMP"s followed. Then the lid is closed.

Within 5 minutes Odie is up and he goes to his locker located at the foot of his bed. The locker CLANKS open and his package of vanilla wafers is pulled out. The package is opened to loud CRINKLES, and then 10 or 20 wafers and he MUNCHED and CRUNCHED away. The package is closed, returned to the locker, which he then CLANGS shut with a loud metallic bang.

Back in bed, he GLUMPS a few more spoonfuls of that crap and then goes back to sleep. But he can't sleep, so he takes out his radio, puts the earphones on over his ears and turns the volume to the max. I can hear the muffled sounds from that fuckin' radio just loud enough to keep me awake. Soon he is snoring away and the earphones have slipped off his ears and are positioned over his nose and the back of his head. I can now hear the words to the songs.

By 3 am, the octopus, the peppers, the garlic, the jalapenos and the onions have processed into the lower portions of his system and now new sounds and odors are emerging from Odie.

So when another room opened, I moved.

My new roommate is Rick. He appears in the attached picture with me. He happens to be a great guy with a wonderful personality, and best of all, no radio.

Food

We have a new food administrator. This guy is absolutely terrible. But he brings good news and bad news. The bad news is that the food is even worse than ever. The good news is that the portions are smaller.

I think this guy's main supplier is BFI (Browning, Ferris Industries). (Those big blue rubbish trucks you see on the road.)

He has cut the budget way back on what he buys. What is leftover from what he serves on Monday night is then made into soup to be served on Tuesday. Have you ever had cream of liver Soup? Yuk!

Because of that Zimmer Bill, the budget has been severely cut. Now twice a week our hot meal of the day consists of a bowl of steam.

The Holidays
Thanksgiving

The guys were all excited about the Thanksgiving meal. The word was that the institution received genuine Perdue turkeys for the holiday. Instead of being from Perdue Poultry Corporation, these turned out to be turkeys used in an experiment at Purdue University in an effort to cure Putrid Poultry Disease.

About 200 guys who ate the meal now glow in the dark. Another 100 or so have red things growing from the front of their necks. Health Services is treating them with large doses of Maalox.

Thank goodness I missed that meal.

Christmas

We had the annual Christmas party for the poor kids of Morgantown. Once again the Jewish inmates did a Chanukah puppet show. It was fun, as again I wrote, produced and directed the skit.

It was also rather sad because the joy of seeing those 47 kids opening their gift packages brought great sadness and loneliness for family and home.

The Christmas meal was 'Cornish Game Hen.' The key word here is 'Cornish.' Instead of being chicken, they took an ear of corn and with clever placement of toothpicks, that piece of corn looked just like a little hen.

Some of the guys who never had Cornish game hen before ate the toothpicks and had very painful bowel movements. Health Services is treating them with large doses of Maalox.

New Year's Day

Just another day here, but the special meal was listed as 'T Bone Steak.' It turns out that the 'T Bone' stands for 'Tyrannosaurus Bone.' An aged steak is usually pretty good, but 3 million years was a bit too much. Health Services is treating most of the guys with large doses of Maalox.

Sports

I finished the badminton season with only three loses, one in singles and twice in doubles. All three were to the same guy, who won it all. He never lost a match all season. I came second in both.

A Book

Everyone tells me I ought to write a book about my experience here. Well, I have one in mind. Although most everything is hard to get, either because of prohibitive rules or because of budget constraints, there is one commodity that is abundant, toilet paper. Someone must have sold the institution 100 million rolls of toilet paper.

The inmates have been very creative in the use of these toilet paper rolls. They are used for every type of cleaning job, for napkins, tablecloths, notepaper and hankies, etc.

The full roll is placed between the radio earphones and a hole about the size of a half-dollar is cut in the middle. You now have a speaker for your radio. A few sheets of toilet paper placed inside the roll will increase the quality of the sound.

If you stuff the empty roll with a very solid core of toilet paper, you can light the paper and use it like a can of Sterno. You can keep food warm with it. It will burn slowly for about 20 minutes.

You can also wrap the ice cream containers in lots of toilet paper and it will insulate it from melting.

Anyway, I thought I'd put all these ideas into a book entitled *A Hundred Other Things to Do with a Roll of Toilet Paper*. What do you think?

Happy New Year all. See you soon.

Love you all,

Jerry

CHAPTER EIGHTEEN

DEAL

We believed the appeal would come as a swift reprieve. But when the holidays ended and we were still waiting, I was reminded of a trip with our kids. Jerry had distracted them from nagging about being home yet by telling them to count to one hundred. When they'd reached ninety-nine and we were still log jammed on the freeway, they'd screamed, "No fair, you said we'd be there." Jerry had directed their attention to the accident ahead. "Sometimes something happens and we have to accept that it won't go our way." After four hours in the car, they didn't care what the reason was, they just wanted the trip to be over. After Jerry's furlough I felt one hundred had come and gone. Jerry's sentence seemed like it would never end. A year later, when word came that he'd lost the appeal, we spoke about it in the same monotone that I'd heard "I am a prisoner's wife." Waiting had become the omen of defeat.

Then, it was the middle of March. It hadn't seemed possible but here it was. Only a month to go until Jerry would be released on April 21st. Fortunately, I was in Cleveland for Andrew's birthday when a halfway house worker called to make an appointment to inspect our house. Unlike Glatz, whose only interest in our home inspection was our financial holdings, this brawny, aggressive woman would peel away the wallpaper if she thought Jerry could hide anything under it. She shoved clothes out of the way in the closets, opened cupboards, inventoried every door in the house and where they led to. She was particularly suspicious of the small attic off what had been Karen's room and the crawl space behind it. "What's with all this mess?" she sneered. "You have to clean it out. We can't have your husband in a home where he can hide things."

"I don't think he'll want to hide his tennis racquet," I said, not making any attempt to hide the sarcasm.

"How about drugs or firearms?" she snapped. "I need to account for how he could escape and all other contingencies. Home release isn't a ticket to go crazy. Your husband will have to prove he can live within limits."

"My husband was convicted of a nonviolent crime that had nothing to do with narcotics. He's a lawyer. Was a lawyer," I said.

She checked off a box in her notebook. "It won't help, your having a bad attitude."

"Look, I don't have a bad anything. I want him home, that's all."

"Yeah," she raised an eyebrow, "so, you'll accept him if he gets home release?"

"Of course. Isn't that what this is about?"

"Some say no. Nothing is given in this business."

In my bedroom, she scanned her list for the next question, sighed and asked, "Where is he going to sleep?"

"With me, here," I stifled a laugh. Her eyes widened. I immediately sobered, "I'm sorry. I'm not making fun of you. It's just that one bedroom has a twin bed and is practically empty. The other has a crib and a toddler bed. This is clearly the master bedroom with a king."

"I don't write the questions I just ask 'em, okay? I've got three more releases to do today, so let's get this over with. Show me all your phones." As I pointed out every line, she explained that there would be no excuse for Jerry not to come to the phone when she called to check on him. No one could claim him to be indisposed and she didn't want to hear the answering machine. If Jerry didn't come to the phone, he would be marked absent, which was a violation that could send him back to, she checked her sheet, "FCI Morgantown. Some guys hate halfway houses, but," she emphasized, "home release won't be any picnic, either."

We were waiting again. Jerry had yet to receive his assignment. An inmate had given him the rundown on the halfway houses within driving distance of downtown Cleveland, where Jerry would be working for Brian as a paralegal. Employment was the lynch pin of the program. Halfway houses were privately owned businesses. Jerry would be required to pay them one-third of his salary. He was most rattled by the rough reputation of Oriana House in Akron, where violent cons were said to harass the white-collars and the staff was tough. Jerry had the option of refusing halfway house and to remain at FCI to serve out the remaining six months. But even if he were assigned to Akron, as dicey as it sounded, he'd decided he couldn't stay at FCI one more second. His eligibility for weekends at home and the future possibility of home release was worth anything. We would be able go to Brian's and baby-sit. Papa Jerry would be behind the wheel again, taking them out on special days, on track to getting his life back.

At the end of March, I met Karen for lunch in Manhattan. We still hadn't received word of halfway-house assignment. Nonetheless, my last trip to Morgantown would be to pick him up. The restaurant was cramped and noisy, reminding Karen of the last time she'd seen Jerry. FCI's population had risen beyond capacity and the visiting room had been unbearably overcrowded. "I can't wait for Dad to be free," she said so loudly, the middle-aged women next to us stopped midsentence and eyed her curiously. Karen reddened with embarrassment. She threw her hair back and turned from them, muttering, "I need to get out of here."

She'd been very guarded about anyone knowing, even those closest to her at work. I said, "We didn't order yet, so let's go." That's freedom, I thought, as we began to cut our way under a fine drizzle through the cobblestone streets of Greenwich Village back to her apartment. "But, he won't really be free," I said.

As if she hadn't heard, she responded, "I'm going to buy airline tickets so I can be with you and Dad when he's released."

Allowing a family to pass, Karen and I split into single file along an ornate iron fence then resumed walking together. Knowing she wouldn't like my response, I said cautiously, "We don't know how his transfer to halfway house is going to happen, let alone where. I don't think it's a good idea for you to come."

"You told me I didn't have to go to the trial and I listened to you, but I should have been there. Now you're telling me no again. You say this now, and then I regret it."

"I didn't keep you from coming to the trial."

"Yes, you did. I feel like I'm always being shut out."

"It's not about shutting you out or letting you in. And you know it. I'm sick of rehashing the hash, Karen."

"Mom, you guys keep making all of the decisions, and not very well I might add. All I know is Dad's getting out and I want to be there. I need to see the place so I don't have to imagine it."

"Do you think they're going to let us in to unpack for him?" I said, exasperated. "I learned that lesson. Dad will be managing on his own."

"Just like he's been managing his sentence?"

"What's that supposed to mean? No one in the history of prison has handled it so well."

"You can't be that blind, Mother. As great as Dad's handling it on the outside, it's killing him on the inside. He puts on a good show. He always has. 'Everything's fine, Kare.' Just read his newsletters. He's full of despair. It's in there. I've seen it in his eyes. He's not like us or Brian. We express ourselves Technicolor, but he… can't."

"Look, Kare, we're so close to the end. We've got to get through halfway house and then we'll all be freed. I've seen him swallowing shame. I know he's suffering. But don't forget how strong he is. We're going to survive. No, more than survive."

We were at my subway station. It began to rain in earnest. I put up my umbrella over both of us.

"You know how Grandpa died when he was fifty-eight? It was from the stress of pretending everything was fine with Grandma!"

"Kare…" I shivered.

"It just worries me— the toll this has taken." Karen blinked back tears.

I said, hugging her, "No one's going to die. He's not Grandpa. He has huge support not only from us but his colleagues and friends too. All of his clients. We're going to be fine. Now go to your haircut appointment."

She declined my umbrella and darted across Seventh Avenue. I headed down to the subway more full of doubt than I would ever admit.

Soaked by the time I entered my building, I opened my mailbox, anxious to get into my apartment to change. I rifled through the mail, disappointed that Jerry's final *'Pen' Pal* newsletter wasn't there. An official looking envelope from the New York Foundation of the Arts caught my attention. Waiting for the elevator to come down from the sixth floor, I opened the envelope and read that the New York Foundation of the Arts was pleased to inform me that I was the recipient of a seven-thousand-dollar fellowship award in drawing. Astounded, I stuffed the letter back in its envelope quickly and stood rooted to the floor, heart racing. I had no recollection of even submitting the prison tape works that I had finished over six months ago. Inside the elevator, I pulled out the letter and read it again, fast, afraid the type might disappear.

I was bursting to tell Jerry. There was little chance of him calling for another hour, and even then it wasn't likely. On Saturdays when he didn't have visitors, this was when he went up to his bunk and listened to opera at the Met. I laid the letter open on the kitchen table, never taking my eyes off of it as I changed into sweats. I paced nervously around the table, wishing the phone would perform a miracle and Jerry would call. Exasperated, I dialed Karen. After the third ring her message came on. Deliberating for a beat, I told her machine my good news. Too worked up to do anything else, I flopped on the couch, waiting for the phone to ring, daydreaming of fame, spending the seven thousand dollars ten times over, and fell asleep.

At 6 PM, the phone rang, waking me. The excitement rushed back when I heard Jerry's, "Hi, hon."

"Jer, I just got the surprise of my life." I rushed to read the letter. "Can you believe it?"

"It's really wonderful. But," he said, "when did you start to make art about prison?"

The award now felt wrong. "I told you. These were the tape pieces with your prison number on them that my gallery didn't want."

"I'm sorry, hon, I just don't remember. But it's really great. And seven thousand dollars is quite an award."

"Are you upset that they're about you?"

"No, of course not."

"Would it bother you if I showed them in Cleveland?"

"No, you should show them wherever you want. I'm just surprised," he said and added hastily, "happy surprised," he paused, "we only have a minute, and I called to tell you that I got my halfway-house assignment. I'm afraid it's Oriana in Akron."

I barely got out, "That's not good," and the line went dead.

~

JERRY'S 'PEN' PALS
Issue No. 11   April 8, 1997

Well my friends, the end is in sight. This will be my last *'Pen' Pals*. Hope you had as much fun reading them as I did living them.

Immediate Plans

1. I leave for the halfway house April 21, 1997. I will be in Akron as there isn't a half-way house in Cleveland.

2. Work in my old office as a paralegal.

3. Have my hearing with the Ohio Supreme Court regarding my "punishment" for my conviction.

4. Get my license to practice back by October 17, 1997, my release date.

5. Get "home confinement" by June or July.

6. Try to get my life back.

Some Things I have Learned During My Time Here

1. As a kid, I had one major dream and one major nightmare. The dream was to have been a fighter pilot during World War II. In my P51 Mustang I was sure I would have been an 'ace.' A few years back I had the good fortune to go to Air Combat U.S.A. in Fullerton, California. There I actually flew an airplane that looked like a small P51 and I fought air battles using lasers instead of bullets. In my very first 'dogfight' my opponent shot me down (we fought five dogfights and I won three.) As much as I cherish that day as one of my favorite experiences in life, the fact that I got shot out of the sky on the very first go-round destroyed my illusions of what real combat must be all about. If that had been for real, it probably would have all ended there for me. Thanks to that experience, I have put that dream to sleep.

Don't need it anymore. It has been satisfied by the fact that I never had to do it and the reality of what might have been.

The nightmare was probably typical of most Jewish kids growing up after WWII. What if I had been born in Europe instead of the U.S.? How would I have fared in the camps? Would I have been a survivor? Now I can put that to rest too. My conclusion is that I would have perished. I did not have the drive that was necessary to survive. I let my despair get the best of me here, so can you imagine what would have happened to me in a camp?

In a magnificent book by Dr. Viktor Frankl, a psychiatrist who did survive the camps, he describes the courage and determination it took to survive. Of the numerous qualities that he attributes to survival, I probably have just two: a sense of humor and family and friends on the outside who have been supportive and accepting, thereby providing a will to go on.

I don't think my sense of humor would have helped much. I probably would have been shot for telling 'stupid Nazi' jokes. But the family and friends might have pulled me through. My problem has been the despair I have felt all these months and the nightmarelike quality of my life. I still can't believe what happened to me and I feel that the inability to accept and move on would have led to my demise.

On his 58th birthday my father died. On my 58th, I surrendered to the Bureau of Prisons in Morgantown, W.V. At first, I was not sure which one of us got the worst deal. Twenty months later, I can appreciate how good it is to be alive.

I have learned that for someone close to 60 years old, I'm in pretty good shape. That was a major challenge for me and I am very satisfied with my accomplishments. I can run five or six miles any time I want and average 9 minutes a mile. I still play pretty good tennis, my badminton got stronger, I still have a decent game of base-ball in me, my ping-pong reflexes are pretty good, I can bench-press my weight, I can do four sets of hammer curls with 30 pounders, my weight is down, so is my tummy, my wind and legs are strong, and I still have the same amount of hair I came in with, but a few more are now gray.

On the negative side, my blood pressure has been up and down, and my eyes have weakened. I now need glasses to read (but not to play tennis, badminton or ping-pong).

3. I have learned to enjoy radio, fresh fruit, religion, teaching, opera, letters from home, pictures of my grandchildren, jokes from friends, writing children's stories, taking afternoon naps, and even how to wash a load of clothes.

I have learned to hate the selfish stupidity and inconsideration of some of my fellow inmates, the total waste that exemplifies this experience, and of course, the m_____ f_____ing food they serve here.

If someone would have bet me on March 1, 1994, that on March 1, 1997, I would be in prison, get up and jog 5 miles in the morning, spend the afternoon at Torah studies class and then hurry back to my room to catch *Aida* from the Met on the radio, I would have bet the farm against any one of those things happening, let alone all of them. Go figure.

The Federal Government

You can't really appreciate our government until you have lived within it. The only rule that seems to apply is, 'If it makes sense, it doesn't make sense.' For the most part, nobody cares, and the people who work here just put in their time, take the money and retire and then take more money.

It is waste at its worst. It's like all other facets of government—whatever they touch, they ruin. Now, with the prison system growing so large, they are ruining that too. The only purpose for a place like this is to provide jobs for people who would otherwise be out of work.

Here is an example. I had to attend a 'pre-release' class. This is designed to help inmates adjust to the outside world when they are within 30 to 60 days of release. It's a whole day thing broken down into about six sessions. The second session was about investing money. Some guy went on and on about stocks, bonds, coupons, etc. The funny thing is that most of the guys have had to forfeit all their funds and property to the government as part of their sentence. While here, they've been making 12¢ an hour, so where are they supposed to get this money to invest? Just a waste of time. But I will tell you something I learned: if you invest your money at 12%, it will grow faster than if you invest it at only 10%. Now you know too, but don't tell anyone else because before you know it, everyone will want to earn 12% instead of just 10%!

But hell, as some poet once said, "My country, right or wrong...." What they don't see is the huge underclass of prisoners and ex-cons who loathe this government. They are so full of venom and hatred that they are dangerous. And they are growing. They cheer the 'real Americans,' the Ruby Ridge people, the David Koreshes and the Timothy McVeighs of the country. And all they want is a chance to 'show' Uncle Sam what 'freedom' is really all about.

I have lived with these guys for the last 20 months. They are classified as 'nonviolent,' but boy, do they hate.

One Last True Life Adventure

A few months ago I needed to have my hemorrhoidal ointment refilled. When I went to the pharmacy, they told me that I needed to be reexamined. So I had to go back to Health Services the next day for my examination. It turns out that I get sent to an examination room with a new, young female PA. I felt terribly embarrassed about having to go through this examination with her so I tried to leave. It's against the rules to leave once you get to the room, so I had to drop my drawers and show her my problems. It was very uncomfortable for me. Anyway, last week I came down with some sort of a cold with a very sore throat. I go to Health Services and the 2 PAs who are working that morning are the doctor from Colombia (the country, not the University) and that same woman. I tell them that I'd prefer to see the doctor, so guess who I get? I walk into the examination room and smile to her and say "Hi, how have you been?" She looks at me and says, "Have I seen you before?" I say, "Yes, don't you remember me?" She shrugs a negative and asks me my problem. I tell her about my cold and my sore throat. She gets a tongue depressor out, says, "Open wide," and looks in. As I am saying, "Ahhh" she is looking down my throat and suddenly says, "Ah, I remember you." I nearly swallowed the tongue depressor. I never realized they could see that far down your throat.

Finally
Thanks for everything. The letters, cards, jokes, support and love have been wonderful. See you soon.

Love always,

Jerry

~

Dear 'Pen' Pal
In the past, many of you have written to me to ask if there was something you could do to help me and now there is. In a few months I will appear before the Disciplinary Committee appointed by the Supreme Court of Ohio to determine the length of my suspension from the practice of law. I would like to be able to present them with letters on my behalf that will provide them with favorable recommendations concerning my character. I would also appreciate you indicating that you still have confidence in my abilities as an attorney and that my return to the practice of law would in no way discredit the profession. Would you please prepare such a letter, address it 'To Whom It May Concern' and mail it to my son, Brian Kraig, Thank you very much for your help and support.

Sincerely,

Jerry

~

A couple of days later, Jerry surprised me with a call at one o'clock in the afternoon. "Only eighteen days," I said, expectancy rushing through me.

"Wait till you hear what just happened. I was getting signed off at the law library, inventorying outstanding books, stuff like that, when I heard my name being called to go to the visiting room. I thought, "Who had come to surprise me?" It could only be a lawyer of record and I ran, excited it might be Brian. You can't imagine how shocked I was to see Craig Morford standing there. When I got to the table, he extended his hand. For the first time in my life, I couldn't bring myself to take it. I'm not proud that I didn't, but that's how repugnant it was for me to see him."

"What could he have possibly wanted?" I slashed my paintbrush loaded with gritty grey across an airline rewards coupon.

"He offered a deal," Jerry said, sounding stunned.

"Isn't it a little late?" I laughed cynically.

"Well, the Feds caught Stockli in Hawaii, of all places. What an ego this guy has. He hired a Concorde to whiz around the world to play golf with his buddies, somehow believing he'd get away with playing in the states. But the Feds nabbed him at customs, charged him with conspiracy and tax evasion, and flew him to Lake County Jail, where he'll be held pending trial."

"It is unbelievable. So Morford wants you to be his witness? It makes me sick."

"They're hoping I'll be the piece of the puzzle that gets Stockli to confess. If that doesn't work, then I'd have to testify."

"I hope you told him you'd have given them Stockli in the first place if you wanted to save your neck."

"I told him, if anyone has the money it would be Stockli, but I don't know exactly what his role was. It was as if Morford hadn't heard me. He's convinced that because I was the 'mastermind' and 'point man' I'm valuable."

"I hate those bastards," I blurted out.

"If I play ball with them, Morford offered me no halfway house, no fine, no probation, and they would recommend my reinstatement to the bar."

"You'd walk out of there and it would be totally over?" I said, suddenly comprehending the enormity of the offer. "But then, you would have served your sentence for nothing. And all that we've been through would become meaningless degradation."

"I just talked to Brian and he said I have nothing to lose now. I was found guilty and if I can get my life back starting tomorrow we should at least sit down with them to see exactly what they expect from me. If I don't have enough to give them, we haven't lost anything."

I felt Jerry's agitation when we hung up. I called Brian. He said, "I don't trust the Feds, but what if Dad can get out free and clear? How could we pass it up?"

"It's like Dad's the starving animal and they're dangling bait in his face."

"You got it, Mom. That's just what they're doing. I'm going to see Dad first and then we'll meet with them."

I hung up with Brian, aching for all of it to be over and thought of Ginsberg and Garfield. We'd be no better than them. I shuddered. I wondered what the statistics would be if the government and the accused played on an equal field.

Brian and Jerry met with Morford, who started off reminding Jerry that his release into halfway house was only two days away. It would be tough, but Morford said if he was satisfied with the quality of Jerry's statement, then it was possible Jerry would never see the inside of Oriana. He wanted Jerry to confess to conspiring with Stockli. He would need to divulge all the details of what they did and most importantly where the money was. But Jerry said he didn't have the answers and Morford began to renege on his offers. The implication was clear: if Jerry didn't sing their song, the deal was off. Morford left the meeting with the admonishment for Jerry to think long and hard about it and baited him by saying, there still was some time for Jerry to change his mind.

CHAPTER NINETEEN

DONE DEAL

The car was loaded with art materials, prison works, books, and most of my clothes. I'd be in Cleveland for the duration of Jerry's time at halfway house. After that, I wanted to get back to New York. Financially, we were scraping bottom and much depended on how Jerry being a paralegal worked out at the office. He wasn't a good enough typist to work the files at that level. And he wouldn't be allowed to counsel clients. Unless he proved to be a valuable asset to Brian, he intended to look for other employment. He predicted that it would take a minimum of two years before he'd get reinstated to the bar, but most likely it would be five, a long time.

Macabee lay curled asleep in the passenger's seat of the car. I scratched the top of his head. "But, we're getting him back, right, boy? Halfway back." One eye opened, a cyclops's approval.

In true FCI fashion, there had been no instructions as to where I was to pick Jerry up. Only the time, 8 AM, I got to FCI a little after seven, knowing I was too early to get in line at the guard house. I'd left Macabee at the motel. Like a remedial student who couldn't learn enough, I'd been voraciously consuming books on imprisonment, and as I had with the first, *The Gulag Archipelago*, if I came across a particularly graphic or illuminating quote, I copied it down.

Having experimented with creating rust panels, I was now embedding male prisoners' quotes into them. I envisioned women's quotes on paper painted like cinder blocks, pressed under chipped and cracked glass, representing the physical and emotional dangers they were exposed to from the c.o.s and other inmates. Juveniles' quotes would be written on chalkboards to suggest that their incarceration could be erased and there was time for them to make better lives. I hoped to have them installed in buildings that dealt with the justice and penal system. With all this research going on, I had let my documentation of Jerry's prison slide. Though I had no particular plans for its use, I felt it was necessary to take photographs.

Taking advantage of this, my last opportunity, I parked on a muddy shoulder five hundred feet before the entrance and began scoping around for a shot. Almost immediately, I was captivated by a triangular, rusty sign with eroded letters that said, 'No trespassing,' dangling like a loose tooth from the chain-link fence. It was so expressive of what I was trying to evoke in the rust pieces that I felt lucky. I thought of the prison tape pieces. It was a great boost to get the NYFA fellowship, but as with Dierdre, the galleries I approached weren't interested, either. Now that I wasn't whizzing by in a hurry to get into the compound, I paid attention to the running track behind the fence and the guardhouse beyond it. Then set off by itself was the cinder block building that housed those in solitary confinement. I changed the camera's settings and was so absorbed, clicking away, that I didn't see the man jogging, who I assumed was an inmate.

"Hey, what do you think you're doing?" the man shouted.

"Nothing," I said, happy to be on the other side of the fence.

"Well, you're taking pictures."

"A few," I palmed my camera, defensively.

"The taking of pictures on the property of a federal penitentiary is against the law."

"I'm on the other side of the prison property's fence, so I believe that makes it public property and therefore fair game."

"Ma'am, I could have your camera confiscated. Is that what you're asking for?" I shook my head no.

"Well then, rewind the film and hand it to me through the fence."

"Are you looking for Brownie points from the BOP?"

"What do you mean?" he smiled coldly.

"I don't get what an inmate has to gain by harassing another inmate's wife. My husband's getting out of here tomorrow, and all I wanted were some pictures to remember where I never want to set foot again as long as I live."

"I see. To set things straight, I'm not an inmate. I'm the assistant warden," he paused, watching me for the impact of his revelation to hit. I obliged as bright red crept up my neck and enflamed my face. His expression softened. "So," he continued, "no photographing is allowed. Understand?" A smile played in his eyes, enjoying the moment. "Now, who is your husband?"

"I think I should plead the fifth." I returned a shaky smile. "But he's Jerry Kraig, out of Carlson."

"I know Jerry. I sat in on a couple of his mock trial classes. You've got a great guy for a husband."

"Thanks." I blushed again from pride.

"I wish you both all the luck. Now, how about taking that camera of yours and finding better sights than FCI?"

"Thank you, I will."

He saluted and jogged off.

I drove off, releasing a loud breath, feeling lucky to still have my film and camera. It was also pretty funny that being Jerry's wife had prevented me from getting busted by the Feds. At 7:45, my car was the only one in the lot. A low fog was rolling down from a mountain in smoky waves around the compound. The personnel change had either already taken place or it was late, because no one was out. I loaded my camera, and through the windshield quickly shot the entrance to the visiting center, the flag flapping in front of the guardhouse, the chapel in the distance, and a panorama of the compound that I'd been taken with on my first visit because it looked like a grid on a board game.

I took my last shot of my clear plastic prison purse with its visible innocuous contents: playing cards, a lipstick, and a roll of quarters for watery cappuccinos that Jerry would never have to have as a treat again. Rewinding the film, I felt I'd run too fast in reverse, and a slight disorientation came over me as though I were back at the beginning, uncertain of so much and so plagued by anxiety I'd driven lost all the way into Hagerstown, Maryland, and almost burned my house down twice. Too real. Unbelievable.

At 8 AM, Jerry waved at me from the guardhouse. When I pulled up, he was holding the same carton he had taken in when he surrendered and was wearing the same sweat suit. Shedding himself of imprisonment for good, he'd shaved his beard for the last time. He threw the box on the back seat of the car and he got in next to me. I ran my finger along his clean jaw. From behind, a honking truck urged us on, and we kissed quickly. Suddenly we were off, almost free and moving forward.

We held hands tightly as I drove to the Holiday Inn, not to pick up Macabee who was at the kennel, but because we needed to be together, intimate and alone. Loving for sustenance. "I'm afraid to ask when you have to be there?"

"At 1 PM, hon, I'm sorry. I really thought we'd have until five. But Oriana isn't known to give slack. I guess we're in for freedom on a choker chain," he laughed. "Ka-ching!"

"It's a three-hour drive, right? So we've get an hour. Better than nothing, huh?" I smiled through my disappointment.

We made hasty love, too anxious to enjoy it. But it was worth everything to hear Jerry whistling as he showered and see him beaming before wrapping himself in a towel, as if he were brand-new. He said, "I ran around like crazy to submit all the paperwork, so I should have my driver's license when I get there. In no time, I'll be driving home to visit and we'll make love all day." He wiggled his eyebrows, "And that's a promise."

~

Oriana was on the edge of downtown Akron, Ohio, an exit away from the Six-teenth Circuit Federal Court, where Jerry had been convicted. It was a crum-bling, red-brick, converted school building. Not realizing the building was multiuse, we entered the door into a jail, where a swarm of scraggly looking people almost filled a drafty, cavernous waiting area. Directed back outside to the other side, where the cars were parked haphazardly, rusty and dented. Jerry and I exchanged alarmed looks. The entrance area didn't promise much better. It was dark and the institutional green paint on the walls was peeling. Rubber mats smelled of grime. A young man, probably an intern, sat at a shabby oak desk. He took Jerry's papers into a room without a door. Though it was a warm day, like the jail, it was drafty and damp, and I rubbed my arms. Jerry put his arm around my shoulders. "It should be called 'No Way House,' I said under my breath.

"I know." Jerry kissed the top of my head. "It's going to be okay."

The aggressive, brawny woman who had inspected our house now extended her hand to Jerry. "I'm Ms. Johnson," she said as Jerry shook it.

He smiled, "How ya' doing?"

She gave me a quick hello, and we shook hands.

"Okay," she rummaged through a file and pulled out a pink form, "this is today's sign-in sheet. For this week of orientation, with the exception of you going to your job, you won't get your sign-out sheets until you earn your privileges," she said, barely masking a sneer directed at me.

"Believe me, I understand," I said.

She smiled, "Good. And you, Jerry?"

"Of course."

"Otherwise, I will get on your neck, and believe me, you don't want that."

"Sure," Jerry said, trying to sound light.

"The situation here is overcrowded. You will be in Room F, on the third floor. Eight bunks." She consulted a diagram. "You're the top, next to the window. You'll have one locker. Since some of our residents can't distinguish their belongings from yours, I suggest you lock everything up, radio, watch, coat, socks, everything. If you're not using it, you're apt to lose it. You will be assigned a housekeeping job. It's the residents' responsibility to keep this place clean." She handed Jerry a packet. "This will answer everything else. Now, if you'll follow me."

"There's one thing the packet can't answer."

"Yeah," she raised an eyebrow, "and what's that?"

"My driver's license. I'm wondering if it's in my file."

She shuffled papers and plucked out a memo. "Not yet." I could feel Jerry's heart drop. "This states that the copy of your license that was sent from Columbus wasn't readable." She looked at Jerry, daring further delays, and then at me. "Then, I suppose you will be driving him to work on Monday?"

"Yes."

"Okay, Jerry, let's go."

Yet another penal institution and another good-bye. I was back in the car on the freeway going home, alone again. Jerry called just as I came back from springing Macabee from the kennel. Word was, depending on the social worker, Oriana would be either tolerable or miserable. Ms. Johnson was miserable. Not only did she have a reputation as a bitch, which I could have told him, but she was vengeful and worst of all, worked an unpredictable schedule that kept her cons on their toes with unpredictable check-ins. It also made it impossible to rely on her for troubleshooting or necessary signatures.

Jerry sounded beaten. The bathroom was all the way down in the basement. The floor was littered with toilet paper and other refuse, soaked in urine. Most of the toilets were blocked. The showers were so bad that Jerry planned to wash up using the sink in the bathroom at the office until he could get home. And he didn't know when that would be. Almost all of the staff went home at night. That's when the gangs took over and the bathroom became their turf. But with Jerry's aging bladder, he could count on being up at least once a night. Dehydration was the only answer; he'd stop taking in liquids at three in the afternoon. He said he needed a mattress pad and several sheets and blankets to layer as much between him and the mattress as possible. It actually looked like it was crawling. Tonight, he'd sleep on top of a sweat suit and wear his clothes or sit up in a chair.

He missed me terribly. He had an appointment with Ms. Johnson to get her approval to be at the office at seven in the morning and work until eight at night. That way we could eat dinner together there, which would be great. He didn't know how he would make it until Monday morning. He was calling from the common room, where there wasn't a pool table or ping-pong, only a couple of tables where the guys ate meals, some vending machines, and the phone. But an inspirational slogan over the watercooler said, "Think of this as the first day of your life, don't mess it up." As he'd done in Lake County Jail, he was back on Snickers.

At 4:30 AM on Monday, after checking the clock all night, I was on the freeway and parked in front of Oriana by 6 AM Jerry was out on the dot, his eyes puffy from no sleep. I handed him a coffee, we kissed, and were off to Cleveland. He was as dejected as he'd been in Lake County Jail. His roommates at Oriana made the guys at FCI look like princes. Two or more guys were up all night, and between farting, snoring, shouting, and verbal harassment, Jerry had hid under his coat, trying to be invisible. It had worked until the guy in the lower bunk had punched his mattress and threatened to climb up there and put him to sleep even though he hadn't moved a muscle.

After dropping Jerry off at the office, I wished I had my studio up the street where I would be able to lose myself in painting until 4 PM, when I had to drive Jerry back to Oriana. Ms. Johnson hadn't bought the idea of Jerry working until eight. On Tuesday and Thursday, though, after he had reported in, he would be allowed to go back out until 9 PM. It was a good chunk of time, but not enough to go home. By Thursday, I had been in the car for such long stretches and so often that I felt as if I were wearing it. And Jerry's driver's license seemed to have disappeared.

Jerry and Brian agreed to meet with Morford again in the federal building, a couple blocks from their office. When I came to pick Jerry up, I was so exhausted I almost told him to give them what they wanted. I just wanted out. But Jerry said they were at the same stalemate, and I kept quiet.

By Saturday, seven grueling days were over. Jerry called, elated; his driver's license had come through. With the burden of driving all day long behind me, I would be able to see Jerry at the office each midafternoon. Behind his desk, he waved me into a seat and continued scribbling notes on a legal pad as he talked on the phone. "It's as if you never left, huh?" I said, as he hung up.

"I wish. I have to be so careful. I'm very nervous. My clients expect me to represent them now that I'm back. They're asking for advice and it's the most natural thing to answer without giving it a second thought. A couple of times I had to catch myself. I have to tell them, Brian will get back to you. It's like I'm not whole anymore. I feel bad. It's actually causing us to handle the same clients twice and we have to pass the information back and forth. Brian's not complaining. He couldn't be better about it. He's trying so hard to make me feel wanted."

"It's only been a week. You'll get into a system."

"But Gene, my being a nonpracticing lawyer and an untrained paralegal isn't going to get the office back on its feet. I'm not an asset. I'm a drain."

"You're not a drain, Dad." Brian said, as he came in and handed Jerry a file. "Remember Mr. Mosely? He only wants you to sign up his new case."

"That's nice. I always liked Henry." Jerry punched in the phone number.

Brian placed his hands on my shoulders. "Mom," he said from behind me, "I want to ask you something. Come in my office."

Brian closed the door and took his seat behind the desk, looking so haggard. I straightened, uneasy in the client's chair. "What's wrong?"

"Nothing," he said, cynically. He slapped at a stack of files. "Look at my desk, I've got more files than Dad ever had, because they're both of ours. He's been back a week, and the phone is jammed with clients and friends welcoming him back. They're arriving without appointments! I know they love him and it won't last, but I don't have a second to be Mr. Chit Chat and I can't be rude. I'm so tired I can't think straight. I need to go away with Cindy and I want you to stay with the kids."

"Of course. When?"

"This weekend. I found a cheap flight to New York and we can stay at your apartment."

"Bri, if I could, you know I would. I feel terrible, but this weekend won't work. We're waiting to see if Dad gets clearance to come home."

"So, he could come home to my house."

"It's not approved."

"Then have the kids at your house," he said so furiously, a vein had popped on his forehead, over his right eye.

My hand clenched. "You have to understand. This will be our first time at home in two years. I need...I'm sorry, no."

"No?" He shouted. "It's always about what you need!" He swiped at the files, causing the ones on top to fall. "Great," he said, glowering at the documents spilled all over the floor. "What about me? What about what I need?"

Jerry came in, startling us. "I heard you all the way in my office. What is this shouting about?" He eyes squinched, as if he were in pain.

"Dad, Mom has had two years in New York to do anything she wants. All I asked her for was this weekend so I could take Cindy away. And she said no."

"I was just going to offer anytime next month," I shouted, angrily wiping away tears with the back of my hand.

"You owe me some consideration, Mom."

"But you're being unreasonable."

"Stop it!" Jerry had turned deep red, his lips white. "I thought our family was finally being reunited and you're tearing away at each other. I can't take it," Jerry yelled, half-imploring and half-outraged. I'd never seen him so upset. "You two settle this." He left, slamming the door.

I went cold with fear that we were being torn apart after we'd come all this way. Through my tears, Brian and I glared at each other in a standoff. Then he said, "Mom, I don't want to fight."

"Me either. I'm sorry. I just can't be everything to everybody." I went to him and kissed his forehead.

"Dad's release from prison into this no-man's-land is making everything tenser. Halfway back is worse. I want him all the way back."

"Me too, Bri. And so does he."

~

Rush hour on the freeway was compounded by construction. I was inching toward the exit as I followed Jerry to Oriana so that he could report in and we could have dinner together. At a table in the food court at Quaker Square Mall, we ate our sandwiches. I was thinking out loud about Brian and how much it would help if Jerry could get reinstated; that the strain Brian was under needed closure. We all needed closure. I couldn't take halfway back anymore. "Is there a way to still strike a deal with the Feds?"

Jerry's eyes widened, surprised. "Maybe," he nodded, "but I'll talk to Brian." He paused. "I think we've reached our nadir where punishment is concerned. I'll see what we can do."

The next morning Jerry called. They had an appointment with Morford and Wooley at 1 PM I was at the office, waiting for their return at two. Brian walked in alone and hugged me. "Boy, did I get an education." Passing the receptionist, he picked up a stack of messages and told her to hold his calls.

"How come Dad's not with you?"

"He was so worked up, he went to court to do some research that I need."

"What happened?"

"Mom, I learned more dealing with Morford and Wooley than I have in ten years of practicing law. It's not possible to make your case with the government, because they have tunnel vision. It's pretty scary."

"Meaning?"

"Meaning the Feds don't see beyond what they want to achieve. They march toward their objectives with methodically placed steps. If you don't get in line, they move on to the next objective. They knew, because we'd called them, that we were coming from weakness. Morford was relaxed, like a cat who's taken ownership of the trap, totally in the position of power."

The secretary interrupted to say a client was waiting. Brian glanced at his watch and said, "Tell them fifteen minutes." To me, he said, "I'll try to sum it up. Basically, we told Dad's story. And they were listening for bells to go off. When they didn't hear what they wanted, they manipulated the events and told Dad what they wanted him to say. Dad was their witness now. I actually felt sick. And I saw Dad tasting his freedom and still trying to hold onto his integrity.

"Morford asked Dad, 'How much money did Reuben pay you to go to the meeting with Stockli in Switzerland?' Dad said only for his expenses. Then it was as if

Morford were writing a script saying, 'Okay, if you were on the stand, Jerry, you would say that you and Stockli devised a plan on how to parcel out the Gemstone money for the accounts. And you gave Stockli the order, which he carried out, knowing full well it was a sham.'

"And Dad leaned back in the chair, thinking, and regarded Morford, who gave him this smirk as if this was the moment he'd been waiting for. I wanted to punch him, Mom. And then he got aggressive. He said, 'How could you not have known, Jerry? You knew we were breathing down Sturman's neck, closing in on him. You knew we had to have something on him. You couldn't be that dumb, so you had to be culpable. Sturman just needed it legal enough and you masterminded it! If you're telling me that you really had no idea that he meant to hide away money for himself in those Swiss bank accounts, you should have. You should have seen beneath the surface. You might not have intended to defraud the federal government but the results were the same. And the law, as you know, says intentions aren't a defense.'

"It was like those words hit Dad like bullets. And he kind of just froze. Oh, Wooley was there too but he'd been quiet. All of a sudden he was leaning toward Dad, saying, 'After your friend Reuben escaped from minimum, we started digging into his documents and inner circle. Jerry Kraig's name came up everywhere Gemstone was mentioned. On every document, from every witness. We couldn't believe our luck. We knew getting you was as good as getting Sturman. Better. You were the link. All those years, trying to decipher Sturman's dirty dealings and it all hinged on you!'

"Then, suddenly, Dad seemed to come back to himself. He said, 'I have to hand it to you guys. All I could see this whole time was you framing me. But now I can see why. You're right, my fingerprints were all over the crime scene. Of course you hunted me down. I should have known what Reuben was up to. I saw him change. He didn't care how he pulled one over on you, he just wanted to taunt you. And he didn't care who went with him when he went down. He maneuvered me around like a pawn and I never questioned him. Gemstone was legal, but only because he never got the chance to use it to hide money. That's why I was certain I was out of the loop' Morford looked at Dad very carefully, like he'd never seen him before. Dad rubbed his face, looking at Morford and said, 'What I've put my family through...'

"Morford said, 'Listen, Jerry, all we need is some leverage with Stockli. He's already shitting in his pants. If we can tell him you remember him commenting on the illegitimacy of the trust, we think we can get him to make a deal, and then we can all go home.'

'And I'd be out of halfway house?' Dad asked.

'It might take a day to get the paperwork processed, but then you'd be out.

Free and clear.' He smiled and added, 'You know, Jerry, I've learned a lot from you during this. Loyalty to Reuben and your belief in First Amendment rights blinded your judgment in your own case, but I'll bet you were a damn good lawyer.'

"Dad stood and offered his hand to Wooley and then to Morford. He said, 'And I've learned a lot from you. Nice work, guys.'

"Mom, Dad saw the whole picture and it was as if he made peace."

"What a meeting, Bri. Again, I'm kind of stunned. It's all so unbelievably real. Here the sentence is practically over and Dad makes a deal. Is it a done deal?"

"Done," Brian smiled. "Now, I'm really putting Dad to work."

A few days passed, and it seemed as if the deal had been a figment of our dreams. There wasn't any paperwork or word that it was proceeding. Neither Morford nor Wooley were reachable. Brian wondered if Morford had played Jerry and gone to Stockli, hoping to come back and squeeze more out of Jerry. Jerry said they'd shaken on the deal and they wouldn't go back on their word.

Jerry woke me on Friday at 7 AM to say he was on his way to the office but he was so depressed he needed to come home to be with me even if it was just for a little while. During the night, he'd gotten such bad cramps, he had to go down to the bathroom. A gang of about ten guys were blocking the door and finally one moved aside, but it had been like begging for each link of a fence to open until he got through. They were having a good time at his expense, laughing and remarking, What's this old guy in for? Things like that. He'd barely made it to the toilet in time.

It was a rainy morning. I smiled at Jerry as he crawled in bed, taking me in his arms. "If the deal doesn't come through soon, I'm calling until I get through."

"My tiger," Jerry said in my ear. "It can't take much longer or I won't have a stomach left."

At 8:45, he called the office to say he'd be fifteen minutes late. Jerry was alarmed by the message that his social worker had been looking for him and that he should call Oriana.

"Of all times to get found out." He dialed Oriana, and then he was listening and he was saying, "Yes, sure, I'll be there in an hour." He hung up. "It's over. I'm released," he said, breaking out in a jubilant grin.

"Oh my God, like this minute? Now?"

"Right now." We kissed and laughed and kissed again. "But get this, the order came in yesterday, but she said she forgot to tell me. I could have been home last night."

"If I weren't so happy, I'd want to kill her. I still want to, but go, get your stuff. Honey, your sentence is officially behind us."

CHAPTER TWENTY

NO CIGAR

Jerry was overwhelmed and embarrassed by his reentry into freedom. He dreamt of presenting himself before the judge in a trial and to his horror looking down to see himself naked. That his parole and fine had been expunged had lifted two black clouds, but unless or until he got reinstated to the bar, Jerry and I were financially back to the early days of marriage, when we couldn't afford to buy both meat and detergent in the same week. We discussed selling the house for some cushion of security. Realtors put a damper on it, saying the market was weak. Our house was in a less desirable neighborhood. And it would require extensive repairs, which I'd so eagerly pointed out to Glatz, to bring it up to code to ready it for sale. We didn't have the estimated twenty-five thousand dollars for the repairs and when all would be said and done, we'd have very little left.

A month after Jerry was home, Jerry was invited to play golf with Joe Sturman at his country club. Jerry wasn't comfortable with such invitations, because he wasn't in a position to reciprocate. But he accepted because he didn't want to hurt his feelings.

I sensed something happened when Jerry called at dinnertime asking me to meet him at a restaurant between Joe's country club and our house. I expected he'd eat with Joe after their game. One of the more troubling changes in Jerry since he'd come home was how obsequious he'd become, a pleading in his voice overlaid with hesitancy when he made an appointment, ordered food, or needed assistance.

At the restaurant, really a diner, before we ordered, he asked the waitress so apologetically for coffee that I thought he had to see a therapist. "Something happened with Joe on the eighteenth green," he said, "that was very upsetting.

"I was putting my putter back in my golf bag and Joe was ranting as usual about his lousy game. He was going on about changing his stance, his clubs, and giving it up altogether. You know Joe…Meantime I'd played a good round and I teased Joe that maybe what he needed was a couple years off playing ping-pong. Joe didn't respond and then, hon, he abruptly changed the subject and asked me how I was getting along

"I said I'm certainly not earning as much as a paralegal, and I'm worried about Brian being overworked, but we were doing okay. Joe pulled out one of his Cuban cigars and lit it, puffing a couple times and said, 'Jer, when are you going to pay back my twenty-five thousand dollars?'

"Honey, at first, I thought I hadn't heard right. I kind of fumbled with my golf glove and said, 'Joe, I don't understand. You donated that money to my defense fund.'

"'I want it back,' Joe said, coldly.

"I said, 'Joe, if you're having financial trouble, I'll do whatever I can, but….'

"This is what I'll never forget. He pointed his cigar at my chest. He said, 'Jer, I don't need the money. I spend more than that on my cigars.'

"I said, 'Joe, how could you jeopardize our friendship over money you don't need? We've been friends all our lives.'

"He said, 'Hey, life moves on, Jer. That's the way it is.'"

Jerry stared down at the menu.

"How could he do this?!"

Jerry crossed his arms defensively, "When we were in the golf cart between holes, he asked if we still had our apartment and if you were going back to New York. I said, yes, I hoped you'd be going back." Jerry rubbed his chin as if searching for his beard.

Interrupting, the waitress came over with her order pad. Without consulting the menu, I ordered a salad and Jerry, a turkey sandwich. Then I said, "Joe loves money too much. He wouldn't forget what he did with it. He knows it wasn't a loan. I can't fathom why he turned on you like that."

"Well, for one thing our foursome is over. There's bad blood because of Garfield. Maybe Joe doesn't want to be reminded of the hit I've taken because of his brother. So, he did the one thing that would sever our ties by putting the blame on me so he would feel justified."

"I think he's also pissed that we still have the apartment in New York. I'll tell you one thing, if I ever have an extra twenty-five thousand dollars, I'm going to have it delivered in pennies and dumped on his front lawn," I said angrily.

The food came but neither of us had the heart to eat. We had it wrapped up and went home.

A week later Jerry received a letter from Joe's attorney threatening a lawsuit if Jerry didn't honor his debt. Jerry was too upset to talk about it. He barely ate dinner, just went to bed and stared at the TV. "I feel sick," he said, when I got in beside him and laid my head on his chest, "to think that he could have turned on me like this."

Brian and Jerry went to see Joe's lawyer, and Brian spread out all of the documents he'd drawn up for those, including Joe, who had contributed to Jerry's defense fund. It stated without any ambiguity, that the money had been donated and would not be considered a loan. Jerry said, "Believe me, if I had the money, I would pay Joe back. I felt demoralized enough at the time to have my hand out, but I accepted the money because Joe had offered it as my friend. Now that he's turned on me, and so heartlessly, the last thing I want is to have taken anything from him."

Waiting for the elevator Brian said, "I don't care if you win the lottery you're not giving that bastard back one red cent."

Jerry never heard from Joe or his lawyer again.

~

Finally in April, a year after Jerry's release, he was eligible to request a hearing for reinstatement to the bar. The date was set for September 1998. Once again Jerry was on trial to prove he was worthy to live his life. We felt it went well. We waited.

In January, Jerry stepped off the elevator and entered the office but it was strangely quiet, not even the receptionist was at the front desk. He poked his nose in Brian's office, nothing. Then he noticed the light on in the conference room and opened the door to a jubilant "Surprise," from the office staff, close friends, Brian, Cindy, the kids, Karen, Alex, and me. Streamers, champagne, and the sheet cake pronounced, "Welcome back counselor." Brian handed him a letter and said, "Read it, Dad."

Jerry hugged me, clutching my shoulder, and read, "The Ohio Bar Association is pleased to announce Jerry B. Kraig's full reinstatement to practice as Attorney at Law in the state of Ohio."

He said in a low, humble voice, "This is the true beginning of the rest of my life. I promise I will do my best to make you proud."

"We are proud already," Karen, Brian, and I said in unison.

CHAPTER TWENTY-ONE

THE LAST SENTENCE

We had six months of happiness after Jerry's reinstatement. We were moving forward. I accepted the offer to use a small area in the artist's studio next door to Margaret's for one hundred dollars a month, where I let loose and began to paint raucous hard, bright abstract spills bursting from spiked and jagged enclosures.

A month before Thanksgiving, Brian and Cindy gave us the wonderful and surprising news that we were going to have a third grandchild at the end of June. Because Cindy was having continual morning sickness, Jerry and I granted Karen's wish for us to have Thanksgiving with them in New York. For the first time since Jerry's release, I planned to stay on in New York for a couple weeks to take care of business, submit another round of slides of my prison art to galleries, still hoping for exhibition, and to spend time with Karen.

Our invited guests crowding around the Thanksgiving table were Karen, Alex, his parents, Karen's friend, and Tony, Jerry's buddy from prison who lived in the Bronx and had no place else to go for dinner. Food and wine accompanied great storytelling. As Jerry and I cleaned up, we relived the pleasure we'd taken in the evening. Next year we would do it with Brian's brood and reveled in the thought of the new baby at the table in a high chair, and with luck, the possibility Karen would be pregnant.

In the morning, determined to overcome sluggishness from overeating the night before, Jerry joined me to walk Macabee along the Hudson River. On Chambers Street, he stopped at a cart and bought a coffee but after a sip said it made him feel queasy and tossed the cup in the trash before we crossed the Westside Highway into the park.

Back at the apartment, Jerry said he could use a little more sleep and went up to the loft bed. I went out on errands and when I got back, I woke him, saying the day was too crisp and sunny to waste. He whistled in the shower and after shaving, announced he felt much better and we hiked up to 21st and 10th Avenue to see a friend's exhibit at a gallery in Chelsea.

But once there, Jerry became pale and broke out in a sweat, saying he had to leave; he thought he must have caught a bug, he felt so lousy. We taxied back to the apartment, and when Karen and Alex came for leftovers, Jerry took a bite of his favorite candied sweet potatoes but said they tasted funny and he had no appetite. He stretched out on the couch, covering himself with the afghan.

"Too much Thanksgiving," Alex sympathized, as he globbed another spoonful of stuffing on his plate. Karen asked Jerry if anything was bothering him at the office. Everything was good he assured her. He'd even tried a tough little case and won. He forced a smile and repeated everything was good, closed his eyes and immediately fell asleep.

Jerry flew back to Cleveland on Sunday night. By the end of the week, he still wasn't feeling great so he went to the doctor, who offered several digestive diagnoses that might be causing his symptoms, but he reassured him there was nothing to worry about and wrote two prescriptions for an antacid and a stomach relaxant.

After I was back home in Cleveland, Jerry's symptoms continued to flit around his digestive tract, seeming to come and go, at times more acutely and at times less. Jerry's battery of tests came back negative, and the doctor concluded that the prolonged stress Jerry had sustained, and was probably still experiencing, was the underlying cause. It might take time, but again he reassured, Jerry's symptoms would disappear just as they had come and prescribed more medications, hoping one would do the trick. But by May, the bloating, acidic stomach, burping, and constipation was causing Jerry more and more distress. I insisted that Jerry ask the doctor to order a CAT scan.

I went with Jerry to the hospital and waited, trying not to imagine the worst. But my worst fear was confirmed. The diagnosis was cancer in his abdomen. I felt as if I'd been slammed into a steel wall. The exact type and stage were yet to be determined. On the way home, neither Jerry nor I cried or carried on. We couldn't bear to let cancer in. This wasn't a black cloud that had fallen down on us from an errant judicial system. This black cloud was inside of Jerry and it could be lethal. We talked about how well Jerry had maintained the habits he'd begun in prison, keeping his weight off by running the track and playing tennis. And outside of a few bouts of nausea, his appetite had returned. He hadn't lost weight. He looked the picture of health.

An oncologist at the Cleveland Clinic ordered a surgical biopsy that nailed down the cancer at stage four, non-Hodgkins lymphoma. On the X-ray the tumor was as large as the state of Alaska. It was hard to fathom how Jerry was making it through the day. Shock prevented us from running out of the hospital screaming. Jerry sat slumped on the examining table , as if he'd been hit in the stomach. His lips compressed in disappointment. But the doctor offered guarded optimism. The cancer wasn't evident in Jerry's other lymph glands and hadn't metastasized to his organs. That didn't mean some cells weren't floating around, he cautioned, but hurried to throw us the life raft that chemotherapy would take care of them.

Jerry's eyes took in those words as if he were saying the cure were inevitable. "It's good, then," he said, "there's hope."

He began eight rounds of chemotherapy two weeks after Danny, a healthy eight pounds, who looked like Andrew, was born on June 30. Andrew and Ali stayed with us for the few days that Cindy was in the hospital, but it proved too hectic and wearing for Jerry. We wouldn't be offering that kind of support again to them anytime soon.

Jerry's protocol was four hours of chemo every week for eight weeks. We were crammed into the freezing, air-conditioned treatment room with three others shivering under blankets in different stages of decline, all draining bags of poison into their veins. It was hell. A hell of forced intimacy; everyone huddled, exposed in his or her own misery. Jerry always smiled gratefully and thanked his nurses, who wore their efficiency like shields. I sat next to him, drawing, my mind absent as my heart cried.

Jerry was sailing through. Our optimism soared. He was handling the side effects he'd been warned to expect with minimum discomfort. We were most relieved that he wasn't afflicted with mouth sores. The anti nausea pills were effective and high doses of cortisone alleviated the worst of his stomach distress. He continued working and playing tennis, which we told each other proved his candidacy to win this fight.

Brian's home life had become more hectic with three children. Just as Jerry had begun to crank at the office, the load was slipping back onto Brian's shoulders. Day to day, Jerry's and my emotions roller-coastered from soaring optimism to plummeting fears. I sublet our apartment to a friend. We were on another ride toward overcoming the odds.

Brian and Karen must have made a pact to be positive. They talked the fight: cancer wasn't what it used to be; by October, it'll be knocked out. Karen and Alex came for a weekend in August, between Jerry's and my birthday, armed with books that claimed miraculous remissions and cures through nutrition. One blamed sugar as the culprit, and we declared Jerry's big sweet tooth would no longer be filled. He took an oath to forgo ice cream at night and his Danish in the morning. I went to a health food co-op and bought every antioxidant in the book: miracle herbs, vitamins, and fruits to concoct Jerry's smoothies, which he drank twice a day even when he had to force them down.

Brian and Karen's optimism was confirmed after the first scan showed that the malignancy had shrunk a good amount. Jerry's hair had begun to fall out, and though he wasn't happy with his balding head, he took it as a sign the chemo was doing its job. His mood picked up with the win of another trial and his stomach problems were still tolerable. He was feeling so good, we visited Debby and Michael at their summer house in New Hampshire's White Mountains. Jerry always had a knack for sending Debby into raptures of laughter and he poured it on, repeating every joke he'd ever told over the years. We reminisced about our Cleveland childhoods. Debby always recalled knowing Jerry before I did. We relived when we went as newly married couples to New York and Michael, as the Brooklynite, had been our native tour guide. Neither prison nor cancer were dwelled upon. We hiked and swam in the pond and planned a winter vacation to cross-country ski after the first of the year.

However, the scan after chemo ended brought grim news. After it's initial shrinkage, the tumor had continued growing. "What's next?" Jerry asked softly. The doctor offered another 'cocktail' that had proven successful. But for this one, because of its high toxicity, Jerry would be admitted. As much as we felt the letdown, hope rallied. Jerry seemed to have given himself over to an unquestioning faith in the medicine. He continued to drink my smoothies, but sugar was creeping back into his diet. At first I was angry with him, and then I gave in. He loved his ice cream sundaes and that had to count as an antidote for something.

In the hospital, I watched over Jerry and the nurses, eagle eyed, double-checking every med, making certain every doctor in the ever increasing team knew what the others were doing, making certain I knew everything that was going on. Jerry came home feeling no worse for the wear. This second round of chemo hadn't seemed to affect him, except for the usual, controllable nausea. Jerry was now taking more pills than there were compartments for in the pill dispenser. The remarkable thing to see was how his body was withstanding such a horrendous blight and still continuing on. But the follow-up scan was unbearably bad. The second round of chemo hadn't shrunk the tumor at all. It was larger.

I read on the internet that the cancer Jerry had was one of the few that adapts to the chemo and actually grows from it. How was it possible that every other person's brother, aunt, mother, husband, and neighbor was in remission? How was it that Jerry was the one who had a lush of a cancer, imbibing chemo as if it were manna from heaven?

I remembered when Jerry was found guilty and was taken out of the courtroom in handcuffs, his head dropped in shame. And I recalled, before that, the shock that had registered on his face when Louie had told him on the phone at Lake Placid that he was being indicted; a premonition, a deep wrenching in his gut that he was in serious trouble. Then, his decision not to take the stand at his trial, and his explanation: a short yet irrefutable, "I don't have the fight in me, hon." I had watched him crumbling in increments. Though in prison his strength had showed a great turnaround, I believed it was his shame, his banishment from his dignity that had grabbed hold of his psyche in some terrible, fundamental way and was now punishing his body. Lymph glands collect and destroy harmful bacteria as a function of the immune system. Jerry's immune system had been under attack from pernicious stress and fear until it became host to voracious cancer cells that thrive on weakness, attack the weakness and if left unchecked, kill the host and themselves.

He spoke of the 'unlucky Kraigs,' dredging up his father having what was considered a minor heart attack and during routine heart by-pass surgery, dying on the table when guys he knew, younger and older, were out on the golf course and tennis courts six weeks after theirs. He dwelled on his mother's severe alcoholism, which had killed her. Two parents who died young. Three uncles had died too young.

Whoever sent the first black cloud seemed to have an endless supply. I covered my head and stayed in bed after I knew I should get up. I saw that the fight had left Jerry. For the first time in our life together I saw his spirit weakening. He was no longer saying he'd win the cancer battle. I said the right words and continued making the smoothies, scavenging for renewed hope in books, articles, and on the Internet, but I was beginning to give up, too. I couldn't see how we were going to beat this thing.

But then we got great news. After a year and a half of trying, Karen called with success. She was pregnant and due the first week in June. We were incredibly happy to look forward to the summer. We laughed: four grandchildren. He was only sixty-one and I was fifty-six. Jerry assembled the crib for Danny, our happy six-month-old grandson, who this year joined Ali and Andrew on their New Year's Eve sleep over. Jerry pushed his strength to roughhouse with them and they were as thrilled, clinking their glasses of blue bubbly soda champagne and enjoying their Chinese food in front of the fire, as they had been two years before.

But the next morning Jerry's stomach was rock hard and distended, and he laid on the couch in terrible pain while I gave the kids breakfast. After Brian and Cindy picked them up, I drove Jerry to the ER. His doctor came to the hospital to read the scan. His bleak expression told of the end. The cancer, he said, gently placing his hand on Jerry's shoulder, had metastasized to his liver.

"He was doing so well," I challenged, as if the doctor had made a mistake. He nodded sympathetically and hot tears pooled in my eyes, burning. But I wasn't going to cry. Now, with Jerry flat on his back and a morphine drip in his arm, was not the time to fall apart.

Regaining his professional tone, the doctor said, there was one more cocktail they could try.

Jerry was admitted to the oncology floor and after a week of more chemo, we knew it hadn't been successful. Brian visited daily, sometimes twice, loaded down with files, messages, and get well cards sent to the office by clients. To escape their anxieties, Brian and Jerry talked trials and cases.

I couldn't have been more steeled or more devastated: denial to hopeless desolation. I carried the sonogram of Karen and Alex's soon-to-be baby girl with me, dreaming of her arrival. Karen and I talked about her incessantly, trying to keep the depths of despair at bay. Karen, too, was suffering mood swings, exacerbated by her raging hormones. She believed her new baby would rekindle Jerry's will to fight, that he'd be there for the birth, and would enjoy walking the baby in the park.

This baby was what he needed to buy time until he could have a stem-cell transplant, which had proved as good as a cure for many cancer patients. Jerry took pleasure in her optimism, but the likelihood of a transplant was slim. Though his bone marrow had been harvested, since his cancer hadn't responded to the chemo he wouldn't be considered to be a candidate until it did. The doctor ordered twelve rounds of radiation as a last-ditch effort. If the radiation worked, a transplant might be possible. Jerry got sick from the radiation, but the cancer had now metastasized to his back.

In Karen's ninth month of pregnancy, Jerry went into palliative care. Hospice made house calls, monitoring his pain, promising a 'painless death.' He accepted the inevitable with graceful resignation, relieved to know he wouldn't have to endure more treatment. On morphine, he was still going to the office, not working much, but enjoying the phone calls and visits from clients and friends. I knew the end was on its way, but I tricked myself into thinking we could keep going in this state of limbo. There was the baby. He had to hold his new granddaughter.

Karen's wonderful boss and colleagues had planned a baby shower for her. Jerry wanted me to go. Brian agreed that I should surprise Karen. She was understandably very depressed. Her father was dying and unable to travel she was stranded far away from him as she prepared to give birth. I flew in the day of the shower and had a return flight the next day. There was marvelous food and gifts, love, and the best of wishes, but it meant everything to her that I was there. There was great joy, the kind of joy that knocked my breath away because I couldn't believe I still had it in me to feel. Debby and her daughter, Alana, Karen, and Alex came back to the apartment afterwards. We focused on the plans for the new baby while we knew the next time we'd be together it was likely to be at Jerry's funeral.

Brian couldn't give up. He haunted the Internet, desperate to find the miracle. He found Dr. Savage, of all unfortunate names, at Columbia Presbyterian Hospital in New York, who said because Jerry was in the end stage of his cancer he would be eligible for an experimental chemotherapy. "He has to do it, Mom," Brian said on the phone.

I called Dr. Savage and asked, "How many patients have gone into remission after the treatment?" None had. "How many have lived?" "None, but the study is small, so your husband has statistical odds."

I dug in my heels, and with my heart breaking, told Brian, "Dad's in no shape to go through anything, let alone an experiment that hasn't saved even one person's life."

Jerry agreed.

Brian called back. "Okay, if there isn't a miracle cure, I'm taking Dad to Las Vegas for the greatest time of his life. We'll stay at Caesar's Palace. There's a golf course that's an exact replica of St. Andrew's in Scotland. It'll be Dad's dream come true. I want to have this one weekend with him for myself. No phones. No clients. No kids. Just him and me."

Jerry's energy welled up from hidden reserves as he packed. The only downside to the trip was that the law required felons to register before Jerry could even check into the hotel. As repugnant as it was, he and Brian got it over with and put it out of their minds. I talked to Jerry three times a day. He'd eaten a steak. He wasn't gambling. He'd napped by the pool and the sun felt wonderful. He'd had a couple of martinis. "Dad's the man." Brian said. "Martinis with morphine. Forget chemo. He's rejuvenated. He played eighteen holes of golf." Jerry said the course had grouse, bracken, and grass as tough as hacking through steel but, "Hon, I was great." He was in bed by eight and Brian was as watchful over him as me. Jerry only hoped Brian would know this kind of love from his children one day. He will, I said, "He's one hundred percent your son."

That was it. When Jerry came home, it seemed as if the cancer had been stoked into a fire that was raging out of control. His energy was alarmingly low. He could barely eat a couple spoons of Jello. There was the choice of a hospice nursing facility or staying at home. We both wanted him home. We converted the den into a hospital room, complete with the bed, a commode, oxygen, a rolling bed cart, and even a recliner with a lift to aid in his sitting down and rising out of it. I was able to get him to the bathroom, which was our last stand at dignity. Then, his body gave out. Bowels, bladder, clarity of thinking. His bones hurt, he said. Even with help, it had reached the point where it was too much for me to handle.

We arranged for Jerry to go to the hospice by ambulance. There was a bed in the room for me. I stayed day and night and helped when I could, but the nurses and aides were wonders of kindness and skill. I watched him sleep. When he was awake, we didn't have much to say and he drifted in and out of consciousness. As long as he could tolerate it, I got in bed with him and tried to soak in his closeness. I never wanted to let go of his hand. I prayed for him to die. I begged, "Please, don't let him continue to be eaten alive to the bitter end."

As much as I asked for his misery to be over and prepared as I was, I couldn't believe it when Jerry died on June 5 at 11:00 AM. Dazed, I left the room and wandered up the corridor, unable to think what to do. A nurse took me by the arm and supported me as she guided me back toward Jerry's room, asking if anything was wrong. "I think my husband died," I said, distraught.

Brian arrived with Cindy and Danny, who toddled toward me and I was holding him, crying, and he was laughing, thinking I was pretending. Next, Karen was with me on the phone. I was telling her Daddy died over and over as she sobbed, "Yes, I know. I know." And then it was as if I found a piece of sunshine to give to her and I said, laughing and crying, "Dad wanted to make sure I would be there for the birth of baby."

After nurses had cleaned Jerry up, Brian and I spent an hour with him, just looking at him, trying to believe death had come and he was gone.

We arranged for a graveside funeral the next day. It was an unseasonably windy and cold morning for June. Karen wasn't allowed to fly, but I had her with me on the cell phone, holding it like a lifeline as I stood at the edge of Jerry's grave, the top of his coffin a hazy gold. Her friend taped the service, my eulogy and then Brian's—a bizarre necessity. I held Ali in my arms as Brian threw the first handful of dirt. She said nodding, "Papa Jerry is dead," as if she understood.

~

I couldn't have withstood a call telling me that Karen was already in labor and the pressure of flying to get there in time. I wanted to go to New York the next morning. Brian understood. He was stronger now than I'd ever known him to be and I was proud of him. It would take time, but I believed he would be fine.

I arrived in New York by early afternoon and that night I invited a small gathering of Karen's and my friends to the apartment. All the talking helped to release some of Karen's grief. She was bursting at the seams in the only maternity dress that fit her. After everyone had gone, she said, "Now that you're here, Mom, I want to have this baby tonight."

It took five more days until we walked the short block to St. Vincent's Hospital for the delivery. Once Karen was examined and settled in the birthing bed, she wanted me with her, so I stayed. She was using a midwife, though should an obstetrician be required, one would be called in. Labor was proceeding fast for a first baby and was as normal as could be. Alex had taken the course and was coaching great as the expectant father.

Suddenly, Karen was seriously bearing down and I felt exhilaration as the top of the baby's head crowned and the rest of her body slid out into the midwife's hands. But to my horror, the baby's face was blue, the blue of Jerry when he died. And she was flopped like a lifeless doll. I was shaking my head, saying, "No, no, no." A thousand hands and instruments descended over the baby. I glimpsed her in a blanket and she was gone. Karen was crying, "What's wrong with my baby?" Someone said, "She just needs some help."

Again I stood in a hospital corridor, dazed. Alex had followed me, and his face was a frozen mask. I didn't care if I was allowed to or not, I entered the treatment room. A team hovered over the baby, working on her, which meant she wasn't dead. Urgency was electric in the air, surreal in the ultrabright overhead lights. I kept repeating to myself, "This can't happen. This can't happen. This can't happen. She is Addie June Nicholas and she has to live."

A kind nurse noticed me and moved aside to let me in. I saw my granddaughter. The respirator was inflating and deflating her tiny chest with oxygen, but her face was still blue. I touched her cheek, terrified, and wondering how long this would go on. Alex had come up behind me. Then, miraculously, the blue of Addie's face turned pink and then a blushing rose, and then full-fired red, like a sunrise bursting alive from the dark of night. The nurse exclaimed, "This child has an angel somewhere!"

A couple hours later, Addie was batting at her respirator in NICU. The doctor said that she's telling us she can breathe on her own. He removed the respirator and Addie gave a quick, sly, newborn grin and fell asleep. I kissed her brand-new soft forehead and said, "I love you, Addie June balloon."

Two days later, Karen and I walked with Alex, carrying their perfect, healthy daughter home. "What joy," I could hear Jerry saying in my head.

It's been three and a half years since Jerry died. Addie has a little brother, Michael Jeremy, whom we call Misha. The Nicholases live in Maplewood, New Jersey, a train ride away. I sold the house and have been living in my apartment in New York, writing and making art. I didn't think I'd get over the attack on the Trade Towers, which occurred six blocks from my apartment. But I've made the transition to feeling as safe as I can and hope every day for a safer future for the children. I visit with my kids in Cleveland and they come to visit me several times a year. Brian's law practice is thriving.

On the anniversary of Jerry's death, the family was all together for the unveiling of Jerry's monument. Brian placed a golf ball against it, and Danny jumped into the ground cover and picked up the golf ball, clutching it like a prize. We read aloud the inscription engraved on Jerry's headstone, "He desired everyone to be happy." Then, Alison wrenched the golf ball away from her little brother, shrieking, "No, Danny. Mom, make him give it back to Papa Jerry."

We all laughed.